*The Place at
the End of the World*

The Place at the End of the World

Essays From the Edge

JANINE DI GIOVANNI

BLOOMSBURY

In some cases, names have been changed because
the subjects are still living in countries
where their lives are at grave risk.

'Hope Wanted: Aids in India' originally published in *Vogue USA*.
'The Place at the End of the World' originally published in *Vanity Fair*.
'Tough Love' Janine di Giovanni © *Vogue*/Condé Nast Publications Ltd.

The following pieces first appeared in *The Times*: 'Goodbye to all That',
February, 2004, Westbrook, Maine: 'Fallen Heroes', August, 2004, 'The Long
Wall', November, 2003, 'Two Rivers, New Jersey', September, 2002, 'Small
Voices in Zimbabwe', March, 2002, 'Dead Men Tell No Lies: Justice in
Jamaica', May, 2001, 'Evil Things Happened here: Samashki, Chechnya',
February, 2000, 'The Battle of Algiers', June, 1998. © Janine di Giovanni,
Times Newspapers Ltd.

First published 2006

Copyright © 2006 by Janine di Giovanni

The moral right of the author has been asserted

Bloomsbury Publishing Plc, 36 Soho Square, London W1D 3QY

A CIP catalogue record for this book
is available from the British Library

ISBN 0 7475 8036 7
ISBN-13 9780747580362

10 9 8 7 6 5 4 3 2 1

Typeset by Hewer Text UK Ltd, Edinburgh
Printed by Clays Ltd, St Ives plc

All papers used by Bloomsbury Publishing are natural,
recyclable products made from wood grown in well-managed
forests. The manufacturing processes conform to the
environmental regulations of the country of origin

For Luca and Bruno

CONTENTS

ACKNOWLEDGEMENTS

People often asked me how I came to live a life reporting from the worst places on earth. The simple answer is that I would be nowhere without great editors behind me. I arrived into journalism by a stroke of fate. I had wanted to be a novelist from the time I was a little girl, but a meeting with Felicia Langer, an Israeli lawyer, changed my destiny. She convinced me to write about life's victims, the dispossessed, the poor, the hungry. The forgotten people that no one cared about.

Some people helped me do that, and to them I am forever grateful for publishing my stories and financing my trips, and, more importantly, supporting me emotionally. But it all has an odd providence. As I said, my route into journalism was not conventional. The short version goes like this.

On a plane trip from New York to London many years ago, an elderly gentleman sat next to me, and did not stop talking. His name was Jo Lustig. He was a producer with a larger-than-life vaudeville personality (he produced Mel Brooks' films) and he took me under his wing. As I knew no one in London and naively believed one got a job by writing letters to the *Guardian*'s Classified Ads which appeared, I believed, every Monday, I was unemployed. No one even bothered to answer my handwritten job applications for BBC research positions or copy-editors at publishing houses.

Lustig called his friends with his 'Hey Boss, the kid can sing!' enthusiasm. He sent me first to Michael Watts, deputy editor of the magazine at the now-defunct *Sunday Corre-*

spondent. In those days – the late 1980s – the big thing in journalism was celebrity bashing. So someone who wanted to write reportage, to go to the ends of the earth, was a rarity. Watts, an intuitive, brilliant editor, took me to lunch, listened to my ideas, and said (and I never knew why), 'You should become a war correspondent.' Watts briefed me a bit about how to write a good magazine piece. 'It's like a complicated puzzle,' he said and introduced me to his editor, Henry Porter, who – if my memory serves me correctly, it was a long time ago – was wearing an elegant pale linen suit and smoking a cigar. Porter was renowned as a gifted and rather maverick magazine editor. He also listened to me talk, asked me some questions, and I left his office with a stack of commissioning notes. I was stunned that he put such trust in an unknown freelancer whose only published demonstration of work was a typewritten graduate-school thesis on Katherine Mansfield and Chekhov, and a few local newspaper articles. When I left the building, I read the commissioning notes that he had signed. The first one was to go to Gaza, a story I had shyly suggested. It was the early days of the first intifada, or Palestinian uprising. Now what have I done, I thought, shaking in my boots. I remember being terribly frightened.

But I went. I began writing, and working for newspapers. A decade ago, I met Gill Morgan, from *The Times* Saturday magazine, who is that rare and wonderful thing – a compassionate editor, a compassionate human being. It was she who gave me the time, the space, the quiet to spend a month researching rape in Kosovo. Or gang wars in Jamaica. Stonings in Nigeria, women in Algeria, and nearly all the stories that make up this book. She taught me how to look at the small story and make it tell the bigger story. But she was also a good friend. When something was too dangerous, she would say, 'I would rather have you safe and alive than have the story.' That is unusual in journalism. My safety, my wellbeing, were always paramount to her, before getting her story. When I would call her from my satellite phone in Iraq, or Chechnya, or Sierra Leone, her first questions were, 'Are you all right?', 'What are you eating?', 'Where are you staying?' Not, 'Where's my story?'

And she also encouraged me to write about the personal things that often made me uncomfortable: the death of my father; the birth of my son. As a truly great editor will do, she drew out my very best writing and my strongest emotions.

Other important people came into my life, honing my skills, helping me shape ideas and making me feel that I was not crazy for wanting to write about places no one cared about: Graydon Carter, Bruce Handy, Alexandra Pringle, Ashbel Green, David Godwin and Kim Witherspoon. Without their faith in me – and on my darker days, I would wonder why – I would be lost.

And a special thanks to Mary Morris, Mary Tomlinson, and Lucy Carrington of News International, and to Chiki Sarkar and Emily Sweet for their methodical eye for detail while working on this book.

Janine di Giovanni
Paris
April, 2005

'Man's inhumanity to man is not only perpetrated by the vitriolic actions of those who are bad. It is also perpetrated by the vitiating inaction of those who are good.'

—Martin Luther King Jr

'Better to light a single candle than to curse the darkness.'

—Chinese proverb

Introduction

What She Taught Me

There are moments in life when what lies ahead of you suddenly comes down to one decision – and that instant, that second, that moment frozen in time changes your life forever. You remember everything about that moment: the lukewarm coffee waiting to be drunk on the scratched table; the way sunlight drifted through a blind; the fading of a dull winter sky.

You can see it as clearly as if there are two doors in front of you. You pass through one. You might have gone through the other one, but you don't. And your life charges forward, like a spirited thoroughbred – on a blind, new racecourse. Nothing is ever the same.

That moment came for me in late December, 1988. I was a recently married twenty-something, drifting aimlessly from postgraduate degree to postgraduate degree with a vague inclination to write. I had no political leanings, no real passions except for a tendency to feel outrage when confronted with injustice: the Ethiopian famine, for instance, or the abuse of small children.

That day, sitting in the kitchen of my then-husband's parents' kitchen in a wealthy Chicago suburb, I saw my life laid out as neatly as a dozen eggs in a plastic container: a few years working; children; a home by the sea; vacations in Europe; sailing trips; collecting art; the pieces of jewellery I would get with each passing anniversary. A comfortable life. Only it did not feel like mine.

I sat at the table aimlessly reading a newspaper. A grainy black and white photograph showed Israeli soldiers burying Palestinian teenagers alive with a bulldozer. The soldiers were so young, but they seemed to be grinning, overjoyed at their accomplishment. The Arabs' faces, however, were fixed with horror as the dirt was slung around their submerged bodies.

My face was frozen with horror, too, as I read the story. The first Palestinian intifada, or uprising, had begun the year before in the Gaza Strip. My husband came from a liberal Jewish family, and they discussed it, along with their trips to Israel, at night over dinner. I would chew my food and nod occasionally and sometimes even listen. So I did know a thing or two about this conflict cursed with blood and vengeance. But I was too buried in my small world of books and dissertations, my small attempts at writing fiction, to know, or care, more than that.

But I kept reading. The story was about another Palestinian teenager who had died during an interrogation by Israeli security forces, and the quest of his lawyer, Felicia Langer, to have his body exhumed. Langer, the newspaper said, was an Israeli Jew, a Holocaust survivor and a dedicated campaigner for the rights of Palestinians.

Since 1967 and the Israeli occupation of the West Bank and Gaza, Langer had devoted her life to defending Palestinians in Israeli military courts. Every morning she got up and faced a gargantuan task, David in front of Goliath. She lost most of her cases. She burst into tears in front of judges when describing how some of her clients lived, or died. Ordinary Israelis hated her; cursed her, spat on her when she walked down the street. They thought she was a self-hating Jew. She was called a communist, a traitor. Her office got bomb threats. Her husband, her only son, got abused.

I re-read the article again, and something inside of me snapped: thousands of miles from the ancient grey stone of Jerusalem, from the Old City and the Damascus Gate, I sat in frozen, wintry Chicago. But I felt this woman's passion, her conviction, and it touched the most remote and hidden part of me. I got up and made another cup of coffee, took one of my mother-in-law's famous homemade chocolate shortbread biscuits and ate while I read the article a third time. Then I got on the telephone, found Langer's office number from International Directory Enquiries, and called her.

I had no idea what to say to Langer once she got on the phone. Since my marriage, I had flirted with journalism, working on a local paper in Boston and later in London, where my husband and I had settled. But because of my marriage, I was in the fortunate position of not having to pay the rent or the bills. I did not *have* to work. My fantasy was to live a spoilt, Virginia Woolf-like, literary existence – without the suicide – before we started our family. To write in the mornings in a sunlit room without the pressure of deadlines, or going into an office.

But the moment Langer answered the phone, my life changed forever. I could see the future I had planned so carefully dismantling, like a child's set of building blocks, but I felt helpless to reach out and catch them. Langer did not seem surprised to hear from a stranger, only extremely fatigued. I asked her if I could come see her. She hesitated and said, 'If you really want to know what is happening in Israel, you must come and see it with your own eyes.'

Some time later, I flew with my husband to Israel. Langer worked out of a cluttered office in downtown Jerusalem. There was a harassed secretary and a few dying plants. She was petite, with pale skin and watery blue eyes which she shielded with Jackie O sunglasses against the Middle Eastern glare. In the car on the way to a prison to visit some of her clients, she handed me a tube of Lancaster sunblock and advised me to take care of my skin. She seemed to know, even before I did, that I would return again and again to this haunted place for many years.

She brought me to the West Bank. She brought me to meet friends of hers, Israelis, who had been imprisoned, the first Jews to be incarcerated under the treason act. She took me to a prison in Ramla to see a client, and burst into tears in the car on the way home because she knew she could do nothing to save him.

She brought me to see a friend in Nablus who had lost both his legs when Israeli special forces planted a bomb under his car. She took me to her home in Tel Aviv and talked about her love for her father, her childhood in Poland and the war. She put me in a taxi to Gaza and arranged for a friend, a man who had been imprisoned and tortured for many years, to meet me and guide me. He was deeply damaged. If you came up too quickly behind him with no warning, he leapt, as though he wanted to leap out of his skin.

And Langer talked. She talked about the passion, the fire, that drove her to find the truth, even though it caused great pain and suffering to her own psyche, and to those around her. She talked about how her son had been tormented at school simply because she was his mother. She talked about the Communist Party, of which she was a member. She grew tearful when she talked about the tolerance and love and support her husband, Moishe, gave to her.

I listened, I scribbled in my notebook. I listened. I read. And when I sat down to write my story about Langer, what came out, for the first time, was something genuine and pure, something bigger than me, something straight from the heart.

'The Embattled Case of Felicia Langer' was the first major piece of journalism that I wrote, for the *Sunday Correspondent Magazine*, a now defunct British newspaper. It was published on November 19, 1989, around the time the Berlin Wall came down: the cover had a photograph of joyous East Berliners waving flags and climbing over bits of rubble. That was another sign, although I did not know it then: the collapse of Communism would play a huge part in my life, moving me in the direction of other crumbling former Soviet-bloc countries, most notably Yugoslavia. But that was further off in the future, and another story.

What happened next propelled me into a life I could not have predicted. The article was picked up by a literary agent, who asked me if I wanted to write a book in the same way, about ordinary people, Israelis and Palestinians, and how they lived. I got a small advance and set off with a small bag. I threw myself into documenting other peoples' lives: sleeping in refugee camps; interviewing teenage terrorist leaders who were wanted by the Israelis; hanging out in kibbutzes and apple farms in the Golan Heights with kibbutzniks; speaking to Israeli mothers whose teenage sons had been murdered by zealots; and having dinner with Druze militiamen and families of 'martyrs', Palestinians who had been killed in demonstrations or prisons.

I went to spend time with new Israeli émigrés from Russia, from Ethiopia. I went to see Americans from Brooklyn who had settled in Hebron, and played with their children. I talked to rabbis and women who had fought in the 1948 war of independence. I saw torture victims, human rights activists. I hung out on the beach with young Israeli soldiers, their faces so fresh that the guns they carried looked as though they were toys.

The book took nearly three years and, by the end of it, I was not yet thirty and an author, but I was also about to become a young divorcee. I don't know exactly why, but the seed that was planted that day in Jerusalem grew – until my need to go to dangerous places and to be in the middle of history being made became larger than my desire to be in a marriage. The fever that convulsed Langer now seemed to convulse me.

'Write about the small voices, the people who can't write about themselves,' she said. Once started, I could not stop doing it. There seemed to be so many places in the world where evil things happened. But the cost of all those stories was huge: the person my husband had married, the naive and rather shy girl in the big white Laura Ashley-style dress, had disappeared. One day he looked at me sadly and said, 'Where is that girl? I just don't see her any more.'

Now I had to work and pay the bills, and by the time my book, *Against the Stranger*, was published I plunged head first into the Bosnian war, an obsession that would last nearly a decade. My literary agent threw a party for me in London to launch the Israeli book during a week that I had come home from Sarajevo. It was odd to stand in a room full of people with faces fresh from skiing holidays and the thrill of London gossip. I had come from a burnt-out shell of a city where there was no electricity, no water, and where my skin peeled off when I removed my clothes after three weeks of not washing.

It was a time that affected me radically, both professionally and emotionally. From Bosnia I went to Africa, to Russia, to Siberia and back to Israel, again and again. Then came Kosovo. Then came Africa again. Then the Middle East, again. 9/11. Afghanistan. Somalia. Iraq. One year, I barely got home to open my post, and my friends joked that they only expected to see me when I walked through the door, like a fainter and fainter ghost. The clothes that hung in my closet looked like strangers. I did not take much into war zones.

I got so good at packing that I could do it in an hour. I could set up my own satellite phone. I learned how to get anywhere on the planet as quickly as possible, and preferably before anyone else did: Chechnya, East Timor, Zimbabwe, Afghanistan, Nigeria, Liberia, the Ivory Coast, Iraq and Israel, again and again. I landed in cities under siege; travelled for weeks with young and hungry militias; slept in freezing tents for weeks and tried to overcome my fear of spiders in the jungle.

One wet day in Conockry, Guinea, trying to bribe my way on to a helicopter going to Sierra Leone, which was about to blow sky high, I had a terrible epiphany: I realised I was the only person trying to get to a place that everyone else was running away from.

But I still got on that chopper, and wrote about child soldiers and civilians whose limbs were amputated by rebel forces simply so they could be grotesque reminders of the war. I fell in love with a three-year-old boy called Victor, a war orphan, and tried to bring him home, perhaps sensing that my own life was too one-dimensional.

But in the end I did not adopt him, as there was another story to go to after Sierra Leone, and who would have taken care of Victor? Because of Langer, I went everywhere to record those little voices that she had told me about – the voices of people who could not speak for themselves – in little black notebooks, then put the words on a page.

Sometimes people reacted to what I wrote and it had some good effect; sometimes not. When I was frustrated, or lonely, I thought of Langer losing most of her court cases yet still getting up, day after day, to prepare another case that would probably go nowhere.

I saw Langer only once after my time in Israel. During the first Gulf War in January, 1991, she was awarded a humanitarian prize in Vienna. One day, her life had changed too. She had left Israel abruptly because she said she could no longer take the harassment, and settled in Germany to teach. I flew to Vienna to see her, and as we walked through the snowy streets of middle Europe she started crying, weeping, over the American invasion of Iraq.

She was fearful for Israel, for the scuds falling on Tel Aviv, for the aftermath, for the future of the Middle East. She must also have been thinking about her future away from the country that she loved so much yet could no longer live in. I hugged her goodbye, but did not see her after that. It was not deliberate. It was simply that I began to do the work that she had inspired me to do, and my life suddenly took on a turbocharged pace.

I spoke to her once or twice, and got news about her from friends in Israel. Does she know she changed my life? Probably not. In a strange way, I was always afraid to see her again. It was almost as though the image of her – of what she represented to my life, how she changed me from that girl sitting in a Chicago suburb to the person I am now – must remain ageless, still as an icy lake, secure and safe.

But certainly, I know that had I not turned the page of that Chicago newspaper, had I not read the article about Langer all those years ago, I might not have passed through the door that I did. I would probably have had the life that perhaps was intended for me. By now, I would have been a fully-fledged soccer mom. I would not have woken up in rooms in Liberia frozen with fear that a rebel army was somewhere near; or cried my heart out because a small boy in Iraq lost both his arms in an American rocket attack.

But instead, I took another path. A few years back, I married a man I met in Sarajevo a decade ago when we were both reporters covering the siege. He is French and I am American, but we speak the same language and I never have to ask him, nor he ask me: *What was it like out there?*

And there are other surprises, miracles really. A telephone call from a doctor in New York one June afternoon as I was crossing the street. I had just emerged from nearly four months in the Middle East, reporting the war in Iraq. I still felt slightly woozy at the American traffic, the shops with all the wonderful clothes, the fact that I could pick up a telephone and it was not bugged.

The doctor said, 'You're pregnant.'

I suddenly had a flash, a visual image of a set of doors in front of me. For the second time in my life I was about to pass through them, totally blank about what lay behind. Or how they would change me.

But that, I suppose, is another story.

ONE: AFTER 9/11

Iraq

The Last Days of Iraq

March, 2003

On Ash Wednesday, a few weeks before war was declared on Iraq, I went to mass in St Mary's Church on Palestine Street, Baghdad. The mass was in Aramaic, the ancient language of Jesus, and around me the Iraqi Christians knelt and prayed for peace. On their faces was etched all the fear and anxiety of the past few weeks as the diplomatic process unravelled and the world fought over whether or not their country would be bombed. A few of the women, wearing lacy white mantillas on their heads, were crying.

Towards the end of the mass, three American peace activists stood and addressed the congregation. Over the past few months in Baghdad, there had been a flurry of pointless peace activities, beginning with the arrival of the actor Sean Penn in December, then a host of human shields from Seattle and Michigan, followed by men of the cloth spreading words of faith. One of the priests, from Washington D.C., said slowly, 'We hope we carry the hopes and fears of the people of the world in the quest for peace.' It was meant to be reassuring, but the congregation looked wary.

The next man came from the Riverside Church in New York and he spoke of Martin Luther King. I turned to the woman next to me, about my own age, deeply drawn in by her own prayers. She was silently mouthing the rosary. When she saw me, her eye seemed to register a plea for help: can anybody stop this?

Outside, the desert sky had grown dark. The mournful wail from the muezzin, the Muslim call to prayer, came from a neighbourhood not far away. But the Christians, who number around three per cent in Iraq, shuffled out of the church and lit beeswax candles in front of a statue of Our Lady.

Suddenly, a group of Muslim peace activists from Egypt appeared with white doves in their hands and a sign demonstrating their solidarity with the Iraqi people. It was an odd moment. The prayer session had turned into a public-relations session with the Egyptian trying to high-five the reverend from Washington. I decided to leave.

My driver, a Palestinian whose family emigrated to Iraq in 1948, was with me. For weeks he had been helping me stockpile food, water, car batteries and medicine in my room at the Al-Rasheed Hotel, and helped me find a secret, safe place to live in the city once the war started. Driving me to church, he said I seemed more nervous in the past few days.

Even though Iraqis in those days before Baghdad fell did not have access to satellite televisions which would bring them CNN or the BBC, my driver knew what was coming: war. But he was fatalistic. A few days before, he arrived with an enormous bag of gum for me to chew during the bombing so that my ears would not pop, and he advised me not to be afraid of the noise, or of the rockets.

'It is written in heaven the day we are going to die,' he said sagely. 'So don't be afraid.'

I said nothing: there was little to say. We climbed into his long 1987 Oldsmobile – everyone in Iraq seems to drive cars straight out of *Starsky and Hutch* – and drove over the muddy Tigris.

'What will happen if the Americans come?' I asked him, breaking the silence. Even though my driver, as well as my government appointed 'minder', had to report back on me and my activities to the Ministry of Information, sometimes on a daily basis, they had both become friends. After two months working inside Saddam's Iraq, I became accustomed to not asking questions, not expecting answers. But sometimes I crossed the line and asked things I knew I should not.

My driver's eyes shifted, the way they did if someone mentioned President Saddam Hussein, or if I asked what happened to the man I kept seeing in the Ministry of Information who had no fingernails. The first time I saw this man, a wizened character who collected money from journalists in a large sack after their official visits, I stared in horror at his naked nail beds. Who had done this? What had this man done to deserve this torture? And how had he managed to survive it, such trauma?

When I asked my driver about the man, he did not answer. I repeated my question, thinking he had not heard. But his face closed down like a steel gate. Don't ask me. He had managed to survive this long without getting into trouble. In those dark days, no one mentioned Saddam's name, no one mentioned the Mukhabarat, the secret police with their thick moustaches and cracked leather jackets who sat all day on the sofas of my hotel and stared brazenly when we passed. No one mentioned the president's evil sons, Uday or Quasay, or his family. Safe things to talk about were the weather, George W. Bush or sanctions.

I tried again. 'What will happen when the Americans come to Baghdad?'

Silence. Finally, he answered. 'We will fight,' he said. 'Every Iraqi has a gun. No one in this country, even if they oppose the president, wants foreigners occupying their soil.'

He turned over Revolution Bridge, over the River Tigris, the wide, muddy river where the great British explorer, Freya Stark, who lived in Baghdad in the 1930s once wrote:

'It is the only sweet and fresh thoroughfare of the town: not clear water, but lion-coloured like the Tiber or Arno. Its low winter mists in early morning, or yellow slabs of sunset shallows when the water buffalos come down to drink after the day . . .'

Now the Tigris is still wide, but it is drastically polluted: tonnes of raw sewage pour in every day, the result of faulty water purification plants destroyed during previous bombings in 1991 and 1998. But it is still grand and imposing; walking near it still makes me realise how ancient Iraq is.

Sometimes, walking by the river, by the old grand colonial houses, by the former British Embassy on Haifa Street – a pale-yellow building with collapsing verandahs which closed when the diplomats fled in 1991 before Operation Desert Storm – I had flashes of life in Iraq before Saddam. Near the river, life continued and war felt distant. The masgouf – grilled carp fish – restaurants were still open and the fishermen pulled in huge silver fish and roasted them over open fire pits on sharpened wooden sticks. Men drizzled the fish with fresh orange slices, and drank bottles of Iraqi beer made with water from the Tigris.

The souks and cafés were full of people, of old men who sat

with *nigilas*, apricot-flavoured water pipes, and plates of the famous Iraqi dates, reading the newspapers and gossiping. And on Thursday nights, the first night of the Muslim weekend, the best restaurants in town – Il Paese, for instance, which served spaghetti all'olio or mozzarella and tomato salad – were packed with well-dressed middle class families. Women with carefully straightened hair, their dark-suited husbands, their well-dressed children.

It was easy to forget that these people, who looked like you or me or like friends of ours, existed. In a country devastated by economic sanctions, where child beggars grabbed the end of your coat and babies died from diarrhoea because of unclean water, it was easy to forget there were people who were educated abroad, who spoke good English, good French, and who looked at America and Britain as friends, not as enemies who would very soon bomb them.

More than the bombing, people were fed up with sanctions which prohibited anything that might remotely be considered a dual-use product – something that can be used to make weapons of mass destruction – to arrive in the country. That included medicine, and strange things like pencils and shoes. 'I don't know who makes up these rules back there in the UN headquarters,' a puzzled Iraqi friend said to me once, staring at his ungainly plastic shoes. 'We used to have the best clothes and the highest standard of living in the Middle East. This embargo is choking us to death.'

This is what sanctions meant: you died of cancer if you got it, unless you were rich enough to afford black-market chemotherapy, which cost around $3,000 each cycle.* A

---

* In most of the countries in which I reported US dollars are the currency of trade.

professional Iraqi earned, in those days, about two dollars a day. It meant you shared books if you were a student, and they were probably photocopied or downloaded from the Internet or smuggled in from abroad.

It meant you read twenty-year-old copies of the *Studio* to get ideas if you were an artist because you could not get new ones. It meant you could not travel or update your knowledge if you were a doctor, a professor, a scientist.

It also meant a strangulation of the intellectuals. On Fridays, the Muslim day of rest, we walked to the book market off Al Rasheed Street. If you got there early in the morning, you saw piles and piles of books in English, French and German, for sale. Copies of the letters of Gertrude Bell – the English woman who rose, along with T.E. Lawrence, to the highest British political office, and died in Baghdad in 1926. Faded orange Penguin Classics, copies of Evelyn Waugh and Somerset Maugham and Truman Capote. Stacks of *Newsweek* from the 1970s, with a photograph of the first test-tube baby on the cover. Encyclopedias of medicine from the 1950s, political leaflets from Moscow, ancient books from the British Consul Library, long disbanded.

People sold books to eat. In the last days of Saddam's Baghdad, they sold them to buy lanterns and supplies for what they believed would be a long war. There was a café at the end of the street, in an old Ottoman-style building that dates before the British mandate, with faded sepia-print photographs on the walls. Inside is a scene out of 1930s Paris, Les Deux Magots. But instead of Simone de Beauvoir and Jean Paul Sartre pouring over the meaning of existence over an espresso, there are Iraqi poets and writers arguing over Italian post-war cinema or translating their poems from Arabic to English.

In one corner was Nasir, who wore a black polo-neck jumper and had dark circles under his eyes; there was his friend Yoahkam Daniel, a Christian film critic, and his friend Sada Bathan, a translator who clutched a worn copy of Truman Capote's *Music for Chameleons*. The two friends met in the café several years before and bonded over their love of books. They call the meeting point at the end of Mutanabe Street their 'sanctuary'. Both smoked heavy, imported French cigarettes, drank sugary tea and discussed Italian post-war cinema.

'Roberto Rosellini!' shouted one.

'Vittorio da Sica!' countered the other.

Sada lost his wife to a routine medical procedure which went wrong. He blamed it on sanctions, but also on the life that has deteriorated around him. He loved his wife passionately, said she was a cross between Sophia Loren and Claudia Cardinale, and his grief hung around him like a mantle. 'I called her Beatrice,' he said, thumbing through the Capote book. 'After Dante.'

The friends compared their lives in 1970s Iraq – 'A rich life, full of travel and money and books and luxury,' said Yoahkam – to the current days, the steady drip of misery, of fear.

'The embargo is suffocating us,' said Sada. He paused. 'But no one can strangle our minds.'

One afternoon during Eid – the Muslim festival of sacrifice which carries on for several days – a middle-aged man with a gentle face approached my table at Il Paese, where I was having lunch with my driver and my minder. He was a former pilot from Iraqi Airways, and he asked if he could sit for a moment. He brought with him a beautiful teenager, his daughter.

'We wanted to welcome you, to thank you for coming here,' he said in slow, careful English. 'For seeing what it is like to live in this country now, in this difficult time.' His wife, who had wide, pale blue eyes and copper coloured hair, waved shyly from the next table. 'It's not easy for us now,' he said. 'We used to travel, meet so many people. Now no one comes to Iraq. Our country is an empty shell.'

When I arrived in Iraq in early December, 2002, war seemed so distant, like a storm that was far off at sea. By early spring, the days were bleaker. Deep in the heart of the city – into old Baghdad, the area of the traders and gold-smiths and market stands that sold shoes and leather bags and copper, and huge pyramids of oranges and tangerines – the mood changed drastically in the days leading up to the war. There were more women shopping with their brothers and their husbands, with huge sacks stuffed with provisions for the war: bags of rice, sugar, tea, flour.

The Iraqi government had given months and months of rations to families, so much that many people complained they didn't have enough space to store it. But buying food, candles, medicine, duct tape or rechargeable lamps gives one a slight psychological triumph over fear and anxiety: it means you can attempt to have some input into something you have no control over.

Those last pre-war days, those last days of Saddam, were dark days in Baghdad. Children were digging trenches in the streets; sandbags were going up; there were more soldiers on the streets. On my bed at the Al Rasheed Hotel, someone discreetly placed a brand new instruction book: *What to Do in Case of a Fire*. It had been freshly printed, the only new thing that I noticed in the shabby, Soviet-style hotel. The instructions might be helpful in suburban America but I doubt they would work during a cruise missile attack. For instance, 'If smoke fills the room, open a window and hang out sheet to drive the attention of rescuers.'

Ten days before Hans Blix, the United Nations' chief weapons inspector, delivered his final progress report to the Security Council – a crucial linchpin in the diplomatic process – I drove to the edge of town and visited the Iraqi House of Fashion. I had thought it was the place where Iraqi women's wear was designed. Instead, the director general, Firyal el-Kilidar, a softly spoken economist wearing an elegant black dress with leopard cuffs, explains that the House of Fashion was a cultural monument, a way of promoting the ancient civilisations of Iraq. Saddam was a sponsor, as was his moody blonde wife, Sajida, whose photograph at the opening of the House of Fashion in 1984 hangs on the wall. She's shaking hands with a very young and nervous looking Firyal. It is the first time I have seen the president's wife: a tall, blonde, pretty woman dressed in an Yves St Laurent kimono-style dress with her tiny dark-eyed daughter, Hala, by her side.

The dresses that Firyal and her team fashioned were exquisite, but they were not for sale. In the old days, pre-war, the dresses and the house models – who had their own gym, their own swimming pool and their own library of copies of *Vogue* from the 1970s – went on a tour of the world, parading in costumes that depicted the ancient Iraqi civilisation. The dresses were staggeringly beautiful: filmy caftans embroidered with real silver; a ballgown made from date-palm leaves; a green and blue silk dress number that suggested Babylonia.

But the place reeked of sadness and disappointment. Firyal, great dark rings under her eyes, put on a brave face. 'This is the best way to show the reality of our country,' she said, adjusting a head-dress on a model. As director general of a company within the Ministry of Culture, she is effectively part of Saddam's regime. But with her soft, motherly face and her fluent English, she did not seem like the enemy. She just seemed like what she was – a grandmother in her late fifties who had worked all her life and was now terrified at what was coming.

The House of Fashion was made from glass. It took a rocket hit during the 1991 bombing and an enormous sculpture of the shards of glass stands in an open courtyard: an Iraqi man playing the flute and a dancing woman joined together. It's a sign of something; not quite defiance, but survival; almost as if to say: you can bomb us and bomb us and bomb us, but we will still survive, we will still have our culture, our history.

'Why can't people leave us alone – let us live our lives?' Firyal said suddenly. She told a long story: her only brother went to live in London, and is now one of the openly active Iraqis in exile, speaking and writing out against Saddam Hussein. Firyal no longer speaks to him, she doesn't understand why he has turned on their country. She prefers the government ahead of her beloved brother. It is typical Saddam propaganda, but when I gently suggest that, she sits up straight. 'There is no pressure to defend Saddam!' she says. 'I've worked within the ministry for thirty years! Everyone is allowed to do what they want.'

When she says goodbye, she tells me that she is so frightened she can't sleep. There are tears in her eyes. 'I will stay here, where else can I go?' she says. 'I will stay at work until I can't work anymore. Then I will go to my home. I won't run away. This is where I belong.'

Then she wishes me luck and goes back to her dresses.

*   *   *

The bombing began on 20 March. Slow at first, in the suburbs. Then closer, hitting Saddam's palaces and Republican Guard positions, lighting up the river. By early April, the electricity went out.

In the south, in the desert, the weather had changed. From raw, low-rising mist on the Tigris, to desert heat. At first, the desert war moved slowly, though the briefings in Centcom in Doha, or in Kuwait City or Amman said the coalition forces were progressing.

'I am a patient man,' said a British general who was in the south with his troops, trying to contain rebel insurgents. His men patrolled checkpoints where they checked civilians to make sure they weren't suicide bombers.

'Remember, we will have lots of surprises in store for the Americans,' was what my friends in Iraq had said, over and over. 'We will not be occupied.' The Iraqis liked to use the words 'quagmire' and 'guerrilla war'. Tariq Aziz likened the winding streets of Baghdad, where Fedayeen paramilitary fighters – most of them recruited from jails and orphanages – could crouch and hide, to the jungles of Vietnam.

The Americans mowed through the desert in tanks and APCs. On 4 April they arrived at Saddam International Airport, which I had flown into many times, and renamed it Baghdad International Airport. I imagined the American marines sitting in the duty-free lounge, eating the plastic cheese sandwiches and drinking the orange Merinda soda, the only thing you could then buy. A day later, the BBC reported that they had made it as far as my former home, the Al Rasheed Hotel.

But it was not an easy war to win. American soldiers with soft eyes, from Texas or Colorado, approach civilian vehicles at southern checkpoints and are met by children with guns.

Prisoners of war are taken. It is said that a girl in Safwan saluted a coalition soldier and was then found hanged a few days later.

The sun drops fast in the desert, the heat drops sharply, and the thousands of coalition soldiers are plunged into darkness. In the base I share with some British soldiers near Basra, everyone uses flashlights at night that have been penned in with red felt-tip. There are eerie flashes of red throughout the camp at night, like martians, and the sound of low thuds, mortars in the distance.

We have to go around with green military bags strapped to our sides: gas masks, spare filters, atropine injections with inch-and-a-half needles to inject into our thighs in case of nerve gas. At 7.15 a.m. every morning, a truck distributes our daily ration packs as well as malaria and nerve-agent pills. There's a decontamination unit next to us. They let us use their cold water showers sometimes, the same showers that will be used if soldiers get 'slimed' or contaminated.

During the day the temperature rises, and rises. There's a bout of some infectious gastrointestinal bug going around and the quartermaster, a thin Brit with a public-school accent and a shrill strictness, lectures everyone about hygiene. We get two litres of drinking water a day, plus a small bowl for washing in the morning. Dinner is rations: Lancashire hotpot in an envelope, eaten with a plastic spoon, or beans. We go to bed early and rise around 6 a.m., when it is still cool.

By 10 a.m., it is full desert heat – 40°C, inside a tank, suffocating gasps of breath. We drive through the desert in Land Rovers and across the flat, lunar landscape. Basra shimmers in the desert heat, surrounded by a cloak of oil fires ringing the city. At the furthest British front-line position a young, sunburnt soldier with a blond crew cut leans out of his tank for a breath of air.

'It's 60°C in here.' His face is ringed with sweat.

Suddenly came the whizz and the dull thud of a mortar landing close by. As it burst, thick black smoke rose like a fat cloud.

'Mortar or grenade?' asked a thirty-three-year-old British reservist, a pretty blonde woman named Nicky, who usually works as a lobbyist in Westminster but has been in Kuwait and Southern Iraq for the past two months. She added dryly, 'If it's an RPG, I can honestly say it's the first time I've been RPGed.'

It turned out to be a mortar, and more rounds came in. Further up the road – past Bridge Number Four in the south-west point of the city which spans the Shatt-al-Basra Canal – another group of soldiers, Irish Guards who had taken position in a former technical college with shattered windows, fired back with rapid machine-gun fire.

A few weeks ago, Iraqi students sat neatly with their books on desks in front of them, portraits of their president, Saddam Hussein, on the walls. Now the school is transformed. It has become the war zone, the furthest front line for British troops, a base with soldiers in desert-coloured uniforms jumping in and out of tanks and armoured vehicles, racing further down the road. The portraits of Saddam have been yanked down from the walls and someone has written, in the fashion of Ali G, the British comic, 'I'm a loser, innit?'

There was a shudder to the hot, still air as rounds came in. The dusty earth under our feet shook slightly. Further on an RPG dented, but did not penetrate, a mustard-coloured Warrior.

There was the rank smell of cordite, then the sound of

more gunfire. 'All fun and games,' sniggered one young soldier. The injured, but not damaged, tank had a dark stain and looked as though it had been struck with rocks. But the rocket had not penetrated the armour, the soldiers explained proudly.

'There's quite a few RPGs around,' explained Second Lieutenant Tom Orde-Powlett, the platoon commander. 'There was quite a lot of noise when it hit, we were aware of it. But there's so many loud bangs going on all the time.'

Underfoot, near the school, the ground was littered with shattered green glass and burnt-out blackened buildings. David Birnie, a twenty-two-year-old from Leamington Spa, lifted his shirt and adjusted his combat trousers to show a three-inch minor flesh wound, bleeding, with a bandage hastily slapped on top to staunch the blood.

'This did it,' he said calmly, taking a chunk of jagged shrapnel from his pocket. 'In that last round of incoming.'

Another Warrior rolled up with a thirty millimetre mounted cannon. A soldier with a shaved head who looked like he should be out raving at a club in Manchester was half hanging out, a startled expression on his face. He had just spied an Iraqi Land Rover moving with an anti-tank gun and, as the Iraqi soldier reloaded, he shot his cannon.

'Got him,' said another soldier with grim satisfaction. 'Took out some Iraqis. But he feels kind of strange, doesn't want to talk about it.'

That day, sixteen days into the battle of Basra, the Brits say they are not besieging the city, but are 'isolating' it from Ba'athist and pro-Ba'athist military elements. All four key bridges which lead into the city centre are secured by British troops and they have taken strategic footholds – houses or industrial sites – from which to launch their operations.

The British forces are battling on two different fronts to secure Basra, but they are still fighting Iraq's armed forces as well as irregular militia troops. There are an estimated 1,000 militia troops reportedly still holed up inside.

'What we did today was rattle the cage,' says one soldier. 'Stir up the wasps' nest. We went in, pushed further, trying to create a response to draw the enemy towards us so we could fight more on our terms.'

The next day we drive out to Basra International Airport, now secured by coalition forces. In my bag, I still have an unused ticket for Baghdad–Basra–Baghdad for February 16, 2003. I never used it and now I look at the gutted airport with a burnt-out Iraqi tank blocking the runway and pock marks of shells everywhere and I can't believe that one month ago this was a normal place.

The wind whips down the runway, scattering sand. There are no civilians, only Desert Rats, British soldiers, who have secured all four strategic bridges in Basra. They talk about hearts and minds and winning the peoples' trust. They talk about 'liberation' not occupation. But later, in the camp, I quietly speak to a young soldier who says to me in a whisper, 'This is all about George Bush's Texan oil friends, isn't it?'

A few days later, Day 18, the Brits go into Basra. Civilians come out with their hands up, the men in dirty dish-dashes, the children scared. The desert outside my camp has wild camels and if you close your eyes, you might imagine that once this was a different place for the Bedouin or the Marsh Arabs who live north of here. But now, it is an army encampment and life in Iraq will never be the same. The place has the bitter and hostile smell of war.

One afternoon, on the way back to our base, we passed villagers fleeing, wheeling trolleys of too-ripened tomatoes grown in soil rich with depleted uranium, and some clothes hastily put together. The trenches around Basra filled with oil flared, a wall of fire, dug by retreating Iraqis in front of an oil-supply line, which they fractured before setting the spillage alight. The British soldiers say their purpose is to obscure aerial or satellite imagery. But the wall of smoke left an eerie light reflecting the sky, painting the houses which flew white flags overhead a milky colour.

It is so easy to forget people lived here. That there was a time when it was not a war. Driving back to camp, further south, in the fields, some peasants still worked the crops in the midst of the smoke and the thuds, as if they did not know there was any war at all.

I am back in Baghdad. The war is over, but the streets have changed; they're full of young soldiers with suntans, from strange small towns in America.

One marine comes to my room to wash the dust off himself, weeks of desert dirt, using the tubs of water I have stored in my dark bathroom. Still no electricity. Another, even younger, comes to my room looking for some food. I give him a chocolate bar. He chews it thoughtfully.

'Miss,' he says, munching on the weird Iraqi chocolate, much more bitter than the candy he grew up with. 'What is this war about?'

The New Iraq

April, 2003

On a clear spring morning, before the languid heat began to rise off the Tigris, I took a walk though Saddam Hussein's newly liberated Republican Palace. The palace was in disarray. Dirty uniforms of the Republican Guard, presumably stripped off in haste, lay in piles. In kitchens fitted with brand new Slovene refrigerators, packets of spaghetti and open boxes of dates were spilled on counters. Shoes were left abandoned and forlorn on the floors. Upstairs, beds fitted with brand new Egyptian cotton sheets were unmade, the shapes of their former inhabitants still visible in the folds.

The palace was finished in the 1990s and was largely unused, like most of the palaces in Baghdad. But everywhere was the scent of wasted money: from the golden fixtures to the sixty-four bathrooms to the frescoes of horses flying to Jerusalem.

In the basement was a darkened movie theatre. Someone had recently watched a version of *Snow White and the Seven Dwarves* as well as a Ukrainian film from 1983. I was with two colleagues and my interpreter and friend, Hala, a Baghdadi postgraduate student of English who had been, more or less, in a state of shock since the first American troops came rolling around the corner at the Palestine Hotel.

As I pointed out the elaborate grounds or the view from the French windows, Hala would wordlessly shake her head, as if in a dream. Second Lieutenant Joe Peppers, a lanky African-American from Chicago by way of West Point, was leading us through the darkened rooms of the palace with a flashlight. He had the air of a reluctant tour guide at Disney World. He pointed out the huge hallways, the ball-room and Saddam's special balcony.

'That's where he stood,' Peppers said. 'Watching people dance.' It was a macabre thought: Saddam poised motionless on the balcony while his minions were forced to dance beneath him.

The palace was now in the first stages of being taken over by American troops. This was going to be the U.S. 'administrator' General Jay Garner's new home, a palace ringed by bitter orange trees; American soldiers were busy setting up maps where Saddam had once dined, and Special Operations rooms where he once mingled with cronies. They lounged on Saddam's soft chairs, plugging in computers and playing board games.

'Whose house was this?' I asked one. 'Saddam's or his sons'?'

'I don't know,' he said with a smirk. 'Now it's our house.'

Later, we climbed into an army Humvee, littered with remnants of MREs, packets of peanut butter and jalapeño cheese spread, and care packages sent from girlfriends, and drove with Peppers out to the palace's private zoo. A lone lioness, depressed, slunk near the gates and then slunk back to her resting place. There was no sign of the other animals –

the six other lions, the peacocks, the sheep. 'Someone forgot to feed them,' said Peppers, who had brought along his M-16 with them in case the lioness, who belonged to Uday, Saddam's most vicious son, attacked.

As we drove back past manicured gardens and an Italian-style swimming pool half filled with green slime, Hala still did not speak. 'So what you think, Hala?' Joe asked. Throughout the tour he had been kind with her, gently asking what she thought of a certain room or a piece of furniture – sensitive that he was a soldier, an occupier, and she was an Iraqi. Hala usually did not answer, still stunned by the sight of an American marine wandering through her former president's palace.

He prodded her again. 'Your president wasted a lot of people's money, right? All this money – your money – to build these palaces.' Hala dropped her head and said nothing.

She had good reason to be in shock. All through the last days of the regime, from January until mid-March, while I had been reporting from Baghdad, Hala would help translate the often scripted words of ordinary Iraqi people – who could not, out of great fear, speak honestly. When we were alone, we talked about her boyfriend or her life, but we had never mentioned the president. Mostly, I did not enquire because I wanted to protect her. I knew she could not answer, and to put her in that position would be hugely dangerous. There was also my own position: all of the state-appointed 'minders' who followed journalists in Baghdad had to report back to the Ministry of Information and ultimately to the Mukhabarat, the secret police. Small, annoying reminders – notes such as 'Yesterday, you wrote that the uniforms of the soldiers guarding the British Embassy were soiled. The Press

Center is not happy with you' – were a warning to journalists that we were constantly being monitored, and that if we were not careful we would be thrown out of the country. Our telephones were tapped, our hotel rooms installed with secret cameras. It was, I imagined, like working in the USSR during Stalin's times.

Now the fear was gone, at least momentarily. For the first time in nearly thirty years, people could say what they felt. But for Hala, it was still too early. She had worked for the government press service, INA, for years and while she did not have a real stake in the regime, she still had her loyalties and her concerns. The day before the Americans arrived in Baghdad, all of the former bigwigs, including the Information Minister, the infamous Mohammad al-Sahaf, vanished into thin air. Hala was one of the few translators from the old days who stuck around. No matter what she thought of Saddam, she was not going to admit it to an American.

In the car, I asked Peppers why he thought America had gone to war. 'Because of September 11,' he replied. He had lost two friends in the Twin Towers; a small twitch in his face betrayed strong emotions. But there was no known link between al-Qaeda and Saddam Hussein, I said. We went back and forth through the litany of reasons the U.S. government had given for the invasion. It was time to get rid of Saddam, Peppers said finally.

Maybe that was up to the Iraqi people, I said.

Squashed in the front seat of the Humvee, Hala brightened. I saw her smile for the first time in a week. Later, after Peppers dropped us off at the entrance to the palace grounds, she told me, 'You said what was in my heart. What is in the heart of Iraqi people.' She paused and looked back at the long road towards Saddam's palace. 'Maybe he was bad and maybe he did bad things,' she continued, her posture suddenly collapsing and her voice dropping to that pre-war whisper that every Iraqi used in the old days when talking about the regime. 'But it was our choice. Now we are occupied by foreign troops. Do you really think the war is over?'

Perhaps the most difficult aspect of the transition, of that murky road between Saddam and post-Saddam, was not the toppling of the statues or the installation of a new regime, but of Iraqi people finding their voice, like mythological creatures that had been silenced long ago and were now suddenly discovering that they could talk.

Before, no one even mentioned Saddam's name. Now, most Iraqis can't stop talking about him, even though the conversations are still tinged with that old paranoia: 'No names please,' said one man who was telling me a story about how it was in the old days. 'We don't know if Saddam's really gone yet. Until we see his body, we don't know for sure.' My driver, Jazz, a former surgeon who made more money driving taxis or working as a part-time cameraman, said in all seriousness that Saddam might be flying overhead in a secret plane, through the skies above Baghdad, taking notes on citizens; activities for later reprisals after the Americans leave. Such is the hold of fear he had over his people.

When I wandered through the newly opened gates of the famous Abu Ghraib prison, outside Baghdad, I saw the reason for this fear: gallows hanging with ropes where twenty-five people were allegedly hung, twice a week.

In another notorious prison, Haakimiya, belonging to the Iraqi intelligence service, there were other reminders: piles of plastic blindfolds and arm restraints and cassettes of interrogations; cells the size of bathtubs where desperate men punched small holes in the wall for each day they were held, or scratched out last messages to their families: 'To my beloved children.' Or even more desperate: 'Don't give up hope.' And the families didn't. All over the city, I met Iraqis who were still looking for loved ones who had disappeared. Silent for so many years, they would begin to weep, all with the same story: one night, for no reason at all, the secret police had come and taken away their son, their daughter, their husband. At first they had tried to find them. Then a firm hand was laid on their arm and they were told to stop. Their loved ones languished in underground cells, or perhaps they were tortured or killed immediately. The survivors never know. I saw them at Abu Ghraib, I saw them at the headquarters of the Iraqi intelligence agency, clawing through burnt bits of paper, looking for anything that would tell them where their prisoner was. Most of them still believe their relatives are alive. Even if it has been decades, they are still hunting. 'I hope my brother sees this picture,' said one man, an engineer, as a journalist took his picture in front of the gates of Abu Ghraib, beneath the legend, 'There is no life without the sun. There is no dignity without Saddam Hussein.' The man tried to stand proudly for the camera, but tears filled his eyes. His brother, a medical student, had disappeared in 1980.

Most Iraqis are relieved to see all this come to an end. Some welcome the Americans. But there are others who believe that if Saddam were still in power order would at least be restored, that the trains would run on time, Mussolini-style. Everyone wants electricity and oil, but instead they have freckled marines with guns patrolling the streets. It's a delicate time, to say the least. And looking forward, there is an urgent question Iraqis are asking themselves: how will they juxtapose their lives alongside the American presence? This is now their biggest concern. Before the war, a professor of modern political science at Baghdad University who has become a friend of mine, casually joked, 'When you come back after the war, maybe I won't have my job. Maybe there will be an American sitting here in my chair.' Don't be silly, I told him, they don't want your job. 'No, but they want our oil,' he said then. Now it is the thing Iraqis say the most.

Iraqis, already traumatised by years of Saddam and crippling economic sanctions, also fear they will lose their sense of identity and purpose under the Americans. And to them, the occupation is a bitter one, at great cost. 'I can't celebrate liberation with twelve holes in my roof,' my professor friend said, and he lost less than many Iraqis who lost relatives or their entire homes.

'It's a very tender situation for us as well,' one marine commander told me. He had taken up residence with his men at one of Uday Hussein's palaces, Azamiya, on the banks of the Tigris. His men lounged on chairs bearing Saddam Hussein's initials and decorated their work space with Saddam's sculptures of gazelles and ostriches, while snipers perched on the roof. 'We're not the police force,' the commander said. 'We've been given guidelines: leave it to the Iraqi police force.' He sighed heavily, this marine who had fought his way up the Euphrates River and whose unit was the first to fight its way into Baghdad under heavy fire. 'We're here not to fight them, but to assist them,' he said. 'But it's not that easy.'

Iraq is a country that has been occupied and persecuted for centuries: by Mongols, by Turks, by Persians, by the British

and, finally, by the repressive ideology of their own people –
the Ba'ath Party. The history of occupation is deeply em-
bedded in their psyche and, like Afghans, they resist foreigners on their soil; it is the root of the anger expressed by Hala,
and by the thousands who have taken to the streets to protest
against the American presence.

This is the task General Garner faces as he takes a long,
hard look at the future of Iraq: not just weeding out the
Fedayeen resistance fighters, or restoring water and electricity, but capturing a people's 'hearts and minds', as his
predecessors put it in South-East Asia so many decades ago.

The day the statue of Saddam came down with the help of
some hefty American marines in Fidros Square, I had run
from the cheering crowd up to the roof of the Palestine Hotel
to watch a group of youths drag the bronze head of Saddam
down a side-street by a rope, like a dog on a leash. 'Holy shit,'
said a marine standing next to me, leaning off the edge,
watching this bizarre moment. 'Holy shit.'

An Iraqi cameraman from NBC was watching too. He
stared wordlessly at the crowd dragging the lifeless head.

That night, in the small third-floor room of my friend,
Melinda Liu, a *Newsweek* reporter, we got tipsy with a few
of the marines from Bravo Company 1st Tank Battalion, 3rd
Battalion, 4th Marines. Among them were the soldiers who
had helped drape the rope around Saddam's neck like a
noose.

Melinda and I had met them in the grim darkness of the
Palestine dining room; the kind manager, who had earlier
gone to the marines asking for protection of the hotel
('Please, sir, we have foreign journalists here') had laid on
an unappetising feast of hamburgers, Iraqi-style, in honour of

the marines, and they were crowing in amazement at the food. Fresh from the desert, they marvelled at the fatty meat, the rancid ketchup, the limp cucumbers grown in soil rich from uranium from the previous Gulf war. They ate and talked and then they pulled local cigarettes out of their pockets and smoked happily.

Later, they came up to the room and took cold-water showers, washing away weeks of grit and sand. They called their wives, their grandfathers and their mothers on our satellite phones.

'Hey, baby, it's me, your husband,' shouted one, out on the balcony overlooking Fidros Square. 'That was me up there on the statue with the rope. Did you see me on CNN?'

'Oh my Gawd!' his wife shouted back in California, loud enough so that we too could hear it through the phone. 'That was you?'

'That was me, baby,' said her proud twenty-seven-year-old husband. Then the marines sat down and started drinking hard. Gin and Coke. The last of a bottle of pre-war vodka mixed with some rancid orange juice. Whiskey and mineral water in dirty, Palestine Hotel bathroom tumblers. They weren't drinkers, but it had been three bad weeks, battling north, through the Basra Road, through al-Nasiriya, through al-Kut, finally taking the turn over the bridge in their tanks that brought them here, to the east side of Baghdad. The alcohol went to their heads fast. First they talked about going home and going surfing in the Pacific Ocean, boards strapped to their cars. Then they started talking about the war.

Sand, bodies, burials, blood, guns. Tanks. The claustrophobia of being inside a tank, inside a chemical warfare suit in scalding desert heat. Fear. What it looked like to see an Iraqi soldier pointing a gun right at you.

The freshness on their newly cleaned faces began to vanish. 'I didn't want to pull that trigger, but the Ex-O' – executive officer – 'made me,' said one, who looked like a younger version of Ben Affleck and was, in fact, a member of the Screen Actors Guild, having had some minor acting roles.

He had been the gunner of his tank, the guy with his head above the parapet, every day, every night. His hand, now fixed around a glass of gin, was shaking slightly. 'It was hard, really hard. Civilians mixed up with soldiers. Soldiers taking off their uniforms. You just didn't know who you were hitting.' The gunner's voice was anguished. Twenty minutes earlier, he had been talking about the glory of the marines.

His buddies joined in. 'My grandfather was in Guadalcanal. My father in Korea. My uncle in Vietnam. And me in Baghdad,' said one. But the gunner was still stuck on one instance when he feared he might have made a mistake and killed an innocent Iraqi. Or possibly more than one.

'I told you to pull the trigger and you pulled it,' said his Ex-O firmly, pouring himself another gin. 'You had to do it. You had orders. There were fighters there, in the crowd.'

'I know,' said the gunner glumly. 'But I didn't want to.'

Another marine talked about discovering pieces of nuclear parts, he said, shiny and new and imported. He talked about a chemical weapons site, allegedly not far from where we were sitting. 'He could have nuked us all,' he said. 'That's what it's all about, isn't it? Saddam's weapons?' No one said anything.

'If you want the truth, I'm not sure what it's all about,' said the Ex-O, mercifully passing out on the bed.

Every war has a human face, a victim who becomes a symbol expressing the suffering and the misery, the heartlessness of battle. Often, that victim is a child. In Vietnam, it was a young girl, running naked down a road scorched by napalm, her terror and agony captured in an indelible photograph. In Bosnia, it was a girl called Irma, who received extensive brain damage when a Serbian shell landed in front of her apartment while she was outside playing. While a few of us hardcore reporters who made up the Sarajevo press corps tried desperately for years to bring the suffering of the Bosnian people into the public eye in the hope of affecting policy, it was a bunch of British tabloid journalists, flown in for a few days, who succeeded in getting the message across by using 'Little Irma' to tell the story of the war.

In Baghdad, it was Ali Ismail Abbas, a twelve-year-old who had lost his arms and had thirty-five per cent first and second degree burns covering his torso, slowly rotting, literally, on the third floor of Saddam General Hospital. A missile had hit his house in the middle of the night while he and his family slept.

Ali was already reluctantly famous, his photograph occupying a two-page spread in *Time*, his pain recounted when I first saw him, lying on dirty sheets with a medieval contraption fitted over his body so that the blankets did not touch his open sores. Not knowing what else to say, I told him, 'You are very brave,' and his face crumbled.

'I want my hands' he said.

Despite the fact that he had been telling his story to journalists and camera crews for a week, Ali still talked to me, grief catching in his voice, about the missile, about his sheets catching fire, about his five-months pregnant mother and his father, both dead, and about his favourite brother Abbas, also dead, and how they liked to play football together. He talked of his six half-sisters – by his father's second wife – also injured and missing. He talked about fishing, swimming, both things he could never do again.

'How can I do that without my hands?' he asked. He began to cry. Hala, who was by my side, told him that there were many things that could be done with science now, many ways that he could get his hands back. She tried to soothe him. 'I just want them back,' he said, trying to muster the last bit of strength in his tiny, ruined body.

The director of the hospital, which lay under siege from looters and was the last functioning hospital in Baghdad, was a Chaldean Christian named Mowafek Gorea. He sat at his desk, exhausted, an untouched glass of water in front of him. A surgeon, he had not left the hospital for twenty-three days and had neither seen his family nor had word from them. Now, he was organising civil protection for the hospital, letting armed men wearing doctors' scrubs to protect it from the crowds outside who wanted to strip the sheets, the machines, the medicines. The hospital is in the sprawling, festering neighbourhood of Saddam City, which before the Saddam days had been called Revolution City, largely because it was home to one million poverty stricken Shias. Hostile before the war, it was now a mini-Beirut. Ali, while tragic, was just one of the many problems Dr Gorea had to deal with.

I asked what could be done for Ali. 'He has had so many promises,' Gorea said, referring to the offers of help Ali had received from other journalists. 'He will die before those promises are fulfilled.'

The American marines, whose rockets had destroyed Ali's life, did not yet know about his plight, and I pushed through the checkpoints to their headquarters at the Palestine Hotel to tell them about it. The medical liaison officer, a man whose task was to try to restore order to the looted and gutted hospitals, was a young and blond petty officer from San Diego named Ed Martin. A GP who had been married only two months, Martin had only arrived in Baghdad the week before and was quickly adjusting to the chaos outside the hotel lobby – the robbers with chairs and office equipment marching triumphantly down the street; the hospitals with doctors under siege or running away in terror of the crowds – and the strange new feeling of trying to walk a delicate balance between being a liberator (the American term) and an occupier (the Iraqi one).

When I told Martin and another marine about Ali, they listened but were apprehensive. One of them said, 'If he's got thirty-five per cent burns on his body, I have to tell you, it's not good odds.'

'I know it's sad,' Martin – who saw that I was trying not to cry – added gently. 'But there's a lot of civilians who have been injured. This is war time.'

I took Martin aside and told him that Ali was now famous and that if he died, it would be a public relations disaster for the marines. Cynical, yes, but it worked. Martin said he would try to do something, even though, he insisted, an evacuation of Ali would be 'way up the chain of command for me'. A few days later, he asked if he could meet with Gorea. I drove to Saddam City, through checkpoints of armed civilians, to deliver the message.

The hospital was in chaos. A crowd of men were unloading corpses from trucks and a crowd, furious and desperate, were shouting, pushing and waving guns and long knives. Every once in a while, a bloody and broken body, caught in the crossfire, was brought through the guarded gates – a sign the war was not over. Inside Dr Gorea's office were two sheiks, one in a black turban, one in white, who were guarding the hospital and who tried to order me out. Gorea wearily let me in and told me to sit. He listened when I explained that the marines were willing to evacuate Ali to a hospital ship, but Gorea frowned slightly.

'You have seen one Ali,' he said. 'But there are many Alis.' Still, he agreed to meet Martin at the Palestine. Then he wrote me two notes, one giving permission to evacuate Ali, and another one that said: 'Dear Sir, Good day. We have wounded people in our hospital. Please do not attack our ambulances. Some armed people are here to protect us. Best regards, Dr. Mowafek Gorea. Consultant Surgeon.'

'Give this to the marines,' he said. 'They keep shooting at us.' He told me that an American tank had rammed the back door of the hospital. 'Next time, knock,' Gorea had told the surprised marine colonel.

Later that day, Gorea and I met outside the Palestine and I led him through the barbed wire and the checkpoints, the barrier between the marines and the crowd of angry Iraqis demanding electricity and water and jobs. A young marine searched him, running his hands down Gorea's soiled white lab coat.

'I don't have a bomb,' Gorea said, trying to make a tired joke. For a second I felt his humiliation: an accomplished Christian Iraqi who was being patted down by a twenty-two-year-old from California, a man who was no longer at home in his own country.

At the meeting with Martin, Gorea looked out of place and very small in the darkened room full of huge marines in desert combat gear. It was immediately clear that something had gone wrong, that the premise of the meeting had been knocked askew. Gorea had changed his mind about evacuating Ali. The boy, he said, was no longer at risk of septi-caemia and should stay in Baghdad where he would not be traumatised by a move. He was cordial but firm; ultimately, he was the director of the hospital.

Martin politely asked questions. Had septicaemia started? Was Ali getting fluids via an IV? What about antibiotics?

'We have everything in the hospital, including a sterile unit,' said Gorea impatiently, ending the conversation. I was stunned. The unit was not sterile. The only sterile thing about it was that visitors had to pull on dirty white boots over their shoes. Anyone was allowed in, without masks. The day before Gorea had told me that Ali's chance of survival were low. He had agreed the best place for him was abroad. What had happened?

Martin, also baffled, reckoned that Gorea's change of heart was due to either pride or politics.

The latter was correct. In the twisted world of post-war Iraq, politics were at work, even if they involved a twelve-year-old boy without arms. The Iraqis, most notably, the Shia sheiks guarding the hospital, did not want the Americans to appear like heroes, rescuing a child that they had brutally wounded. 'Why should they appear as good guys?' one Shia who was guarding the hospital would say to me later.

'Don't you think the Americans want this chaos?' Gorea asked me sheepishly. 'So that they can appear like heroes making it better?' He asked me, as did many Iraqis, why the marines were not protecting the museums or the national library, instead only guarding the Ministry of Oil.

Ali eventually did get out. Martin came to my door at the hotel late one afternoon, smiling brightly, and said the military ambulance was on his way to pick him up. I genuinely believed Martin had worked so hard on Ali's case not for the sake of PR, but out of humanity.

I rushed to the third floor of Saddam General, past the belligerent armed sheiks and the crowds of weeping relatives, and saw Ali as he was being led away, surrounded by cameras, an armless media star with a green shower cap on his curls. I searched and searched, but Dr. Gorea was nowhere to be found.

I left a few days later, driving through the western desert, during the early morning light. I was tired after nearly four months of non-stop tension. When I left, I had no way of knowing how far Baghdad would descend into anarchy. When I would return, fourteen months later, it would be wearing an abbaya and not being able to travel to certain parts of the city for fear of being kidnapped. Most of my friends were gone. There were no more long afternoons eating grilled fish by the Tigris. There was just the thud of distant mortars and the constant sadness of the defeated city.

The Fate of Iraqi Women

September, 2004

Shortly after the fall of the Taliban in November, 2001, I was stopped on Chicken Street in Kabul by three young women wearing sky-blue burkas. They were friendly and curious. They wanted to know why I was not wearing something that covered me from head to toe.

I responded by asking them why they were still wearing burkas. The Taliban had been gone for weeks, I reminded them. Behind the grey mesh that covered their eyes, I saw their admonishment.

'They explained that it was for safety. It was either that, or stay at home and disappear from society.

I kept thinking of that day in Kabul when I returned to Baghdad, a city I once knew well, after an absence of fifteen months. During that time I had become a mother, and my Iraqi women friends had become enslaved.

Iraq had once been the most progressive country in the Middle East in terms of women's rights. An outspoken British Arabist, Gertrude Bell, had drawn the map of modern Iraq in the 1920s, gaining unprecedented access to sheiks and chieftains and inspiring an entire generation of Iraqi women who saw her as a feminist icon. And there were other role models: the first Women's League in the Middle East was established in Iraq in 1952, and Iraq was the first Arab country to have a female Cabinet Minister seven years later.

But forty-five years on, that progress has been brutally halted. It is partly due to the lack of security and the lawlessness on the streets since the fall of Saddam Hussein. It is also due to the rise of radical Islamists, formerly suppressed under Saddam, who regard the new Iraq as a synonym for promiscuity. They seek a return to the tribal ways in which men dominate society and women are treated like subversives.

'It is terrible to say,' one of my friends, a philosophy student at Baghdad University, told me wearily as she pulled a veil over her head to go out on the street, 'but women's lives were actually better under Saddam.'

It is a loaded statement, but there is some truth to this. By September, 2004, the streets of Baghdad are so unsafe that few women come out of their houses. There are calls for sharia – Islamic religious law – to be written into the Iraqi constitution by major Shia clerics. University women are harassed on campus for not wearing a veil.

Honour killings, though radically reduced in neighbouring Jordan, have risen dramatically – up to one a day throughout the country. Prostitution, once punishable by beheading under Saddam, has soared, and with it unwanted pregnancies. Then come backstreet abortion clinics, like something out of 1950s England.

Healthcare under Saddam suffered due to economic sanctions, but the clinics and maternity units I visited that specialised in women's care seemed worse off than before the war. According to Hana Edwar, a Christian Iraqi who runs al-Amal, an NGO focusing on conflict resolution, breast and ovarian cancer are on the rise.

Economic conditions are desperate. Although most Iraqi families get government food packages each month, every family I visited complained that they had had a better quality of life before March, 2003, and many of the women suffered from anaemia and typhoid.

But far worse is the sense of fear for personal safety that did not exist before. People feared Saddam and his gruesome sons, Uday and Qusay, and quivered at the sound of his name, but ordinary Iraqis could still walk down Haifa Street without fear of getting kidnapped or blown up by a car bomb, which is not the case anymore.

Now, women are afraid to leave their front gardens. Children, particularly girls, are not being sent to school. Kidnapping is the gravest anxiety, not only for Western journalists and contractors, but also for ordinary Iraqis who are being nabbed by opportunist thugs looking for easy cash. Christians are particularly vulnerable as they are perceived to have more money. There are rampant stories of women abducted and sold as prostitutes in one of the Gulf states or Yemen.

What startled me most was how the quality of my friends' lives had dissipated with the so-called liberation. One sweltering afternoon, I drove to a leafy western neighbourhood to visit friends, a forty-five-year-old British-educated chemical engineer called Sajeeda.

Before the war, I had frequently visited their home and eaten dinner with Sajeeda, her husband and her three daughters. Their comfortable house, set back in a lush garden, was respite for me from the paranoia of working in Saddam's Ministry of Information. But since the war, Sajeeda's husband had gotten a job working for a Western company as a translator. His Shia neighbours, increasingly fuelled by Islamists, accused him of collaborating with the coalition forces and sent him written death threats. He fled to Jordan and communicates with the family via email.

Sajeeda copes alone and complained bitterly about it. She had aged rapidly since my last visit, and warned that if her neighbours spotted me, I was not only putting myself at risk of kidnapping but putting her and her girls in great danger. So we arranged the visit with military precision. I arrived in an abaya and she stood at the front gate and whisked me inside the courtyard the minute my car door opened.

Sajeeda then recounted stories of her women friends being mugged, attacked or threatened for walking on the street. Her eighteen-year-old daughter tearfully told me her best friend had been kidnapped in March. The rumour going around her school was that Iraqi gangs took young girls to Kuwait to sell them as sex slaves, and the teenager clung to me in tears. Her mother begged me to find her a place at an English university in the winter. 'Otherwise, I am not sure I can protect her,' she said.

Hana Edwar said that these cases were typical, that assassinations, muggings, attacks and abductions on women were commonplace since the fall of Saddam.

'The security is terrible for me, women and children,' she said. 'The perpetuators want to terrify: people have to come under their umbrella to be protected. They control people by making them afraid.'

The morning we met, two friends of Edwar's, young

Italian aid workers, had been kidnapped when armed men stormed their office in broad daylight. Edwar was noticeably agitated.

'No one is safe anymore,' she said, motioning to the streets where angry mobs were moving towards a mosque to stage an anti-coalition protest, which would eventually turn bloody. From behind her gated house, Edwar served coffee in elegant little cups but described how more women were forced to wear the veil.

'They feel they must wear one,' she says. 'Or they stay home. It's horrifying because it exiles our women from public life.'

Given the grim prognosis, there aren't many Iraqi feminists wandering around Baghdad. So it is almost shocking to find Yanar Mohammed, a forty-two-year-old who wears jeans and red lipstick instead of an abaya, working out of a dusty office on al-Za'ain Street. Mohammed is one of the leaders of the Organisation of Iraqi Women's Freedom, which tries to help women who are under threat from honour killings.

It's a brave thing to try to do. But there is a price to pay for this courage. Mohammed can't go anywhere without bodyguards and she has had so many death threats that she has lost count of them.

Aside from the jeans and the sleeveless T-shirt which exposes her tanned arms, Mohammed's crime is that she has set up safe houses throughout Iraq for women who have run away from families planning to murder them. Most of the women simply fell in love with someone outside their tribe, or got pregnant before they were married, bringing shame on their families. The stories that Mohammed tells are predictably terrible: of women mutilated and hacked up by their own brothers, their heads thrown out on the street for everyone to see, their hands amputated and proudly displayed as proof of their murder by their fathers.

'The men are then applauded not only by their families but by society, as keepers of the family honour,' Mohammed says bitterly. She feels the number of honour killings in Iraq has risen dramatically since the invasion because of depravation, poverty and isolation due to years of economic sanctions.

'That, combined with years of Ba'athist repression, has ended the heritage of the Iraqi women's movement,' she says.

She says that, ironically, more women are returning to wearing the headscarves that even their grandmothers chose not to wear. And more are returning to the traditional arranged marriages.

'When I was younger,' she says, 'my mother wore miniskirts. She married my father for love. Now, we have the veil. And a return to tribalism.'

Mohammed feels the only way to counteract this suppression of women is to raise awareness, to open more shelters, to get more support from other women.

But in a country where women are afraid to come outside, it is difficult. The day we met, Mohammed spent the day accompanied by her bodyguards, putting up posters around Baghdad for a demonstration calling for safer streets for women. Last year, at a similar rally she organised for International Women's Day, more than one thousand women turned up. This year, Mohammed thinks only a handful will come. 'It's just so unsafe outside,' she frets.

Mohammed is right. The day of the demonstration, she gets a sad turnout. A handful of women join her, then rush home.

A few days later, I go to visit one of the former members of the Iraqi Governing Council, Dr Salama Khafalji, who now is a member of the Iraqi Assembly and has been credited with helping to negotiate the first Najaf truce.

A forty-six-year-old former dental surgeon, Khafalji lives in a bunker rather than a house: The entrance is guarded by burly men with Kalashnikovs and one must navigate through sandbagged tunnels to find the door. A shot-up car sits in the driveway, glass still spread across the seats, along with dried blood, the windows blown out.

It is a painful reminder of the attack on Khafalji's life as her convoy drove from Najaf to Baghdad last May. Khafalji lost a bodyguard in that attack, and her beloved seventeen-year-old son, Ahmed.

'He was trying to protect his mother,' she says in her book-lined office, her face still a map of grief. 'He was trying to save me, and he died.'

Khafalji does not know why she was targeted, or why, for that matter, her colleague in the Governing Council, Aquila al-Hashimi, a former French professor, was murdered last September. 'There is no order, no law,' she says quietly.

When I ask Khafalji why she was nearly assassinated last May, she replies that she suspects it is because she is a woman doing a man's job and because she is trying to rebuild Iraq.

'These people who are against peace want chaos,' she says.

Later that day, I visit a maternity ward in Sadr City, the festering Shia slum where an American gunship had fired on crowds the day before. Inside the filthy maternity ward, three women have just given birth in the middle of such violence. One has a little boy, two others have tiny girls.

'It's an easier life for the boys,' said one of the exhausted mothers – who gave birth without the benefit of an epidural because there are none.

But others have some hope. 'Remember that we Iraqi

women endured the darkest days of Saddam, so maybe we can get through this,' Sajeeda told me when I left her house. Hana Edwar is hopeful that once security returns to the streets, the veil will become obsolete. 'When things get normal, women will take off their veils,' she said.

Edwar also points out that at the Iraqi National Conference held in August, twenty-five per cent of the nominees were women. 'That's unique in Arab countries,' she says. 'Out of one hundred members of the National Assembly, twenty-five are women. It's something great.'

And when I say goodbye to Sajeeda's nervous eighteen-year-old daughter, she says she wants to go to school in England so she can come back to her country with some lessons of life.

'I'm never going to let a man dominate me,' she says defiantly. 'I'm going to be strong, and teach other women to do the same.'

The Professor from Baghdad

February, 2005

In the strange, dark days before the war in Iraq began, I met a professor at the University of Baghdad. Mahdi was a scholar of modern history and political science, an Anglophile who had studied at the University of Reading in the 1980s. His speciality was the British occupation of Iraq. He had a BBC accent and wild, frizzled hair: the caricature of a mad English professor.

After a short conversation, he invited me home to meet his wife and three daughters. He wrote down an address and drew a map of the northern neighbourhood of Adhamiya on the back of my notebook. This was a shock. Even the government-appointed 'minder', who reported my activities back to the Ministry of Information on a daily basis, was stunned. In those days, few Iraqis mixed with foreigners. For a quarter of a century, Saddam had driven twenty-five million people into desperate submission: most were frightened simply mentioning his name. A foreigner at home was unthinkable.

But Mahdi was warm and cheerful. He had a prized

collection of British documents from the 1920s, he said, and his wife had learned how to cook in England.

There was nothing remarkable about our exchange except that we were not in a normal place in normal times. An invasion by US forces was inevitable. All of Baghdad was terrified. As I was leaving, I passed a dark hallway heaving with surplus supplies: sacks of beans and rice, wool blankets, plastic water containers.

'It looks like you're ready for a long war,' I said.

Mahdi laughed, with a knowing confidence. 'They'll never get to Baghdad' he said. I left. In another time, we might not have ever met again.

But we did. And within weeks, Baghdad was sealed off by a ring of Saddam's elite Iraqi troops protecting it against foreign invaders. Bombs began falling on the capital, pelting government buildings, communications centres and, unfortunately, markets where Baghdadis did their shopping. The city of Scheherazade slid into chaos. And so did the lives of its inhabitants, many of whom had lived double lives for many years. This is what happened to Mahdi.

His old life, old secrecy and the fierce loyalty that kept the Saddam machine oiled and running for more than two decades would fall away. He would be exposed as a powerful Ba'athist, not just a simple professor who loved all things British. The bright, friendly house where I ate dinners and sipped tea and discussed Iraqi history would disappear, and the family within would cease being Baghdadis.

Life would never be the same again.

Adhamiya is one of the oldest districts of Baghdad, established after the burial of Iraq's greatest imam, Abu Hanifa An-Nu'man. Originally inhabited by Sunni tribes who came to protect the imam from Persian invaders, it was nearly all Sunni Muslims before the war. Now it is rife with insurgents, former Ba'athists and die-hard Saddam supporters.

There is a strong link between Saddam and Adhamiya. He had built a palace nearby, and many of his lackeys lived in the surrounding neighbourhoods. He was last seen by the local population on 10 April, 2003, standing on the roof of a car outside a coffee shop called Al Nu'man, calling on his followers to never give up.

After the fall of Baghdad, Adhamiya became the site of fierce fighting. In the tense days immediately after the statue of Saddam was toppled, I remember the crackle of gunfire and rockets from American helicopters. The streets where I had walked were covered in rubble and broken glass. Terrified residents cowered in doorways. The little shop where I had once bought sweets for Mahdi's four girls was boarded up and deserted.

But in February, 2003, there was not yet fighting and the winding street where the family lived looked pleasantly suburban. Neighbours were polite teachers, doctors, an airline pilot for Iraqi Air. Inside the house were two dogs, four neat little girls speaking perfect English, a roast chicken laid on a neatly set table. I sat with Fatima, the seven-year-old, on my lap and watched Iraqi news.

Aliya, Mahdi's wife, was a former chemical engineer who had given up her job shortly after Fatima was born. The couple had met through their families; it was an arranged marriage, Mahdi told me later, but there was real love between them. Together they left for England in the 1980s, and taped to an old photo album, Mahdi proudly showed me a fading Polaroid of the two of them on a foggy street. They were wearing raincoats and holding their eldest daughter, Aqila.

The family were devout Shias – rare in Adhamiya – and when they drove me home in Mahdi's new Peugeot, Aliya abruptly pulled a headscarf over her hair. 'Not at home,' she said, by way of explanation, 'but on the street, always.'

In those days, Saddam's paranoia had reached an all time high. It was difficult to operate. My hotel and office were bugged. A minder followed me constantly. My phone line was tapped. If I tried to have a conversation with someone in a hotel, we had to turn on the television so that music drowned out our words. It was exhausting and terrifying. The Mahdis, in the midst of this madness, symbolised a normal family life for me. We met in local restaurants or I visited them at home. I trusted them, and in Baghdad in those days, it was difficult to find trust.

My days with the family were different. I would sit on the floor with Fatima as she coloured and felt like I was not in a city that was about to be destroyed. Or I would lie on the bed in the pink bedroom with the poster of the Backstreet Boys taped to the mirror, where Zeinab and Aqila slept and talk to them about their friends, their books and clothes. I listened to Aliya fret about how to keep Zeinab, who was fifteen and diabetic, calm during the bombing raids, and how we could preserve her insulin if the electricity was cut.

And I worried about them. One afternoon, I came to visit with a small generator as a gift, but Mahdi proudly told me that he had solved the insulin problem.

'I'm digging a hole in the garden with my neighbour,' he said. 'It will be so deep, we'll hit water. Then we can lower her insulin down with ropes.' It touched me that a professor who could quote obscure English politicians from the 1930s had to resort to a medieval measure to keep his sick daughter's medicine intact.

I suppose that if I were not so involved with the family – their daily life and their concerns and grievances – I might have been more observant and suspected there was more to this family than I thought. But the fact was, I simplistically believed that they were too kind, too generous, too loving, too normal to be Ba'athists. Ba'athists to me were evil, and this family was anything but that.

I felt on a very deep level that I could trust them. So much so that as life at my hotel grew more paranoid, and children began appearing on the street filling sandbags against the coming bombing, and there was talk that foreign journalists would be rounded up and shot, I asked if I could come and hide with the family.

Mahdi hesitated – it was a dangerous thing to ask an Iraqi to hide a foreigner. But his face softened. 'Of course you can,' he said.

When I think back carefully, I remember the slight look of panic – or was it fear? – that crossed his wife's face.

Like everyone, the family calmly began to prepare for another bombardment. Food, tea and soap issued by the government was being stored in a cupboard under the stairs; empty 7-UP bottles were being filled with water. There was a small oil cooking stove to make bread; there were batteries for the radio and extra blankets and flashlights. The windows were being re-enforced with tape and breakable items stored.

But despite that, the last few days of Saddam's Baghdad seemed weirdly alive. The souks were full of people buying aspirin and bandages. The churches and mosques were full.

Saddam was on television urging civilians to dig shelters in their gardens. There was a last-minute rush of weddings, a faux optimism, and the joyful dancing music played late into the night.

'Maybe it won't happen and we can go on with our lives,' Zeinab said, tearfully.

'Oh, it's gonna happen,' Aqila added.

A few days later, the bombs began to fall.

In the days after Saddam fell, I tried to find the al-Windawis. But their neighbourhood had been heavily bombed and was on the route that the Americans took when they rolled into Baghdad in tanks and Humvees at forty miles per hour. The day before, I had driven to Adhamiya, but there was still fierce fighting: some Fedayeen holed up in a mosque. I abandoned the car and set off on foot through glass-en-crusted alleys, but got turned back by the whirl and screech of a fighter plane about to launch an air strike on the neighbourhood.

The next day, I found the house. Mahdi was at the gate. His hair was standing on end; he was dressed in rumpled clothes. But he was smiling.

'Oh my God, it's you!' he said. The family had spent the last days of the bombing in the countryside and he was examining the damage to the house: twelve holes in the roof. The dogs were still alive, he said, and no one had been hurt.

Inside, Fatima was lying on the floor, oblivious to the protective sheets still hanging over the furniture, drawing. She was in exactly the same place I had left her the last time I saw her, but the difference was her artwork. Before the war, she had made me elaborate drawings of women with stick-out, 1950s style skirts, or gigantic daisies.

'Draw me a lady,' I said. She smiled, but kept drawing a soldier with a gun and what looked like a gunner.

Aliya stood above her, frowning. 'Fatima, what about the ladies?' she said. 'Can't you draw something else?'

Fatima ignored us both. She kept on drawing bombers.

Aqila was in the garden. She had lost one of her closest friends during the bombing, and was angry. 'I went through the bombing of 1991 and 1998, but this was different,' she said. 'It was the end of something.'

Upstairs, the frilly bedroom was the same. She handed me a diary that she had kept during the war, a plain, wire-bound school notebook, written in Arabic. We sat on the bed for a few hours as she translated her words. It started out about her sense of chaos as she and her family fled the house; her sense of sadness at losing her friend. Then it showed the fear she felt for the future, and the sense of losing her old life forever.

APRIL 12

I see an American soldier, he's around my age. He's got beautiful sunglasses. When I get close, I see he is really handsome. But at the same time, he is my enemy. I tell Dad that if he comes near us, I hope he will be friendly – but I think he's probably a monster. What's inside of him? Is he afraid of us? Does he think we want to harm him?

Mahdi took me to a friend's house, a vast stone and brick ranch-style villa. Inside, a wide screen was lit up with CNN and I watched, in amazement, as Wolf Blitzer reported from Kuwait. Where had this family obtained a satellite dish? I was shocked. There was even a fax machine in this house, totally unheard of for ordinary Iraqis who were not connected to either the regime or the black market. When I asked the friend, he did not answer directly. 'There are ways to do everything,' he mumbled.

As if to prove he was just like everyone else, Mahdi's friend told a story about a friend who was on a trip to the Far East and casually mentioned to a stranger how rough life in Iraq was. When he got back to Baghdad, he was stunned to be hauled into prison, beaten, interrogated and thrown into jail. Saddam was everywhere, the man was telling me. Even in a pool in a nice hotel in Singapore.

Later, I would understand what he was not saying: that it was far easier to swim alongside Saddam than to try to go the opposite direction.

Meanwhile, Aqila was becoming a reluctant celebrity. Shortly after excerpts from her diary appeared in a famous western newspaper, an editor at a prestigious publishing house contacted me in Baghdad. Beth (not her real name) wanted Aqila to continue her diary, to describe life not only during the war but in the newly occupied Iraq. She wanted to promote Aqila as an Iraqi Anne Frank. Such a book had real potential.

It was exciting news and I drove to the family's house with my Thuraya satellite phone and let Mahdi speak directly to Beth, and to a literary agent in London who agreed to represent the family.

Within weeks, Aqila was offered a publishing contract for more money than I earn in a year, more than her dad earned in ten. At the same time, Baghdad was rapidly descending into anarchy: looting; revenge crimes; the nascent insurgents beginning to stage attacks. Mass graves were being discovered and families were hunting down the people who had turned in their disappeared family members to the Ba'athists. I watched people claw the dirt at Abu Ghraib prison, believing their loved ones were still alive in some secret vault under the ground.

At the al-Kinder Hospital, I met doctors who were running away leaving wounded patients bleeding on stretchers in the hallways, in Saddam (now Sadr) City, I watched the mullahs take control of the neighbourhoods, and people arming themselves with guns against street to street fighting. Roadblocks were being hastily set up by renegade militias: anyone with a gun had power.

At the end of summer, Aqila was going off to America, to write her book and to study at an Ivy League university.

In retrospect, she must have known that her old life – the one that was comfortably padded by Saddam – was going to come to an abrupt halt.

The first sign of trouble came as Aqila's book neared completion. The final manuscript was not what the publisher had expected: the journal of a young girl in a war-scarred country. Instead, someone – and Beth believed it was Mahdi – had been standing over Aqila's shoulder dictating fierce political rhetoric. Most of it was anti-American, and did not fit in with the Anne Frank image the publisher wanted.

I sent Mahdi an email and gently prodded him to let Aqila write the diary by herself. He emailed back, joking that he was 'too much a teacher'. He said he was working with two producers at an American television network. A few weeks later, he wrote to me asking to help him get a UK visa. I was sure the publisher would be happy to oblige their star writer's father.

But when I phoned Beth, there was a terrible silence.

Then she broke it. 'We're not sure we want him here,' she said, sounding pained. She said a letter had arrived at the office from an Iraqi civilian warning them that Mahdi was not a professor at the university – but a former agent in Saddam's regime. One of his brothers was an important general. The two of them had caused suffering and pain to ordinary Iraqis. They were not like Anne Frank's hunted family at all – in fact, they were the hunters.

I remember reading that letter in my little office in Notting Hill, thousands of miles from Baghdad. I was three months pregnant and emotionally worlds apart from my old life in Iraq. Still, my first reaction was shock. My second was to feel slightly ill, as though – and the cliché really is true – I had been punched in the stomach. My third was to feel a cold rush of fear, real fear. How much had Mahdi known about me? Had he played me from the beginning, from that first meeting at the University of Baghdad? Was I watched more closely than I thought?

And I was angry. Betrayal is a strange thing, especially when deep trust is involved. And for reasons I still do not understand, Beth had not told me about the letter for several months. She rather naively disregarded the writer as a jealous Iraqi. 'You've got to take this information seriously,' I said, trying to control my anger. 'Do you understand how serious this is?'

'Even if it is true, the daughter is not responsible for the sins of the father,' Beth responded calmly. But she sounded wary.

Part of her problem was that the publisher was overexcited about Aqila's book and was hailing it as 'a very personal account of what life has been like for ordinary Iraqis during the recent war and its chaotic aftermath'. They were hoping for big sales, especially amongst school children and teen-agers. But if the rumour was true, the family were far from being ordinary Iraqis. And Aqila's dad worked for the equivalent of the Gestapo.

When I saw that the publisher would rather not deal with the issue, I turned to a private security contact, a former British officer working in Iraq, to see what he could find. It took him about a week to get back to me. His message was short and curt: 'Our man was truly a general in Security Service (Al-Amen Al-A'ma). He has also a brother who is a high-ranking army officer . . . Sorry that I could not confirm that he was not involved, I have chatted to my agent and it would be obvious that he was up to his neck in supporting the regime etc etc.'

I trusted my source, but I did a second check, through a well-connected Sunni friend. I asked her to go to her cousin, a high-ranking security officer. I told her to just mention Mahdi's name.

'He's my colleague!' her cousin shrieked. 'We worked together at the Security Service for years.'

I phoned Beth again with the information. She said coldly, 'Most Iraqis had to do what they did to survive.' She did, however, ask Aqila to note in her introduction that her father worked for 'the government'. But there was no mention of what he had actually done during the Saddam years. There was no apology or reference to the widespread and hideous human rights abuse that had occurred under the regime of which he was a part.

I suddenly remembered Mahdi's neighbour with the wide-screen television. I remembered how surprised I was that an Iraqi professor had singled me out, invited me to his home. It now made sense that he was connected to the regime and had the immunity to invite a foreigner home. I remembered how Mahdi had left Iraq to study in Britain at a time when Saddam allowed few Iraqis out of the country. Clearly, when he returned, he had a debt to pay.

Journalists make mistakes, but usually we trust our instincts. It was my instincts that kept me alive when Grozny fell in February, 2000, and I needed to get out of Chechnya before I got slaughtered by Russian forces. In Bosnia, my colleagues and I stayed alive only by trusting our instincts about whether to travel down certain roads or not. I was angry but also baffled: how had I managed to let myself get so taken in? Perhaps he was a better agent than I was giving him credit for; an arch manipulator.

I was still unclear exactly what he had done. If he had been an informer within his neighbourhood, he could have been responsible for the deaths of dozens, perhaps hundreds of people. I thought about all the Shia families I had seen after the war first discovering the news that their disappeared relatives were dead and buried in mass graves. I remember asking one of the mothers of a man who never returned home if she ever found out how he died. She said what was worse was that she did not know who turned him in.

'You never knew who you were talking to in the Saddam days,' she said.

I wondered if Mahdi could have done things like that, even if he was forced to for the sake of protecting his own family. I decided, I hoped, he had not.

After the fall of Baghdad, the security services disintegrated. Documents were shredded or stolen or wound up in the hands of anti-Saddam Iraqi National Congress members who were hoping to put together cases in the war crimes tribunal. The highest officers disappeared, some slipping over borders; others were absorbed into the community. Some flaunted their old connections. One Mukhabarat officer who worked in the Ministry of Information ended up working for a right wing American television network.

One sweltering afternoon, I went to a building I never thought I would ever enter. I had a meeting with a colonel, a head of the new Mukhabarat, the new intelligence service. I rode up an elevator which reeked of stale cigarettes, with a group of silent people. I wondered how many people had ridden up this same lift, terrified, and never come down.

At the top of the building, the colonel came out to greet me. He had strange eyes. A former dissident, he told me he had led an anti-Saddam group inside Iraq and finally had to flee to the north for several years. After taking me to his office, he suddenly became fidgety. 'It's not secure,' he decided, and brought me into a small kitchen where we sat on a camp-bed.

The colonel talked about raiding suspected insurgents and breaking up kidnapping rings. I broke in to ask him about my friend. Without giving his name, I asked what he probably would have done in the Saddam days.

The colonel's eyes flickered. 'If he was inside the regime, enjoying all the privileges, he probably had to denounce people to keep himself in good favour.' He shrugged his shoulders. 'You're looking for excuses. I think you will find that no Ba'athists were good Ba'athists.'

Another evening, I met with one of Mahdi's former colleagues from the Security Service. It was a hot night and he drank a 7-UP and kept wiping his sweaty brow. He actually grew nostalgic talking of the old Saddam days.

'I don't even have a pension,' he complained. 'That old life, gone with the wind!'

He knew Mahdi well. He said the professor joined the security service in the early 1970s, that his former title was Director General, that he taught cadets about security, and that he did research within the Al-Amen Al-A'ma.

I asked him to clarify 'research'. He did not answer.

'Investigating subjects,' he finally said. Did he mean inter-rogation? He changed the subject.

'He was kind of a professor, he did not lie to you,' the man said. 'The government did send him to England to finish his studies, but in return he had to give something to the government.' He educated a lot of agents on security issues, the man said. Then he added, 'He didn't do anything like killing or torture.'

Once he started talking, the man was happy to continue. The family had long ties to Saddam, he said, so it was natural Mahdi would follow suit. One of Mahdi's brothers, Ali, was a famous general brigadier in the Al-Jaish Al-Iraqi, the Iraqi Army.

He also remembered a heated argument with Mahdi where the professor later apologised. 'He wasn't vicious,' he said. 'I think he was more interested in scholarly pursuits and just got trapped in security services.' Before he left he shook my hand: 'You know, I am sure he genuinely wanted your friendship, was not spying on you or anything like that.'

The next evening I had dinner with Saddam's former translator. I mentioned Mahdi. The man stopped eating, fork midway to his mouth. 'You mean the policeman?' he said.

'I thought he was an academic,' I replied.

'My dear,' he said calmly. 'He might have been an academic in his spare time, but he was a famous policeman. Everyone knew that.'

The thing about delving into the years of Saddam history is that everything is opaque. It gradually unravels, but even then, there is little transparency. So much remains buried. I still had no idea what Mahdi actually did, and what repercussions his actions might have had.

Outside of Iraq, people had theories. Toby Dodge, a leading British authority on Iraqi politics, supposed that Mahdi 'would have been at the very least aware of and probably culpable for, and could even have committed, some of the worst crimes of the Saddam regime'. But the writer Said Aburish, who once reported to the office of Saddam about the relations between Iraq and the United States, in the 1980s, was more thoughtful. 'Your friend was essentially a secret policeman. But what exactly does a secret policeman do?' Aburish sighed. 'It's a vague term. Like the rest of Saddam's past, we will never know.'

After the war, I did not return to Baghdad for fourteen months. I was tired of the difficulty of working in Iraq, trying to decipher truth from lies. Mahdi had hurt me deeply. But I had personal reasons: one year after the American bombing of Iraq, I became a mother for the first time. Gradually, my anger at Mahdi lessened. We kept in touch, but I did not confront him; I was waiting for the day we would meet again.

His life, meanwhile, was not going well. Like many Iraqis post-Saddam, the once comfortable family had serious money problems. Mahdi's job at the American network only lasted a few months. Aqila's money was in a special trust set up for her future. Her father, meanwhile, had to sell his Peugeot, and considered selling the house.

Aqila, with the help of an American reporter who had promoted her on their *Morning Show* as the 'new Anne Frank', knowing full well what her father had done during the war, left Baghdad in August, 2003, while the city was exploding with car bombs. She entered America knowing she could not go home, because of visa restrictions, for several years. Her English was becoming perfect. She said she was beginning to forget her Arabic. She did not want to watch television reports from Iraq.

Adhamiya became wild. With each attack on Fallujah, there were incidents in Adhamiya. Many of the residents were imprisoned. Kidnapping occurred with alarming frequency – of ordinary Iraqis perceived to be wealthy and of pretty girls like one of Zeinab's friends, who was snatched off the street as she walked home from school.

In January, 2004, Mahdi left for Jordan, finding his old neighbourhood no longer safe to live in. Whether or not he received actual threats because of his old life is unclear; he hinted to me that he did 'because people think I work for the Americans'. Aliya, however, insisted that her husband did not receive threats. 'He just thinks bad things can happen.'

In Amman, he rented a one-room apartment and took a job writing for a website. He was living off the sale of his car. At first, he could not afford to bring the entire family to Jordan: Aliya was left alone with the two youngest girls in the big house. They slept huddled together in one room downstairs and never went upstairs, where the twelve bullet holes still remained. The dogs were given away to a cousin.

*   *   *

I went back to Baghdad to try to find out the truth about Mahdi. I was still haunted by what I did not foresee, long ago now, at that first meeting.

He was sitting on a chair in the lobby of the Hotel Intercontinental when I first saw him. He looked older, tired. He was also not alone; he was accompanied by Aliya's younger brother, who was still living in Baghdad. This meant I could not ask him straight out if he worked for Saddam.

We sat with black coffee and cigarettes, dodging the real issue. Instead, he briefed me on the security situation. He warned me not to go to Adhamiya. He told me to wear an abaya – a head-to-toe garment – when I went out, and not to linger too long on the street. He joked that if I got kidnapped, he had a good contact in Fallujah.

In Baghdad, I was often the only foreigner in the restaurants. My driver and translator and I ate lunch quickly to avoid the uncomfortable stares. We left the hotel at different times so that, if we were being watched, we did not follow a schedule.

I wondered what had happened to all the old Ba'athists. One autumn morning, I attended a de-Ba'athification class, where former Ba'athists were to be reformed, supposedly into law-abiding democratic citizens of the new Iraq. It was a few days after the two Italian female aid workers had been kidnapped and in the taxi, Mary Pat Nunan, a *Voice of America* reporter, was casually showing me how to programme the GPS of my Thuraya phone and then transmit it to a special kidnapping hotline.

The de-Ba'athification class took place in a musty classroom with old blackboards. Three times a week, for three hours, a few dozen men and women met. They sat holding notebooks, waiting with bored expressions for the teacher to begin the lecture. The professor, a pudgy man called Ali Furaji, had lived in Germany where he belonged to a group called 'Enemies of Saddam'.

Another afternoon, I met Mahdi's children and their mother in a safe location in central Baghdad. They had changed. Zeinab was now eighteen. She had grown tall and very beautiful, but she was unbearably tense, like a wire about to break. Her mother told me that, when she had taken her final high-school exams, she had had a sugar diabetic seizure. 'She was so nervous, she just passed out.'

I wanted to visit their home, to get a sense of their new life, but they were afraid the neighbours would see a foreigner entering the home. 'It will make our life worse,' she said. Finally, we agreed I would lie down in the back of the car and Aliya would open the gates of the house at a specific time. We planned it with military precision.

In less than two years, everything had changed. The pretty house where Mahdi had reared his family for more than two decades was quiet and ghostly; the upstairs bedrooms were dusty. The garden was unkempt, and the electricity had been out for more than twenty-four hours. There was a sense of staleness in the house, and of sorrow.

In the kitchen, Aliya was cooking vegetables for lunch. Chicken was too expensive. I went to take a call on my satellite phone in the walled garden. Zeinab came out, crying, begging me to come inside.

'It's not safe!' she said, tugging on my arm. 'It's not safe!' I tried to calm her, but she broke away, angry. 'You don't understand!' Then she sat and sobbed. She never saw her friends any more, she said. She never left the house. She was afraid of getting kidnapped and sold as a sex slave in Kuwait. 'It's true, it happens!' she shouted. She told me she liked

Moqtada al-Sadr because he fought Americans. She said she missed her father. She saw no future for herself, but she did not want to get married. Her country, her family, she said, was destroyed.

I wanted to ask Aliya about her husband's double life, because I often felt close to her as a woman and as a mother – but whenever the talk grew close to the old days, the Saddam days, something changed in her eyes. I decided she was still scared: for herself, her daughters, her husband. And even though she was an engineer with a Ph.D. who spoke several languages, I knew that at heart she was a traditional Shia woman. She would never betray her husband.

Ironically, I never had to ask Mahdi about his former life. He casually did it himself, over dinner in Amman.

'When I worked for the government . . .' he began, launching into a long story about the secret police.

I sat back, aghast. It was almost anticlimatic. For nearly two years, I had played the confrontation in my mind, and here he was, talking about his days as a Saddam agent in the most casual voice. 'I thought you were a professor,' I said coldly.

'I am an academic,' he said, calmly. 'But I had to work for the regime.' He launched into a vague description of his job at the Al-Amen. His title was General Director of Environmental Security. He gave minor details, like an accountant; he said he was in charge of 'smuggling'. He worked seven days a week and was paid about thirty dollars a month. He supplemented his income by lecturing at Baghdad University, where he was paid fifteen dollars a lecture.

He says he joined the Ba'athists in the 1970s because, 'If you wanted anything in those days, you had to.' Besides, he added, Ba'athist then was something cool – a pan-Arabic socialist movement, not a word synonymous with dictatorship. 'Saddam was nothing in those days.'

He had personally met with Saddam several times, but he said he had done no denouncing, no spying on neighbours, no acts of violence. In fact, he said, he himself was denounced in 2003, just before the war, as a 'Shia fanatic', and lost his government posting.

'Because I was often on foreign television because I could speak English, I was denounced as a collaborator,' he said grimly.

I sat back in my chair suddenly feeling exhausted. I remembered the de-Ba'athification classes. Professor Furaji had told me there were three types of Ba'athists: the diehard followers of the cult of Saddam; those who actually believed the philosophy of Ba'athism; and the third group, those obliged to join so they could obtain education or jobs.

I reckoned Mahdi fell between the second and third camps. Not a big fish, not a war criminal, but not someone who bravely stood up to evil. Just a grey man.

For that, I suppose, on some level he was paying a price. He was in exile, forced to leave his country because, ironically, instead of seeing him as a Ba'athist, his neighbours wanted to kill him because they thought he was supporting the Americans. The man who had lived a lie was now in danger because of a lie.

And he was aware, more than anything, that he might never be able to go home again. 'Did I ever tell you about my grandfather's post office?' he asked. He told a long story of his grandfather, Ali, who had founded the first post office in Baghdad in 1918, under the British occupation. He rose up to become Director General. He spoke seven languages and lived in a huge house in Baghdad where he entertained in the old Pasha style. Mahdi and his five brothers, all of whom grew up to be influential men in the Iraqi Army, were reared on past stories of glory and honour.

And now, at fifty-seven, he was marooned in Jordan. Was he paying penance? No, because he still did not think he did anything wrong.

The final piece of the family puzzle lay in America, with twenty-one-year-old Aqila. Driving to meet her one autumn day, I thought being in America for her must be like being a Parisian sent to study in Berlin during the occupation of Paris in World War II. I wanted to ask her that, but more than anything, I wanted to ask her about her father.

I met her at her dorm but she was not allowed to be alone with me. She was shadowed by two 'advisors' from her university who would not let me ask her personal questions. It was oddly like being back in the Saddam days in Baghdad. Under their cold observation, she unpacked the roast chicken I had brought her. When I mentioned Baghdad, they both stiffened. One shook his head.

Did she want to go home? I asked. Not really, she said blandly. She was focused on perfecting her English and her organic chemistry. She never watched the news. She did not want to know about the insurgency. We could not discuss her father's old job. It was an utterly depressing meeting. Somehow the old, feisty Aqila, confronting American soldiers with sunglasses, had disappeared to blend in, chameleon-like, with the banality of her college dorm.

Some time later, away from her 'minders', I emailed her

about her old life. I knew that Aliya had finally left Baghdad, too frightened to stay, taking the children with her to join Mahdi. I knew he still felt depressed and directionless, and frightened that he was being hunted down. Money was running out. He could not find a job.

But I did not know what Aqila felt about it, so I asked her. Did she know about her dad's work? Did it ever trouble her? Did she know what was going on during the Saddam years?

I don't know what went on in her head when she read the emails. Was she proud of her dad? Did she despise him for what he did? Or was she totally unaware?

She never wrote back.

Afghanistan

The Place at the End of the World

November, 2001

The flat barge that carries passengers across the Amu Dar'ya, the river that separates Tajikistan from Afghanistan, takes less than ten minutes, but the journey is into another world. The Amu Dar'ya, also called the Oxus, was the former boundary between the Russian and the British Empire, and even now, eighty-two years after Afghanistan's independence from Britain was established, the land around the river has a feeling of being on the edge of the world. In the darkness, the only light comes from the full moon and from fires burning on the banks of the Afghan side. Soldiers huddle around them, casting strange, distorted shadows.

It is three weeks since the attacks on the World Trade Center and the Pentagon. American forces have been massing in this part of the world, some kind of action is expected soon, and the Russian soldiers who patrol the Tajik border and check passports by flashlight at the barge dock are jittery. On the other side of the river, the passport control is a shack in which three Afghans sit cross-legged around a petrol lantern, their automatic rifles resting on their laps. The man checking passports leans forward, points to my hair, and shakes his own head violently. This is northern Afghanistan, not under Taliban control, but I am still supposed to wear a headscarf; I forgot.

It takes two hours by ancient Soviet jeep to reach Khoje Bahauddin, an outback town in the province of Takhar that has become the provincial seat of the Northern Alliance since Taloqan, the Takhar capital, fell to Taliban troops last year. There is no road to Khoje Bahauddin, only tracks in hardened dust. The Jeep shivers, sputters, and finally grinds to a halt after an hour, in the middle of the desert. As the driver argues with a companion about how to fix it, I fall asleep, huddled against the cold metal of the Jeep.

When I awake an hour later, back on the 'road', I recall a conversation I had two decades ago in a post office in Parioli, an affluent Roman neighbourhood. I had met an elderly man. We were both waiting to use the public telephones. His clothes were shabby and foreign, and he had the troubled eyes of someone who was far from home. I asked him where that was. His long face sagged.

'I come from a country that no longer exists,' he said after a pause. 'You see, I come from Afghanistan.'

I understand the impact of his words only now that I am here, in a country of many sorrows, a country that has been buried alive by outside invaders, by war, by famine, by history.

Afghanistan, peopled by dozens of frequently antagonistic ethnic groups, is one of the poorest nations on earth. Its modern history begins with the invasion of India by Nader Shah of Persia, after which the Mughals lost control of all their territories west of the River Indus. In 1747, after Nader Shah was assassinated, a twenty-three-year-old member of the Durrani Pashtun tribe, the country's largest, fought his way back to his homeland and founded a kingdom in the territory that would become Afghanistan, establishing himself as King Ahmad Shah Durrani. The Russian czars had designs on Afghanistan but were thwarted by Great Britain, which took precarious control of the region in the early 1840s and then again in 1879. It was the British who in 1893 first drew the modern border between Afghanistan and Pakistan (which was then part of India), in the process sundering the homelands of some Afghan tribes. But the British never had much of a handle on Afghanistan, and after a third attempt at taking control, in 1919, they finally gave up.

Afghans are proud of the independence they won that year, but strategically they remain highly vulnerable, surrounded as they are by Iran, Pakistan and China, with Russia and India on the near horizon. The country's recent history has been one of conflict and treachery, beginning with the peaceful Soviet-assisted overthrow of King Zahir Shah in 1973 by a cousin of his, former Prime Minister Mohammad Daoud. A subsequent Marxist coup and increasing unrest among Islamic nationalists provided the pretext for the 1979 Soviet invasion. On Christmas Eve that year the Red Army seized Kabul's airport, and four Soviet motorised divisions rolled over the border. The country soon descended into a savage war, one in which teenage Russian soldiers fought against mujahidin fighters – Afghanistan's anti-Soviet, US-backed shock troops. This was to be the last great stand of the Cold War, and the scars of this ten-year conflict still cut deep into the Russian soul, that nation's version of Vietnam. As the late Russian journalist Artyom Borovik wrote, 'Afghanistan became part of each person who fought there. And each of the half-million soldiers who went through this war became part of Afghanistan – part of the land that could never absorb all the blood that spilled on it.'

By the time the last Soviet tank rolled back over the bridge separating Afghanistan from Uzbekistan in 1989, the country had been devastated and was ripe for a series of new battles in which rival warlords and the country's nominal government fought over the last remnants of Afghan nationhood. By October, 1994, vulnerable to anyone who would promise its residents a better life, the southern city of Kandahar fell to an obscure militia of religious students, or Taliban, led by Mullah Muhammad Omar, who called for 4,000 volunteers from Pakistan. Some of the Taliban (the plural form of the singular, Talib) were former mujahidin, but the majority were young Koranic students drawn from the hundreds of madaris (Islamic theology schools) that had been set up in Afghan refugee camps in Pakistan.

By 1996, 1.5 million people had been killed since the 1979 Soviet invasion. Weariness, fear and desperation opened the doors to the Taliban. In September, 1996, when Kabul fell, they were first welcomed as liberators. But the world watched in horror as Najibullah, the Communist ex-president, was tortured and killed. (Like many Afghans, he used only one name.) Slowly and methodically, the Taliban plunged the country into their vision of seventh-century Arabia, of life in the immediate wake of the Prophet Mohammed. This was a new agenda for Islamic radicalism. Afghanistan was declared 'a completely Islamic state', and the door to the West, to progress, to any kind of advancement, was abruptly slammed shut. Life under the Taliban became life behind a shroud. Girls were banned from schools. Women were forced to wear burkas – head-to-toe garments even more extreme than the traditional Muslim veil – in which they could barely see or hear, and were more or less ordered to stay at home. Men were commanded to grow beards long enough to grasp in one's hand, or else be imprisoned. Television, playing cards, music and photography were banned. If a woman's shoes made too much noise, she would be beaten, because this was said to incite lust in men. Intellectuals were repressed and jailed. Public executions, stonings and lashings took place to the glee of the Taliban soldiers, who provided security with their Datsun 4 × 4s and Kalashnikov assault rifles. Money poured in from Arab benefactors.

Gradually, the Taliban, most of whose members are Pashtun, took more than ninety per cent of the country. The intellectuals who could flee did so; the ones who could not chose to live underground and drew as little attention to themselves as possible. The remnants of the government that had been pushed out of Kabul by the Taliban in 1996 began to form a loose opposition under the command of Ahmed Shah Massoud, the son of an officer in the old royal army. Massoud's troops, the Shura-e-Nazar, had been the strongest force during the war against the Russians. Now, he re-formed his largely Tajik and Uzbek army, dubbed the Northern Alliance or the United Front, along with the men of other commanders who were intent on laying aside their rivalries and banishing the common enemy – the Taliban.

For six years, the Northern Alliance worked alone, with some assistance from Russia and Iran, but it was largely ignored by the West. Massoud tried to rally support, but aside from France, where he was a popular, romanticised resistance figure, no one in Europe or America took much notice of the Afghan opposition. On September 9, 2001, two days before the attacks on America, Commander Massoud met with two 'Belgian journalists' in Khoje Bahauddin at the alliance's headquarters. One of the journalists – they were, in fact, North Africans and are suspected to have been members of Osama bin Laden's al-Qaeda terrorist network – carried a video camera, inside of which was hidden a bomb. Leaning forward, one man posed a question to Massoud: 'And what will you do with Osama when you get him?' Massoud moved to answer, and the cameraman detonated his device. Massoud, who was called 'the Lion of Panjshir', was dead, and with him went the West's great hope of a charismatic leader who could stand up to the Taliban.

In Khoje Bahauddin, when I finally arrive at headquarters late at night, one of Massoud's former bodyguards, Nasir, a young soldier from the Panjshir Valley, leads me with a lantern to find a space on the floor to sleep. In the morning, he smiles and shows me where to find water that a donkey had carried up from the river below the village. He sits quietly with me, staring at the blackened room, a bombed-out shell, where Massoud was killed. The blood of Massoud and the suicide bombers is still splattered on the wall.

In the next room, I eat breakfast with the soldiers who guarded Massoud. We sit on the floor, and they share their bread and tea, motioning for me to take more, and to dip the bread into Russian cream that they pour from a carton. 'Eat, eat,' says one. 'Before the . . .' With his hand, he play-acts firing a gun. 'Before the fighting.'

When I point to the blackened room, the soldiers grow silent. 'They killed our leader,' Nasir says, the gentleness of his face suddenly turning to something hard, something vengeful. 'Now we will fight them until we die.'

Front Line, The Kalakata Hills,
Northern Afghanistan, 7 October

It's some 20 kilometres from Khoje Bahauddin to where Northern Alliance forces are massing for an expected offensive against the Taliban. The front runs along a thirty kilometre line, trenches dug into dusty hills. But before you get there you pass a cemetery. Mounds of earth, dried to dust, are neatly lined up, covering a large field. There are no markers, but under each one is a body, a reminder that war is hardly a new phenomenon here.

In Afghanistan, the average life expectancy for a male is forty-six years, and the soldiers here are so immune to living in a state of war, so immune to seeing death and mutilation, that when a round of automatic gunfire bursts over this frontline position no one cowers inside the trench. Instead, they run towards it, laughing, howling, raising their guns over the trench. A tank shell is fired from a nearby hill, and the thud silences them for a moment. But they seem totally untouched by fear. The ability to value their own lives seems to have disappeared.

The shooting stops around midday and the men begin to pray. They are largely uneducated. Many are refugees who fled the Taliban as their troops gradually moved northwards from Kabul, taking more and more Afghan territory. The alliance has held on to roughly ten per cent of the country, in the northern provinces, and fights with what little equipment it has – a few helicopters, old Soviet weapons, hunting rifles.

And yet, according to military observers, its men are some of the bravest fighters in the world. Russian soldiers feared them and called them *dukhi*, or spirits, because of their ability to ambush and run away, hide, disappear.

Some are old enough to have fought in the former king's army. Some of them fought with the mujahidin. Some of them fought with the forces of former President Najibullah. All of them fought, sometimes against one another. Now they are united against a common enemy. 'It was a mistake that we made, fighting each other,' says one commander, Isak. 'Now people must agree with us – we have to make a strong government.' Like a lot of the commanders, he is grateful for, but slightly suspicious of, the attention that is now being paid to his country. 'Before the bombing in New York, we fought the Taliban, and no one knew us, no one cared, no one gave us help,' he says. 'Now there is an attack on America, and people want to know who we are.'

Mazar-e-Sharif is a strategically crucial city in the North, the capital of the Northern Alliance before it fell into the hands of the Taliban in 1998; it is about one hundred miles from here and the ultimate goal of the coming offensive. For the time being, the front lines are only being reinforced. Hanging off the backs of old Soviet trucks, more soldiers arrive, some in battered American-made fatigues, others wearing traditional Afghan dress – knee-length shirts over baggy trousers – along with padded grey parkas and slip-on black shoes caked in dust. Over their shoulders they carry old Kalashnikovs, around their waists ammunition. These are hardened fighters, and yet there is a strange innocence to them. Unaccustomed to seeing a woman without a burka, which is traditional in the North though not mandatory, they stare at me as if I were a television set and gather in groups, whispering and holding one another's hands – a common sight among men in Muslim countries. They make me eat lunch with them, 'a soldier's lunch' of rice, beans, grapes and nan, the flatbread that is a staple in the Afghan diet. During the meal they talk, and the talk is always about war.

The '*dushman*' – the enemy, the Taliban – have reinforced their own front lines with Chechens, Pakistanis and other recruits who have come to fight the jihad. 'Foreigners,' the Northern Alliance soldiers snort with disgust. 'We are fighting foreign forces, Osama's forces,' they tell me, quick to point out that bin Laden is not an Afghan but an Arab. To compensate for the Taliban's strength, the Northern Alliance now claims its ranks have swelled to 12,000, and its spokesmen claim that the enemy troops are defecting, more of them crossing the lines every day.

I leave the front to visit Commander Dagarvol Shirendel Sohil, who oversees a Northern Alliance defensive position on top of a hill in an area known as Al Khanum. Below this position is an abandoned mud-hut village. The people there, fearing the sound of outgoing tank shells, fled when fighting began in the area earlier this year.

'Our soldiers are stronger,' says Commander Sohil. 'Up until now, the Taliban were supported by foreign money. Now they have a choice. Join us, or die.' At the foot of his camp, which is littered with empty 100-millimetre tank shells, are Greek ruins dating back to the time of Alexander the Great, yet another foreign invader. It is a surreal sight to see an old Soviet T-55 tank near an ancient Greek urn.

'You forget, this was a beautiful country,' says my translator, Ahmad, a twenty-four-year-old Afghan whose father was an important mujahidin commander. He was killed fighting the Russians when Ahmad was two years old. Ahmad's twelve-year-old sister was killed during the war against the Taliban. He swallows these tragedies with a shrug of his shoulders. 'Yes, it is sad,' he says, 'but I am used to it by now.'

Ahmad lost his childhood. Like many sons of the Afghan élite when the country was under Communist rule, he went to Russia to study when he was eight, along with his two younger brothers. They were meant to go for one month, to absorb Soviet culture. But one month became four, four months became a year, five years, ten years; the boys were housed in an orphanage.

'After President Najibullah fell, they forgot we were there,' Ahmad says casually. His mother had no idea how to get her sons back; they had no idea how to return to their country. 'At first, we were too small, then we forgot what it was like to be Afghan,' he says. He was twenty-two when he finally saw his mother again last year. At first, she did not recognise her eldest son; then, when it was clear who the stranger standing in front of her was, she burst into tears. He had to relearn Dari, the language spoken by most Afghans. Two months after his return, Taloqan, his city, fell to the Taliban. He fled; his mother stayed. There are no telephones, no communications, so he has no idea how or where his mother is now.

Ahmad takes my map, bought in London, and points out our location at Al Khanum. Underneath, written in red, is 'Excavation of Greek ruins'.

It is odd to think of this country as having had Hellenic life, having had civilisation. But farther south on the map there are markers for more former tourist attractions; near the city of Charikar, 'Picturesque Bazaar, Ceramics', and closer to

Kabul, 'Climatic Health resort'. Through the Paghman mountain range, near Bamian, there are two sites of interest. One offers 'Scenic Beauty, differently coloured lakes'. To the east, marked with a star: 'Giant Buddha sculptures'. But a word has been added underneath: 'destroyed'.

The map does not say when or by whom. It was, of course, the Taliban, who last March dynamited the ancient and monumental stone Buddhas, remnants of the country's layered history, in pursuit of their completely Islamic state.

From the top of the hill, the Kokcha River winds down throgh flat rice marshes and past a series of Northern Alliance positions. Crossing the river, I return to the line, to a position near the village of Jilin Hur. Here, the soldiers move on horseback, and the biblical landscape swirls with dust. The Taliban are about a mile over a hill, and you can see the Northern Alliance's mortars land on the Taliban positions, sending up plumes of smoke. Their trenches, dug into a hill, look like a seam on a dress; around the seam are buttonholes where Northern Alliance shells have landed. When return fire rips past, I crouch in the trench, then lift my head to see shadowy stick figures – the Taliban, the soldiers tell me – manning their distant position.

Night falls. I am returning to Khoje Bahauddin with soldiers and some other journalists. We cross the Kokcha by military truck, which wades through the river, the water rushing up to the bottom of the door. The sky for the first time seems clear. The dust storms, which were preventing helicopters from bringing supplies, have quieted. There is a stillness to the air. It is perfect bombing weather.

After a one-hour drive over yet another series of ruts that passes for a road, bumping over holes gouged into the dry earth, I am back in the alliance headquarters. The soldiers and the officials are gathered around a television intermittently powered by a generator and tuned to CNN. On the screen, there are snowy images of white lights blinking over Kabul.

'Bombs,' says one soldier, and the others lean forward. It is the first night of the US and British attacks. We watch in silence. Though the allies are attacking the Taliban, there is no jubilation here among the Northern Alliance troops. Someone asks the soldiers if they are happy. 'They're bombing the Taliban,' someone says. 'But they are also bombing our country.'

Dasht-e-Qala, Northern Afghanistan, 8 October

This grim village was once surrounded by farmland, but there has been no rain here in the North for three years, and so there is no harvest. Fields that were once full of wheat are now pale dust-beds, caravan routes for donkeys and camels. There is hardly any fresh food for sale in the area's markets; beggars and children covered in scabs and dust pick the remains from rice bowls and beg for nan. An orange is a strange and foreign thing.

Entire towns are emptied, most of the inhabitants having fled the fighting, the famine, the disease. Tuberculosis, cholera and malaria are on the rise, and with the heavy snows expected in about six weeks' time, the few aid organisations that are here are fearing the worst. If it were not for the Agency for Cooperation and Development (ACTED), a French non-governmental organisation that distributes wheat, no one would eat.

Most of the international charity organisations, except

ACTED, left after September 11, but a team of German doctors have arrived. 'It is an emergency,' says Rupert Neudeig, whose group is trying to establish a clinic here before winter closes the roads. 'I say "clinic", but it will only be a shadow of what you think of as a clinic,' he explains with resignation; the reality is that saving this country is a Sisyphean task.

In the bazaar at Dasht-e-Qala, men sit drinking green tea, and a lone child carries a bag in which she stuffs pieces of fat and rice that have fallen on the floor of a kabob café. Like clinic, 'café' is too grand a word. It is a dusty room where the men sit cross-legged on the floor, and plates of meat, seared on iron sticks, are placed in the middle with a stack of nan. There are no women in the bazaar, let alone the restaurant.

There is a group from Kabul; refugees. One of them, Khaled, comes over to practise the English that he learned in secret – a very expensive course, he says, which cost $10. 'Everyone wanted to learn English in Kabul,' he says, 'so they could run away.' Khaled hated life under the Taliban, hated the fact that he could not listen to music, could not meet his friends, and had no hope for a different life. At seventeen, he could also not grow a full beard. When the religious police caught the barefaced teenager on the street one day, they threw him in jail for a week.

'I told them I wasn't old enough to grow a beard, but they didn't believe me,' he says. After that, he didn't walk around the city so much.

Here in the North, people listen to Radio Mashhad, broadcast in Dari from Iran. That country, with its mostly Shiite Muslim population, is no friend of the Taliban, who are predominantly Sunnis. Radio Mashhad gives locations of the allied bombing raids: Kabul, Kandahar, Mazar-e-Sharif.

With the bombing, however, there is no chance of aid being delivered from Pakistan.

Because there is nothing, people make things from nothing. In the corner of the bazaar, a metalworker named Ustaboba is fashioning shovels, hinges and nails from the remnants of 100-millimetre shells. He buys three shells for $1, sells a shovel for $3 – a war profiteer. What he is doing does not seem so odd to him. Before him, his father did the same thing, using shells from the Afghan–Soviet war. And besides, he cannot imagine a life without war.

Khoje, Bahauddin, 9 October

To be a woman in Afghanistan can mean a life of constant struggle. Or it can mean that you simply don't exist, that you are invisible, that you live through a burka.

The first thing I notice about Farahnaz, a refugee from Kabul, is the way she walks through the dusty courtyard of the relief agency where she works. She is proud and defiant, her head high, not dropped low like those of the other women – the very few women – I have seen since I arrived in Afghanistan. The second thing I notice is that she is not wearing a burka, only a headscarf. As we talk, the headscarf falls off, and under it she has a shiny ponytail and a smooth, high forehead.

On 8 March, International Women's Day, Farahnaz founded the country's first women's centre here in Khoje Bahauddin. If this were not Afghanistan, a land bound by tradition, that would not be extraordinary. But to have a women's centre in a country without women's rights – the Northern Alliance is only slightly better than the Taliban on this score – is unthinkable. Still, she tries. She wrote to the provincial governor for help in teaching local women the Koran and basic healthcare. He responded by closing down her small women's centre. Now she conducts meetings in secret where women can study English and hygiene.

Her husband was threatened by the local government because of her work. 'I went to the authorities and said, "If you have something to say, you say it to me. I am running the centre, not my husband."'

Her husband supported her in this, even though he did not support her when she refused to wear a burka. This was because she had spent years wearing Western-style clothes when she studied electrical engineering in the Ukraine. Even her husband's fury could not convince her. 'I couldn't see, I couldn't hear, I kept falling down!' she says of the burka. 'And more important, I must set an example to other women.'

If you are a woman in Afghanistan, even in areas not held by the Taliban, you are lucky if you get to go to school. And even if you do, the resources are limited. There is only one university for women in the entire country, in the city of Feyzabad; it is so badly equipped that medical students who finish there are not skilled enough to operate even on corpses.

But before the wars ravaged this country, life was different, at least for the élite. When Kabul fell to the Taliban in 1996, Farahnaz, her husband, and their two children, a boy and a girl now aged seventeen and ten, fled to Pakistan, where they stayed for nearly four years. Farahnaz learned English, studying alongside her children. The family returned to Taliban-controlled Afghanistan last year, but soon fled again, this time by donkey, to the North. For three months they were trapped in an obscure valley where they had only rainwater to drink. Farahnaz watched mothers feeding babies the dirty water; she watched the babies get sick, and she tried to do something to help, to teach them.

Finally, she arrived in Khoje Bahauddin, where she realised she was one of the few educated women. She told the local women that there was another world where women went to work outside the home, and that they could free themselves through education.

Talking to Farahnaz in her small, whitewashed home, I realise how lonely she must be, how she must feel like an alien, how out of sync her ideas are with those of the other women here, most of whom simply accept the miserable fate that life has dealt them. Farahnaz looks down at her lap. It is lonely, she says, but there are small satisfactions. There are now one hundred women in her group. 'I can't help these women economically, but I can help by opening their eyes, giving a different vision of the world.'

Down the road, at a small women's workplace run by ACTED, a group of women, most of whom are war widows or married to men unable to work, have formed a collective that sews clothes and quilts. For each article of clothing, they get five kilos of wheat.

They all sit cross-legged in front of ancient Chinese Butter-fly sewing machines, and when I enter the room, they stare and giggle. One of them grabs my hand. 'Taliban! Taliban!' she says, squeezing it so hard it hurts. She pantomimes holding a gun at her head. 'Her husband was killed by the Taliban,' explains the director, Fahima Murodi, who is the mother of seven, four of whom are girls, and has a master's degree in economics from a Russian university. Despite her education, and the fact that she says the most important thing she can do for her daughters is to fight for their education, she still wears a burka.

'But we want change. We want things to be different,' she says. 'We want to be free! We want to develop ourselves. But it is hard in a place where there are no opportunities for girls to be educated after the age of fourteen.' Then she takes me outside to meet another girl working there, who has a plastic leg because she stepped on a land mine. Both her parents were killed in fighting. She has no brothers and sisters, so the village helps look after her. The girl, Asyla, rolls up her long dress to show me her leg. She speaks a few words of English. One of them is 'war'.

Back at her home, Farahnaz insists to me that she is not going to give up. She says this when her daughter, Vida, a miniature replica of her mother, enters the room. The child speaks perfect English and tells me she wants to be a doctor when she grows up because she wants to help her country. Then she recounts a long story about the Taliban beating women, growing more excited with the injustice of it all, and I look at her and wonder what she will be like in ten years, and how different the country could be if more mothers produced children like this.

As I leave, I ask Farahnaz what it feels like not wearing a burka. She got stares at first, she says, when she went out without one. Now she gets few looks, because the people in the village know how much she does to help people. 'I think they respect me,' she says. 'Some of them call me Mother.'

Front Line, Qur'ugh, 10 October

It is a hot autumn day, and the news is that Northern Alliance fighters have taken two strategic villages close to Mazar-e-

Sharif and are now six kilometres from the city. The allied bombings are moving closer to the Taliban front line and its infantry. Dr Abdullah Abdullah, the Northern Alliance's foreign minister, says this is a new phase of the war. Something is turning.

Yesterday, to get to the front here in Takhar, I crossed the Kokcha River on a frightened, shell-shocked horse with rope for reins, led by a teenage horseman. Today a military truck arrives, and I catch a ride in somewhat more comfort. I sit in the front, between two soldiers who sing quietly under their breaths – religious songs, for Allah, they say. We take a dirt road that leads to a different front line. From there we get out next to a bridge by a turn in the river and walk. A commander, not pleased by my presence, says, 'We are close to the enemy. If you get injured, what happens then?' An outgoing tank shell explodes somewhere, and I say nothing. The walk continues through rice-fields and a field of bursting cotton plants, and someone says not to stray off the path.

'Mines,' he says.

The lush cotton-fields look surreal in this otherwise wasted landscape. A soldier bends down and picks up one of the soft, fuzzy plants. When he gives it to me, he laughs and rubs it against my cheek. The soldier in front of me is barefoot and carries a light machine-gun. He is seventeen, shy, does not look in my eyes, but he is singing in Dari as we march single file.

At the front, the dushman are close, so close that one of the soldiers points to a moving object and says in an excited voice, 'Taliban!' We crouch and watch the *dushman*, and the commander tells us to go quickly now, because they have spotted our position. So we walk back from the trenches, through a field of rice, another of cotton, past donkeys and soldiers on horseback and blooming trees. We pass a lone grave next to the river, a commander's. Women have come and wrapped tattered, coloured cloth around a tree. 'So we don't forget him,' one tells me.

We arrive at a command post. The soldiers there make us drink green, sugared tea and eat coconut biscuits from Iran. Outside is a small oasis of flowers: pink gerberas, what look like red dahlias. One of the soldiers has a tame blackbird, a pet, on his shoulder. On the wall, in charcoal, they have sketched a beautiful woman inside a heart. She has long eyelashes and does not wear a burka or veil.

The colours of the day darken. Across the river, the hills where the lines are seem to fade in the dying light, and the sky shakes slightly with a shell falling somewhere. I think of a group of young soldiers I saw earlier in the week, who had scrawled something on a wall. Ahmad had translated it for me;

We wait for tomorrow
For the victory against the Taliban
Our brother Talib
Sold our country to the foreigners.

Next to the command post is a small triage hospital, two beds under a tarp. There is one blanket, and the medical supplies consist of a box of ancient field dressings and a bottle of Russian disinfectant. That's it. When someone is injured, they have to carry him across the river, by donkey or horse, and then drive an hour to Khoje Bahauddin over the tracks that jar every bone in the body, even if you are not injured.

'All we can do is stop the bleeding,' says the triage nurse, a young boy of eighteen or nineteen. 'We just stop the bleeding.'

I'm driven back over the river to the front, into another night of bombing, this time near Taliban infantry lines. Some of the alliance soldiers are angry because they don't know if their families in Mazar-e-Sharif, Kabul and Taloqan are dead or alive. I can't keep the image of a bleeding soldier being carried by donkey over the Kokcha River out of my mind, and then I realize the bleeding soldier is really an analogy for this country. I have never been in a place so stained with its own blood. And all we are doing, all we can do, is stop the bleeding.

Learning to Dance:
Women after the Taliban

December, 2001

Near Chicken Street, three burkas paused in front of me and peered out from the netting that covered their eyes. From behind the muffled blue nylon cloth, one spoke.

'What's your name?' she said, in halting English. 'What are you doing here?'

Her friend, hearing the foreign words spoken out loud, began to laugh. It sounded strange to hear something joyful coming from behind the burka, even stranger to hear a person speaking.

It was one week after the Northern Alliance liberated Kabul. One week since the Taliban were 'driven from town with a lash', in the words of the radio announcer Jamila Mujahid. One week since the barber shops were crowded with men lined up to have their beards shaved; one week since these three friends came out of their dank basements where they had languished, for five years, unable to work or leave their houses unaccompanied by a male relative.

Now they walked around in the sunshine with their arms

entwined. Now they spoke to my driver, a young man in his twenties who was so shy around them that he could not lift his eyes from the pavement and look into the place behind the burkas where their faces were. Now, in the shop in front of us, there were packages of hair dye modelled by blonde Swedish models in scanty tank tops, and dolls with garish red and white polka-dot skirts.

Now there was such a thing as a woman. Before, during the Taliban, that creature simply did not exist.

The four of us stood on the corner sizing each other up. I realised it was the first time a woman in a burka had addressed me after many long weeks in Afghanistan.

'If you want to talk to me,' I said, 'you have to take off your burka.' I had meant it to be playful, but the three burkas recoiled slightly.

'Why?' said one.

'We can't,' said another. 'It's not safe yet.'

But the third, the bravest, the leader of the gang, rolled back the nylon, and behind it was a young girl in her twenties called Sahaila. She had dyed blonde hair, pink lipstick and blue eyeliner. She had a job now, a medical technician. She had a face, and she stared at me defiantly, a smile twitching the corner of her lips.

'Ah, you see', she said, 'I am a person after all.'

Things are changing. The radio is back on. There is television. There are things for sale in the bazaar, strange, forbidden things. Books. Condoms. Hair dryers.

People are coming back to life, and most of them can pinpoint a moment when their lives began again. A lot of them say the moment they knew the Taliban were really gone was when they heard Jamila Mujahid's voice on the radio.

For years, the thirty-six-year-old journalist had always been the 'Voice of Afghanistan' on Radio Kabul, speaking out from her studio perch during the time of Soviet-backed Babrak Kamal, during the time of the Russian invasion, during the time of Mohammed Najibullah, during the time of the mujahidin. Opinionated, defiant, outspoken, she criticised the regimes, the politicians, the armies. She had no fear. She was relentless.

'I was critical of them, always critical of their backing from foreign countries – America, Iran, Pakistan,' she says. 'I just told the truth.'

Then, horribly, one day her voice disappeared. At noon on 28 September, 1996, Jamila stepped outside her apartment and followed a crowd through the streets of Kabul. The Taliban had arrived in the capital, a city which had been gutted and ravaged by four years of a brutal civil war.

When they first appeared two years earlier, the Taliban acted against a mujahidin commander in Kandahar who had reportedly raped and abducted three women. So no one was really sure whether or not they would be a good thing or a bad thing. Like most people, Jamila saw this as a return to a safer life and she welcomed them, saw them raise their white flags, and thought, 'Thank God, at last we will have peace.'

But that bright September afternoon, she turned a corner and saw the former president, Mohammed Najibullah, a puppet of the Soviet regime, tortured and dangling from an elevated traffic island near the Presidential Palace. He was bound and drenched in blood. Jamila's own blood froze.

'I just wanted the war to end. Then I saw him hanging in the centre of Kabul,' she says quietly, 'and I knew nothing had changed. The fighting was not over.'

Within hours after taking over the city, the Taliban began barking orders to women on Radio Afghanistan, to cease attending workplaces and to move outside the home only when necessary and only then with a male relative. Schools were closed.

Radio Afghanistan became renamed Radio Shariat by the Taliban, and for five long years, Jamila was silenced. The Taliban took her off the air and, like other women, she was not allowed on the street unless accompanied by a male relative. Very quickly, and very quietly, her life as she knew it disappeared.

She tried not to fall into a victim trap. After working all of her adult life, she retreated to her grim concrete flat in Microrayon, a Kabul suburb built during the Soviet days. She fought against the confinement, the 'internal exile'. She wrote secret poetry. She looked after her husband. She got pregnant twice, gave birth, raised her five children. She fought depression, isolation and loneliness. Sometimes her anger was so big that she hit her children, lashing out in her rage. She went to a doctor who told her the only cure was to go back to work, an impossible feat.

For someone who had lived a life of total freedom before, and who had been raised by a feminist mother, it was agony.

'It was horribly painful for me,' she says now. 'Like a free bird put into a cage.'

Some days, she retreated to the basement of her block of flats and, behind blankets, she and the other residents watched smuggled video casettes from India. But it was hard for her to watch a life beyond Afghanistan, and to remember her old life – books, intelligent conversations, a working life.

'My world shrunk,' she said, 'to four walls.'

Instead, she wrote, harbouring her thoughts and frustrations in small notebooks. One black day when she felt completely and utterly lost, she wrote this.

On a piece of old and torn paper, which was mixed with dust and mud, there was written the word Freedom.

I was crossing this way, even though my eyes did not work well under the burka. But suddenly, I saw this word. At first, I crossed this way, but I didn't know what happened that I returned back and picked this paper up.

On the black sheet of paper was the word Freedom, written in big and white letters.

It made a strange feeling on my heart. I cleaned it from the mud and held it up correctly in my hands so not to tear it. I looked at the word many times, God knows how many times.

I was taking a nap when an acquainted voice interrupted me. I couldn't see sideways because of the burkha. A sister asked, what are you holding in your hands that you are looking at so deeply? I answered her, laughing, this is Freedom! But she answered me with surprise. 'What do you want to do with it? We saw this word so many times in our school books, but what is it?'

I smiled and said, yes, we have read this in our school books but have we really known it?

And now, under the burka, do I really know freedom?

Jamila had given up hope for any freedom, and she felt the years slipping by. Then, during the holy month of Ramadan, the Northern Alliance, backed by US-led air strikes, began their offensive. First the North fell, then Kabul. At 8 a.m. on 13 November, Jamila was woken up by a knock at her door. 'The Northern Alliance have arrived!' a neighbour told her. It did not seem real. But by noon, she was seated in her old chair at the Radio Afghanistan studio. She shook as she sat down and took out her notes.

'People of Kabul, blessings,' she began. Her voice shook. 'The Taliban have been driven out of town with a lash . . .' People, hearing the familiar and yet forgotten voice, began to cry, realising the years of repression were over. Hundreds of people phoned the station to congratulate her.

'Those men, the Taliban, I don't think they were born from their mothers to behave as they did,' she says now, looking down at her Western clothes – a veil instead of a burka, a shapeless black skirt, flat shoes. They are not fashionable, not even modern. But they are clothes nonetheless, not the dreaded, stifling burka.

She produces a photograph of herself in the 1980s during the days of the Najibullah regime, and there she is in a miniskirt and heels and pale lipstick. Next to her is a friend, Commander Roser, wearing combat fatigues. 'Ah, she was a brave one. She had 200 armed men fighting under her command.' Another is wearing a long dress.

'What I am trying to show you,' Jamila says, 'is that we were people before the burka.'

It is a different world now. While Afghanistan has never exactly been a leader in female emancipation – especially in rural areas where a different way of life prevailed from the urban élite in Kabul – there was dignity for women. Women gained the right to vote in the 1920s and the government had begun strongly supporting women's education and employment in separate institutions, even while keeping women in purdah. In 1959, Prime Minister Daoud Khan announced the voluntary end of seclusion in the home and removal of the veil for women. In the 1960s, the Afghan Constitution called for female equality. By the early 1990s, according to a US State Department report issued in November, 2001, seventy per cent of the schoolteachers in Kabul were women, as well as fifty per cent of government workers and forty percent of doctors.

When the Taliban arrived, all that progress was erased. 'After 1959, women in ever increasing numbers took education and professional careers for granted, a trend that escalated after 1978,' wrote Nancy Hatch Dupree, an Afghan expert, in an essay composed while the Taliban were still in power. 'Now that momentum has been abruptly halted.'

'We grew up free, women doing what we wanted to do,' Jamila says, staring hard at the photograph. 'All that disappeared when the mujahidin came in 1991.'

The mujahidin, the holy warriors, are often forgotten for the hideous abuse they heaped on Afghanistan during their years of power. 'The Taliban, after all, did not just spring from hell, they sprang from Afghan culture strained through hell,' writes Tamin Ansary, an Afghan woman living in California.

During the 1970s and 1980s, in the urban areas, Afghanistan's pro-Soviet Marxist leaders pushed forward an aggressive programme of women's rights that irritated the nation's Islamic mullahs and other conservative factions in society. They rightly or wrongly associated the women in miniskirts going to university and holding down men's jobs as an influence from the atheist and all-consuming Soviet Union. They rejected the movement as an ideology of infidels, as a betrayal of all things Islam.

When the mujahidin arrived fresh from fighting the Soviets, they were startled by the freedom that the women of Kabul had, walking around bareheaded, working, appearing on television without their faces covered.

According to Nancy Hatch Dupree, the soldiers assumed it was their right to have complete sexual control over women who dared to live in a male world. 'Young, immature mujahidin who had grown up on the battlefield under the influence of conservative leaders marvelled at the unveiled Afghan newsreaders on TV and concluded they must be promiscuous and – Kalashnikovs ready – waylaid the ladies at the studio gate saying, "tonight you are mine",' Hatch Dupree recalls.

To the mujahidin, there were two kinds of women: good girls who stayed at home behind a veil, and bad girls who walked the streets brazenly, mingling with men in public places. Many of those mujahidin grew up to be Taliban. The others were recruited from the teeming refugee camps of Pakistan, where frustration and rage were fed to them as easily as tea and nan bread, the staple diet of Afghans.

Now, five years after the nightmare, on a cold, clear Sunday night in Kabul, Jamila walks back into Radio Afghanistan, takes off her burka and hangs it on a peg. TV has just gone back on the air and the studio smells like an abandoned place. It is a shabby place, with ancient, out-of-date equipment. A few technicians stand around watching an Afghan soap opera of three men sitting in a field cracking jokes. Another group stare at Chaplin's *The Tramp* on a monitor, their mouths open in astonishment at the moving images, even if it is nearly one hundred years old. I wonder what they would do if they saw the computer wizardry of something like *The Lord of the Rings*. Probably have a heart attack through shock, I decide.

Jamila has come to read the nightly news, and underneath the burka she is wearing a skirt and sweater, fishnet stockings and flat black shoes. She's back at work, after five years, getting paid nothing at the moment, but soon, when the money comes into the studio, she hopes she'll get $10 a month. 'That doesn't matter, you can't imagine how happy I am,' she says, sitting down in front of her microphone. 'I'm not interested in gifts or money, I'm interested in my country and my people.'

'When the women of Afghanistan hear her voice, they become happy,' says the station director, Ahmed Shah Nabizullah. 'They believe that things are changing. In every country, you find a voice that people identify with. In Afghanistan, that voice is hers.'

But despite all this, Jamila worries about a shift in society, that five years of the Taliban have altered the psyche of the Afghan people. 'It will take a long, long time for them to adjust after five years of this repression,' she says. 'Too much pain has happened. Not only have women's lives changed forever, but so has the mentality of the Afghan male.'

She still wears a burka to the market, because she is not yet sure that the time is right to take it off. She is afraid that if she goes to the market barefaced, the men will react violently, angrily. She remembers too much the rapes and attacks. She is afraid, like many people, that now that the elastic band of security and repression the Taliban instilled in the people has snapped, the country will descend into chaos and anarchy, like the days before they arrived.

She is afraid. She does not know what will happen.

Because of the large number of men killed in two decades of war, women make up about sixty per cent of Afghanistan's 26 million people. During the Taliban reign, nearly all Afghan women – aside from female nurses who were needed to care for Taliban wives – lost their jobs. The Prophet

Mohammed twelve centuries ago improved the status of women: Islamic law made the education of girls a sacred duty and gave them the right to own and inherit property. He even decreed that sexual satisfaction was a woman's entitlement.

The Taliban took those things, and everything else, away.

This is what else women lost. Their public baths. Their right to medical care. Their voices. Their schools. As many as 7,700 female teachers were out of work. 8,000 female undergraduates 'dropped out' – i.e., were forced out – of Kabul University. Their confidence. The psychological impact of the Taliban years on Afghan women was extensive. According to author Michael Griffui, a former UN advisor to Afghanistan, 'a survey of 160 women . . . disclosed that ninety-seven per cent showed symptoms of major depression and seventy-one per cent reported a decline in their major health status.'

According to a report published by the US State Department in November, as many as 50,000 women who had lost husbands or other male relatives during the civil war had no source of income under the Taliban. To earn a living, or to earn a crust of bread, they begged on the streets. You see them everywhere; they attack your car, pounding with their small fists, begging for money to feed their children. They surround you on the streets, crying, pleading, from behind the burkas. It's their only chance of survival.

They lost their health. Even tuberculosis, a disease that is primarily more apparent in males, went shooting up in women during the Taliban time. The cause, according to doctors in Kabul who treated the women, was largely because they were confined to dank, bacteria-breeding spaces and forced to stand cooking in front of wood fires for hours on end.

In a grimy dirt street near the Hotel Intercontinental, an Afghan friend took me to the saddest place. This was the 'National Tuberculosis Institute', a shabby house where eight women lived, caring for each other. None of these women were old, but all of them looked ancient. There was Bulbul, who at forty had borne eleven children and was so thin that her skin hung in folds from her body. She arrived in the capital from the Panshjir Valley when she was so sick she could barely stand. There was Bibi Awasha, who said she was 'maybe thirty years old', who had lost an eye from the disease, and who arrived when her TB was in a secondary stage, too late to be cured.

There were no doctors when I arrived at the clinic, no nurses, only an elderly caretaker and the women who had brought some of their family with them. On the filthy walls were posted hand-drawn warnings: to cover their mouths when breast-feeding; and reminders to stay clean; to wash sheets and towels frequently. But the place, their only refuge, was a filthy, teeming mess.

Dr Abdi Mohammed, the head of the World Health Organisation, says that the oppression of women during five years of Taliban rule has resulted in a huge increase in the number of cases of TB. 'Women account for seventy per cent of the cases,' he said, making the country one of the few places in the world where the rate of the disease is higher in women than in men.

Because of confined conditions, the bacteria bred quicker and thrived in the dirty, claustrophobic homes. Early marriage and close pregnancies weakened the body's immune system, making most of the women more vulnerable.

'Also, the women work harder than the men,' Dr Mohammed said. 'They can spend ten hours a day minimum in the fields, harvesting and collecting. Then they cook and spend three or four hours breathing woodsmoke.'

If they did get medication, if they somehow managed to get to a doctor and try to make themselves better, many of them sold their antibiotics – which cost around $200 a year – on the black market.

'If you had to feed your children, you would probably sell your own medication too,' says Dr Gino Stride, an outspoken and courageous Italian surgeon who runs Emergency, a war trauma hospital situated in the middle of Kabul which had been closed down by the Taliban – because they did not believe the male and female patients were segregated enough – and re-opened after the liberation. 'That, I am afraid, is the sad reality of the healthcare system in Afghanistan.'

The mental state of the women, post-Taliban, is equally shaky. In the Kabul Psychiatric Hospital, another grim Soviet-style building, men and women are treated for heroin addiction, depression, psychosis, schizophrenia. With the dark hallways, the smell of urine and faeces and the wailing that never seems to stop, it could be something out of a Dickens novel.

But it's better than it was before. A psychiatrist, Said Abdullah Ahad Ahora, says the Taliban years were a nightmare for him.

'I was not allowed to speak to the women working here,' he says. 'Fifteen stayed on, as assistants, but only to treat the wives of the Taliban.'

Up the cold stairway, down a dirty corridor, a young woman crouches on a bed, her fingernails painted pale pink, rocking back and forth uttering incoherent phrases. She looks more like a bird than a human being. The room is freezing cold and the girl. who is called Shufga, which means blossom, is bundled in sweaters and a purple skirt and heavy socks. Her face is young, but lined with pain. Her father, Karimshah, is there, a farmer from the Shomali Valley north of Kabul, which suffered fierce fighting and carnage. Farms and villages were burned. Bodies were stuffed down wells. Cattle was slaughtered. Karimshah says that she is suffering as a result of years of war trauma.

'Six days ago, she stopped talking, went into another world,' he says. 'Our house was on the front line. She was terrified of the Taliban, of the noise, of the bombs.' For months, he said, as the fighting got worse, she stopped sleeping and eating. One day, she announced, 'I want the Taliban to go. I want the war to be over. I want to be free.' The next day, the young girl they knew disappeared behind a curtain of madness.

The doctors, not knowing what to do, have heavily sedated her. In Afghanistan, they still treat depression with electric shock, but they haven't given that to her yet. They diagnose her with 'acute psychosis' and feed her pills from a large brown bottle which she swallows dutifully. Sometimes she looks to the door and says, in a druggy voice, 'Are you my brothers?'

Her doctor, Said Abdullah Ahad Ahora, says, 'She doesn't know what she is saying.' But the British reporter I visit her with, Sam Kiley, is convinced she has suffered some trauma such as rape, maybe by a family member, and has retreated into another world to protect herself.

The doctor denies this. 'During the Taliban, we had many cases of grief. Teachers were forbidden to teach. Students were forbidden to learn. Women could not work. Of course they became depressed. You take a girl who is studying at university, who grew up with freedom and liberty, suddenly forced into a burka, and they get depressed.'

Shufga does not listen to the analysis, the explanations. It does not matter to her anymore. Her head lolls back, her eyelids flutter over glazed eyes and she draws her hands together like claws.

What will happen in Afghanistan? Jamila Mujahid believes that if 'Afghanistan unites, it can heal itself'. But it is a decision, she believes, that must be taken on by the educated people. 'And most of the educated people have fled,' she adds somberly. 'I am not sure they will return. Who would want to come back to this damaged place?' The ones that are left, she says, have no money and no power.

The Bonn Peace talks last November featured three women, Amina Afzali, an Iran-based activist, Seddighe Balkhi, who was also based in Iran, as well as a third woman, Sima Wali, another woman who lived in exile. More were promised to be included in the *loya jirga*, the traditional Afghan council, or general assembly. But the appointment of these women was not a popular choice in Kabul. The women I knew in the capital were angry, saying they came from wealthy, well-connected families and had not lived in Afghanistan during the Taliban years, opting for the comfort of Europe and Pakistan.

All over the regions I travelled during the war – Kabul, Jalalabad, Feysabad – even the remote northern outposts like Dash-e-Quala, women were sniffy about the difference between women who had stayed and lived under the heavy mantle of the Taliban and the ones who fled. Even RAWA, (Revolutionary Association of the Women of Afghanistan) which attracted so much media attention in the West, was targeted as an organisation which had been run outside of Afghanistan.

'It's not so difficult to fight for rights when you are not there,' said one. 'The real challenge is when you are inside, working under the oppression and trying to change things. That takes bravery.'

'If those Afghan women living in exile in Europe had been living in my position, they would have gone crazy,' Jamila Mujahid says. 'There were times when I felt like I was going crazy. But I resisted it.'

On 22 December, Hamid Karzai, the head of Afghanistan's six-month interim government was sworn in, promising to make more changes for women. The new administration opened a Department of Women's Affairs, and named women as heads of two of the government's twenty-nine ministries.

All this appears fine on paper. On the ground, change happens slowly. 'It will be a long time before the rights of women are restored,' says Kabul's most famous underground feminist, Soraya – *nom de guerre*, Parlika – a fifty-seven-year-old economist and former General Secretary of the Red Crescent Society. She chose the name Parlika because it was the name of a woman working for the Prophet Mohammed.

She first came to prominence when she began a women's organisation in 1992 in Kabul during the time of the mujahidin, when seven armed factions controlled the city and the fighting was intense. Rape, abduction, torture, looting and discrimination were every day occurrences for women. Women could not leave their homes because they would have to pass through several armed faction checkpoints, risking everything. Soraya remembers days spent locked in her house, her radio and television looted by the soldiers, without even a spoon to drink her tea. 'They took everything.'

The mujahidin would say, 'Give up your daughters, or we will kill you.' She explains: 'So families had no choice. I remember, there was this beautiful young girl who came to me and was so disturbed by the rape, she threw herself out the window. I can't describe in words the suffering of that time.'

Soraya – who was imprisoned for three months during the Russian invasion, was tortured with electric currents, was handcuffed for weeks on end, and still has scars on her arms where the guards stubbed their cigarettes out – decided to help women the only way she knew how. She informally organised a group which focused on the needs of women, orphans and widows. She continued during the Taliban years, organising secret schools, having to change her name and move from safe house to safe house so that she would not get caught.

'I had to be so careful, not just for me, but for other women,' she says. 'Many members were caught and beaten by the Taliban.'

Now, Soraya is trying to help women post-Taliban. The day I visit, there is supposed to be a demonstration of women throughout the streets of Microrayon, but it is cancelled 'for security reasons'. No one knows the security reasons, least of all the fifty or more women who crowd into her flat, begging her to help them find jobs. They sit on the floor, crowd in her corridors, in her kitchen. They wear burkas and hold out their hands, pleading, grabbing at my clothes as I squeeze pass them. The air is full of desperation, anger, sorrow.

'Please, please, help us,' they say. I try to talk to some, but too many cluster around, shouting, begging, shouting. It becomes claustrophobic. They see a Western face and they think you can do something for them, let them out of their prisons. You are their only ticket out of hell.

One woman, Shura, explains the desperation. She says, 'For five years, we could not recognise each other on the street because of our burkas. Now we can be together, and try to fight.'

Another woman, Kandigul, a sixty-year-old widow, comes up to me with a map of pain stamped on her face. Tears run like rivers down her face. Her entire family was displaced during the war, and she begins to tell a story of death, destruction and poverty, ending with a plea: 'Where can I put my name down for a job?' she asks. 'Where can I find a job?'

Another, Nadia, grabs my arm, pinching it hard as I move towards the door. 'Don't leave!' she commands. 'For five years, we have been sitting at home. Now, where can I get a job?'

In the end, I have to go. But it is with that horrible feeling I get in the pit of my stomach every time I am reporting somewhere like this, feeling powerless and useless in the face of other people's misery.

Afghanistan has changed a lot since that late autumn, early winter of 2001. A new government. So-called democracy. Cell phones and Internet cafés.

But all of these things are superficial in a sense, a Band-Aid on a bullet wound. To change a medieval mentality stamped on the psyche of a society will take far more than building bakeries, enforcing curfews and opening health clinics.

'The only way to restore peace is to educate Afghan men and women,' wrote Nick Danzinger, the British author of books on Afghanistan.

It's an obvious statement. But the reality on the ground, on Chicken Street in Kabul and in a girls' school in Jalalabad that I watched being reopened, with teachers still whipping the students with long branches from trees, is a long way from the armchair punters in London and New York. Everyone thinks they know what is best for Afghanistan. The reality is that this country is a fatally wounded place, badly bleeding, that has left its mark on the next generation. It is up to them in what direction their country will go, and how they will break down the traditional tribal and family values that keep women in the dark ages.

For instance, in the Kabul Central Police Station, a place that bears the legacy of years of torture and beatings, there is a nineteen-year-old girl called Feriba who sits in a darkened room in the Women's Section. This is where all the women under the Taliban who were tried for crimes like adultery, escaping from their families or kidnapping children were held.

She's wearing a white dress, like a bride, but she will probably never be a bride. The man she loves, Said Ahra, is in another section of the prison. They are there for their own protection. If they leave, Feriba's family will kill them.

During the Taliban years, the teenager was promised to a friend of her father, a wealthy Pashtun with strong links to the Taliban. She rebelled; she had fallen in love with twenty-three-year-old Said Ahra and the two lovers would often meet secretly in the garden of her house or when she came out on her balcony, like Juliet, while he waited underneath, telling her how much he loved her. They got caught.

She says in a heated voice, 'My father said, you will marry this man! And I cried, no I can't. My father said, you will marry him or I will kill you with my own revolver.'

Finally, her father dragged his headstrong daughter to prison, along with her beloved. Under the sharia law imposed by the Taliban, they were sentenced to five years in prison. The two languished for six months, meeting secretly when sympathetic guards brought them together, or passing love poems. They were released when the Northern Alliance liberated the town on 13 November.

The story then progresses into something out of *Arabian Nights*. When Feriba returned home, her father grabbed her by the hair and announced that she would marry another rich man, or die. 'He said he would kill Said too,' she says. Then her father relented.

According to Said, who I met in the men's section of the prison, 'He said if I had $3,000 I could have her,' he says. 'He knew I didn't even have $30.' The lovers were doomed.

A few days later, Feriba waited until night fell, found her lover and the two of them went back to prison.

'We are here for our own protection,' she said, and added that they were trying to get legal rights to marry from a judge. But she doubted it would ever happen. 'Said sends me messages: don't lose yourself. Remember I love you.'

She sits in the sunlight in a courtyard of her prison and stares up at the blue sky. Kites, once banned by the Taliban, are flying somewhere in the distance. Some things have changed here, but many have not, and Feriba is aware of this terrible irony.

'I know it would be easier to follow the tradition, to marry the man my parents want me to, and live a life of unhappiness,' she says, playing with her long fingers. 'Maybe now that the Taliban are gone, things will change. But you can see the problem – my family hold my fate.'

Her warder appears. She has to go back inside to the dank

cell. She turns back. 'The problem is society, but also Said. I just love *him*. It's in my heart. I can't explain why I do.'

The questions surrounding the future of women in Afghanistan are big ones. How to rebuild a society and what form should the government take: a secular democracy, an Islamic republic based on the Iran model, or something in between? Who will apply the rights of women in the new society? The women who have stayed in Afghanistan, and who did not go into exile, are aware of how strong the traditional Islamic culture is. They are aware of how hard it will be to break that mould, and to move forward in a traditional and, one can say, backward, patriarchal and conservative country.

Above all, there should not be too much interference from outside. All the women I spoke to voiced concern about Afghanistan, a country that has always prided itself on resisting foreign intervention since the days of what historians call 'The Great Game', essentially Britain and Russia's attempts to overrun it. They are quick to blame all of their problems, all of their internal strifes on Iran, Pakistan, Russia, the United States. During this healing time, they do need money and an economic lifeline. But they want to emerge from their chrysalis at their own speed, of their own accord. Even Dr Abdullah Abdullah, the thoughtful and charismatic Foreign Minister, told me over dinner in Kabul that change will come slow when it comes to women.

'In the short term, Afghanistan will emerge from this as a socially conservative Islamic society,' wrote Tamim Ansary. 'And if it does, it should not be confused with restoring the Taliban. If left alone and allowed to heal, Afghanistan will evolve. Social change imposed from the outside cannot produce a healthy society.'

The next generation, the ones who will be responsible for pulling this place out of the seventh century that the Taliban tried to recreate, are still shell-shocked, still trying to find their way around in this new world where they are not beaten for showing their ankles or making too much noise with their shoes lest they incite lust in the hearts of men. But it is not easy.

One night, two of the three burkas that I met near Chicken Street invite me to dinner at one of their houses. They are young struggling medical students, it turns out, who have finally resumed their studies after a five-year hiatus of sitting at home. It is Ramadan and, after the sun sets, I go to Sahaila's family house which lies down a dusty dirt road in Kabul. I am worried and embarrassed because I know that they will have spent all the money they have to prepare a feast for me, but it will be insulting to them to bring food or offer money. Instead, I shop in the bazaar and find jewelry for the three girls, lavish costume jewelry that to me seems happy, colourful and garish after years of Taliban grey.

When I arrive, they are thrilled with their presents and put on the earrings and the necklaces. 'We weren't sure you would come,' they say excitedly, making tea, taking my shoes and bringing me slippers. 'My father said if you were honourable, you would appear. And you have.'

They flocked around me. Sahaila's father, Hashim, is a kind, softly-spoken man who speaks fluent English and once worked for the UN as an agricultural specialist. In the old days, he travelled on seminars to Britain, America and France. Now he is starved for information on the outside world. He has not worked for several years and shows me around the house, shows the markings from shells and artillery fire that have pockmarked the walls. When you think about bombs falling, you don't think about them falling on houses, on people like this. But they do.

When the feast arrives, it is clear the women have spent all day cooking. Traditionally, it is served on the floor, but they do not eat with me; they just sit on cushions, serve and watch. Hashim tells stories of life under the Taliban. Their mother does not join me.

'She is too shy,' says Sahaila, who on this occasion has removed her burka and is wearing trousers and a sparkly jumper. Her friend, Karishma, is wearing eyeshadow and jeans.

The girls act like teenagers. They play music on a cheap cassette player: Ricky Martin and the soundtrack to *Titanic*. They are crazy about *Titanic*, a bizarre trend that occurred during the Taliban years when everyone watched the smuggled video over and over again in secret basements. The girls keep asking if I know Leonardo di Caprio, and I spare them the misery of telling them about his supermodel girlfriend, Gisele.

Instead, I try to ask them what they hope for the future, what they want to do with their country, but they are more concerned with the first step, understanding popular culture and what they have missed by all the years of seclusion.

'*Titanic* was the only video I saw for a year,' Sahaila says, getting back to her favourite conversation as a way of telling her own tale. During that year, and all the other dark ones when she was not going to medical school, she studied secretly, at home, carefully reading an English dictionary and trying to practise her vocabulary with her father. She was a lot luckier than most. She had a father who was educated and modern enough to believe a girl should be too.

But bad things happened. Hunger. Sickness. Isolation.

Death. On a small table is a photograph of a young woman with the darkest eyes. Something about the photograph looks sombre, and Sahaila catches me looking at it. 'My sister, she's dead,' says Sahaila. It's her older sister who died in childbirth, the fate of 1,700 per 100,000 Afghan women who give birth.

Karishma's eyes fill with tears; she says her friend had just graduated from law school before the Taliban arrived. 'She never got to see the end of them.' According to the World Health Organisation, one woman in Afghanistan dies from pregnancy-related complications every thirty minutes. Afghanistan rates second highest in the world for maternal mortality, next to Sierra Leone.

This family, who I am laughing and drinking sweet tea with, are victims of a bland statistic.

Hashim's face sags. He says, 'I tried to save her. I drove her all the way to Pakistan, but it was too late.' He shakes his head. 'She had the most beautiful character.' Then he looks at his younger daughter, as if to lighten the mood of sadness and says, 'This one is more feisty.'

The feisty one, Sahaila, is tired of sorrow and darkness and living underground. She suddenly stands up, picking up the empty dishes of food with her, a signal that the conversation is over. She changes the cassette to something Latin-sounding and sways slightly to the beat. Karishma looks up at her, startled by the provocative moves.

'Do you know how to dance?' Sahaila asks. 'I never learned. Now maybe I am going to start.'

The Battle of Tora Bora

4 December, 2001

If you like this kind of thing, the bombing is spectacular

The B52s fly between 20,000 and 30,000 feet, but some days there are AC130 gunships with 25-millimetre Gatlin guns. With binoculars or a strong camera lens, you see this: a grey blur moving through the sky slowly but menacingly. Then you see the fine white line that it leaves behind in the blue sky, a perfect clean line as neatly drawn as a child's first alphabet. The morning a surrender was demanded of al-Qaeda fighters by 8 a.m., war planes began circling in the early morning light, methodically drawing figure-of-eights and widening circles.

When the bombs finally drop the mujahidin stop laughing and look reverently at the valley where they have fallen. The hills look like they are on fire with a burst of orange explosion. Then comes the crash and, sometimes, the shake of the earth.

The smoke curls into the sky like a mushroom cloud, grey

and fierce. You drive deeper and deeper into the White Mountains, and get so close to the bombing that the cloud is almost overhead. After the explosion, the cloud hangs and lingers delicately for a few minutes then dissipates into the air, scattering the sky and the ground with thick, choking dust.

These are the weapons they use: Joint Attack Direct Munition – JADMS – satellite-guided bombs that cost $20,000 and are attached to the tail of a conventional 1,000-pound and 2,000-pound warhead launched from fifteen miles away and an altitude of 45,000 feet; CBU-87 cluster bombs; cluster bombs that split open and release more than 200 mini-bomblets hung by parachutes; 500-pound bombs; 1,000-pound bombs – 'bunker busters'; GBU-15 manually guided or satellite bombs; a 15,000-pound 'daisy cutter' that destroys everything within a 600-yard radius.

This is what it feels like to be under aerial bombardment. You see the planes and you hear the whirr of the engine. Or maybe you don't see anything because you are running to take cover. In a cave, in a ditch, in something that might offer you some protection. If the crash is near, it is so loud that you cover your ears and try to protect your head, but it might be too late.

Your skin gets punctured by white-hot shrapnel that imbeds itself into your flesh, or your vital organs. You are lucky if you die quickly. The daisy cutter is more cruel. It acts like a petrol bomb and sucks the air out of your lungs. You suffocate. It might take time to die.

Most of all, you feel like you cannot hide. That the bombs will seek you out and swallow you up. You feel like you are in a doll's house and there is a giant on top, smashing his hand again and again into your room.

Afterwards, the al-Qaeda fighters who got captured talked

and wept about the defencelessness they felt as they lay under the bombs. How the bombs kept coming, even when they could take no more. How they killed everyone around them, wiped out the trees, the animals and the birds. The trees were on fire. And how they could not stop hearing the crash and not stop seeing the bombers, even in their dreams.

The people who drop the bombs, the American soldiers, are young, probably in their twenties. From the ground underneath them, I try to imagine their faces and what they are thinking when they drop these things that kill the enemy. One morning, scattered among the unexploded bomblets is a canister. One American soldier had taken out his magic marker and wrote this on the side of the canister before it dropped out the side of the plane:

> For those whose dreams were taken,
> Here are a few nightmares
> This is gonna shine like a diamond in a goat's ass.

The al-Qaeda are supposedly the enemy, but I try to imagine their fear. The relentless bombs. How they found them even in their caves, in their trenches, dugouts. The ones who survived kept seeing and hearing them. Even in their dreams they kept hearing the bombers.

The Bombs, 4–21 December, 2001

> *Guided by satellite, the military's newest 'smart bomb' is designed to hit its target with great precision in any weather.*
> *The system is not without risk, as was evident Wednesday in Afghanistan, with deadly results for the U.S. military: three*

soldiers killed, 20 others wounded when a bomb carrying 2,000 pounds of explosives landed about 100 yards from their position.

'Sometimes things just don't work out perfectly,' Rear Adm. John Stufflebeem said at the Pentagon.

The Associated Press, December 6, 2001

Sometimes the bombs miss, then they hit villages. Sometimes people are killed and we don't hear about it and it reminds me of a macabre journalist's joke. If 1,000 people are killed in a rainforest in Brazil but there are no reporters to witness it, did it really happen?

In Jalalabad, the only hospital is a reeking, filthy place, with dirty blankets and peeling walls. The emergency room is a stinking pit with cubicles separated by grimy sheets, and a mujahidin wounded fighting near Tora Bora vomiting from pain while a crowd of children watch.

There are fifty-seven people here today wounded by errant bombs. Fifteen this week have died. One of them who is not yet dead is this small boy lying on his side. He's called Patient Number Ten and he hasn't woken up since the B52 dropped the bomb that fell on his house five days ago and killed his father, his three sisters and eight other members of the extended family living in his house.

Patient Number Ten is lying in a filthy bed with a bloody rag on his head and a dirty syringe in his arm. His hands are curled like claws, his arms are wrapped in more bandages, all soaked in blood. Sometimes he turns over and moans in pain, and sometimes, his nurses say, he calls out for his mother.

The doctor watching him speaks some English. He tries to be helpful, but when he speaks to the boy his tone is harsh, maybe because he knows Patient Number Ten is a goner.

He's had surgery to remove the superficial bits of metal from his skull, but the deeper bits still remain lodged in his brain.

Patient Number Ten, whose name is Zahid Ullah, is eight years old.

The doctor tells me to go and see his mother to find out what happened the day the bomb dropped. Down the hallway with bodies on dirty stretchers, up the stairs to the women's ward is his thirty-two-year-old mother, Gouhar Taj. She's got a baby, five-month old son Nasir, curled in her arms and she is in shock; she can't remember which of her children is living and which is dead. Her left eye is missing and is nothing more than a hole; her face is marked by deep brown wounds. She pulls back the thin blanket and shifts Nasir to show her left leg, which is broken.

She tries to explain what happened, but when she talks she makes little sense. Her words come out slow and slurred. 'All we were doing was eating dinner,' she says, watching me with her one good eye. 'We were drinking our tea when it happened.'

There were seven of them sitting down to eat, Gouhar says. It was the holy month of Ramadan and everyone had been fasting during the day. When the sun set, she laid bread down on the floor for Iftar, the breaking of the fast, and the children were so hungry. She got the tea, got the glasses. Then an explosion threw her across the room.

When she looked down, there was blood all over the place, on her leg and face. She scooped up two of her children – the baby Nasir and her two-year-old – and ran outside.

There, the village she had known all of her life, Agam, was transformed into a place she did not know. People were screaming, picking up bodies, clutching their clothes, moaning in agony. Cars arrived to take the wounded three hours by car, over bumpy tracks to the hospital in Jalalabad. By the time there was a car for Gouhar and two of her surviving children, the villagers had already begun burying the dead. They buried ten at night and ten more in the morning. She still did not know her husband was dead. Maybe they buried him then, she says.

Lying on her side, Gouhar – who is illiterate and who married when she was fourteen – says she doesn't know why, in fact, Tora Bora is getting bombed. I ask her about Osama bin Laden. Her brow wrinkles. She has heard the name, but she doesn't know what al-Qaeda is, and she has no idea where New York or Washington are.

All she knows is that her husband is dead, along with her three daughters, and that she is now a widow, which is possibly the worse thing that can happen to a woman in Afghanistan.

She says she is too tired to cry. She says, 'I don't know what to do. I lost my husband, my daughters and a part of my body.'

She wants me to leave, so she sends me to the next bed, to her sister-in-law, Mustafa Jan, who is nursing her six-month-old baby, Rahim. Every part of her body, including her breast, is razored with shrapnel wounds. Her face is an oozing wound and Rahim has a bandage on his bald head.

Mustafa Jan is twenty-eight and was in the house when the bomb dropped. Now she's a widow too and her two children, Shahla and Zanub, are covered in bandages and have tiny broken arms. Shahla, who is two, is sitting in her own urine and no one is there to change her; she keeps screaming and screaming, while her mother cringes with pain as the baby nurses on her wounded breast. She says her son, Esmatullah, will tell me what happened.

He's nine. He's got a bandage around his eyes; the doctors aren't sure the extent of the damage to his optic nerve. Right now he can't see, but he moves his hands as he talks to this stranger, me, and tells me how my country bombed him.

'It was getting dark. Then the plane came and there was something loud. It was so loud my ears hurt. Then I saw nothing. Someone came and picked me up.'

I leave him and his mother who is still nursing the baby with glazed eyes, deadened with pain. The chief surgeon is outside. His eyes burn with something too: rage. He says that Osama is in the mountains, but these people live in the villages. 'It isn't their problem,' he keeps repeating to me, over and over. I tell him I am sorry. In light of the pain in the room nearby, in light of the fact that an entire family is destroyed because of a computer mistake from the bomb, it sounds hollow and empty.

Offensive, The Milewa Valley, 12 December, 2001

It still smelled like death. Trees that had been hit by cluster bombs were still smouldering, amputated at the limbs, their strange stunted arms reaching towards the sky. Tins of food that the al-Qaeda fighters may have eaten that morning lay in front of their positions. Strange things that showed how they lived, how they died. A shredded uniform hanging from a tree, someone that had been vaporised by a bomb. A packet of cheap Iranian strawberry biscuits. Paper scrawled with Arabic writing. Manuals for guns.

In front of one cave, a fire still burning where someone had made their morning tea.

It did not seem possible that, hours before, al-Qaeda had

lived here, fought here, lain on their stomachs in position with their guns poised at the ridge below. Died here, or ran away. The deserted, barren place where they fought back with mortars, tanks, long-range missiles, is empty. More shredded clothes; a bloody shoe. There is something apocalyptic about the place.

In the rubble, one mujahidin called Osman stands in front of a cave. His cheap brown plastic shoes are falling apart; he says that he has been awake all night and fighting this last battle since 9 a.m. He rubs his eyes with exhaustion.

'They're gone,' Osman says. 'The Arabs have run away.'

Now, nothing human remains, but the air was heavy and strange, as though the phantoms of the fighters were still somewhere in the trees. Osman talks about booby traps the Arabs have left behind. He leads the way, gingerly, one foot in front of the other, looking for mines, across a flattened hilltop, past a stream. A burnt-out car; some more scattered uniforms.

There was still smoke from the bombs, and there were more remnants of how these fighters had lived for the past few weeks. They left behind pieces of gym equipment – green plastic barbells, boxing gloves, weights – and in the middle of the field they had constructed a primitive chin-up bar. Inside the dankness of the caves, there were scattered documents in Arabic, old tattered notebooks with scores and Kevlar helmets. Pillows and mattresses where they slept.

Near the burnt-out remains of a shack, a soldier pointed out a ruined position. He said Osama had lived here. 'This was his house, his place.'

The sun lowered in the sky, the soldiers gathered their blankets around their uniforms and prepared to break their fast for Ramadan. In one valley that had been gutted by bombs, a dead tank was left abandoned in the middle of the field. Now, an old mujahidin was standing near it, oblivious to this object of destruction. He was facing East and praying.

Mop-Up, Tora Bora, 17 December, 2001

In the end, the fighting grew fierce. The cold came, spreading across the valleys, more snow falling on the whiteness of the peaks that led towards the Pakistani border. The border was sealed, with gunships and troops. They said that al-Qaeda were cornered.

The bombing was harder, more intense. The sounds were different. Vacuum bombs, bunker busters, petrol bombs that made it impossible to breathe. A mujahidin holds his hands to his chest to demonstrate. 'It makes your lungs . . .' He moves his hand. 'Explode.'

Small units of mujahidin moved closer to the higher caves, so close to the bombs falling that they saw the trees lit up by fire. It became so cold that they pleaded over the radio for blankets to be sent up by donkeys. They had no food and were running out of ammunition; it was Ramadan and they were growing weaker and weaker from fasting. One commander snapped, 'My men have not eaten in twenty-nine days.' Another mujahidin, reached by radio from his position, pleaded for the end of the battle. He said the cold was unbearable.

'Our hands are so stiff we can't fire,' he cried. 'Ask the Americans to use gas and it will be the end of the story.'

The Americans are in the sky and American and British Special Forces are on the ground, but they are not alone.

There's three mujahidin and former anti-Taliban commanders leading three separate militias here, working alongside them. They are meant to be united, deploying their individual militias up different sides of the mountains, but like everything in Afghanistan, their roles are unclear and their loyalties are divided. This is a country where betrayal in battle is so common that to find a commander who has not switched several allegiances during the twenty-two years of fighting is to find an odd man.

'We don't fight for ideology,' a mujahidin who had first fought with the Communists, then the anti-Communists, then flirted with the Taliban, then the anti-Taliban, laughingly told me. 'We fight for whoever gives us the most.'

The three here are clearly battling it out for power. Haji Zahir, the youngest, is the son of Haji Abdul Kadir, the governor of the Nangahir province and the new Minister for Reconstruction. His father is an elegant, articulate man whose family for generations have been part of Afghanistan's landed gentry, but have also been linked to the opium trade. When he first arrived back in Jalalabad in November after spending the Taliban years in exile, Haji Kadir brought with him a flowing white turban that he had not put on since he had been forced to flee over the Pakistani border. That night, he put the turban back on his head and moved back into his stately home that the Taliban had just vacated.

Zahir's uncle was the late Abdul Haq, who was closely aligned to America during the Soviet war, and who was captured and hung by the Taliban in October. Like his uncle and his father, Zahir is a fighter. When he holds his Kalashnikov, it is with the certain assurance of a man who has lived all his life in war, but his militia is said to be the weakest and, in the end, he will vie and scramble for control.

The second commander, Haji Zaman, is closest to the Americans. He lived in France and the USA for years, and can rattle off all the states he has passed time in. His French is perfect, but heavily accented. It is Zaman who meets with the Americans as he has the best English and the best contacts, but he still has the air of a man who is terrified of being pushed out of the circle. He had allegedly been given $100 per soldier in addition to food and clothes. But Zaman was also rumoured to have had close links with both the Taliban and al-Qaeda, and therefore sympathies and interests to let them escape as bloodlessly as possible.

The third, Hazret Ali, is a grizzled former Northern Alliance commander and therefore a stranger in these eastern, largely Pashtun-dominated parts. He is thought to be the best fighter with the best militia. But he seemed to be completely drawn out of the circle involving the Americans, and he frequently complains of the decisions the others make.

All of them keep sending more men up the mountains. Every morning, when the pink light rolls behind the ridges, the reinforcements go up the dirt paths that led to the parallel valleys, packed in the back of flat-bed trucks, wrapped in their patus, their thin brown Afghan blankets. They go up cheering and waving their guns.

At night, when the sun went down and the time for Iftar, the breaking of the Ramadan fast, approached, a different group came down, bringing the dead, small bodies, wrapped in bloody green and pink quilts. In death, these packages seemed too small to be men. The lumps they made under the blankets did not seem big enough to define a life.

Sometimes the mujahidin travel with foreigners. American and British Special Forces arrive and dress in Afghan clothes, but carry M-16s and grenade launchers. Sitting behind the tinted windows of four-wheel drive vehicles, they hide their faces.

One Sunday as Ramadan was nearing its end, Haji Zahir stood on a peak and announced that the battle for Tora Bora had reached a turning point. 'There will be no more negotiations because there are so many dead,' Zahir announced. He said he and his men had captured dozens of al-Qaeda prisoners and that the battle was nearly finished. But as Zahir gloated, machine-gun fire from an al-Qaeda position across the ridge sprayed the place where we stood, the acoustic of the bullets ricocheting through the air.

Zahir ordered everyone to move to a safe place, but dangled a carrot to reporters. He said he had prisoners, that he would present them the next day. He said it grinning happily, as though this victory ensured him the coveted place in the Americans' affections.

The soldiers leaned against a stone hut that had been their position that morning with exhaustion and the weariness that comes with days on end of battle. Another soldier, Commander Shah, said the battle was nearing an end, that the fields higher up were littered with the dead bodies of al-Qaeda. 'There are five in one place, ten in another, so many in different places.' One of his mujahidin fighters said there were guts and intestines of the dead split open on the ground.

Despite the fact that, the week before, two plans for surrender negotiations had failed, Commander Shah insisted this time that the 'real surrender had begun'. The al-Qaeda, split into isolated groups, could only contact each other by radio now and were surrounded in their caves by the Special Forces and the mujahidin. On the radio, some were crying in Arabic, pleading not to be handed over to the Americans. Some became more fanatic as the end of the battle drew closer; they killed themselves rather than be taken, ripping pins from their grenades as the mujahidin entered the caves, blowing themselves to bits and surrendering to the fate of Allah.

The next morning, ten kilometres from the front line, the American bombers still flew overhead, but the Arab prisoners were brought down the mountain. They did not look like the devil to me. They looked hungry, scared, lonely, far from homes in Yemen, Lebanon, Syria, Egypt. The ones from Afghanistan had their hands behind their backs, tied with red rope.

The mujahidin, who were trying to take credit for the victory over Tora Bora, led them out of a timber and mud shack and paraded them in front of a penned-up crowd of frantic journalists waving cameras, notebooks and tape recorders. They hid their faces and stared at the ground. They looked as though they had not eaten for a long time, cheekbones sunken, eyes like dead men.

At first, the twenty-two prisoners were led one by one to a makeshift wooden bench in the yard and made to sit amongst crowing chickens. At first, I wrote scrawled notes. Number One: striped shirt, defiant expression. Number Two: limps, looks like bullet wound, older, grey beard. Number Three: no shoelaces, stares at the ground.

Watching their humiliation was painful, but they had become more than prisoners of war. They were the only tangible evidence of Osama bin Laden, symbols of everything that had happened on September 11.

As one was pushed forward, he stumbled. His face was a grimace of fear. I stopped taking notes. I muttered, to no one, 'Isn't this a violation of the Geneva Convention?' A reporter in front of me, whom I have known for a decade, was angry.

The night before, he had seen parts of the video in which Osama bin Laden learns of the fatal damage of the September 11 attacks in America. 'He was gloating and gleeful,' my friend said. Now, he has no sympathy for the al-Qaeda fighters, even if they were only foot soldiers. 'Did they show mercy to the people who were killed in America?' he raged. 'Did they think of the Geneva Convention when they joined al-Qaeda?'

In the yard, one of the prisoners dropped his head in his hands. He said he did not want his family to see his photograph, to know that he was a member of al-Qaeda.

He was led away. The grotesque circus was almost over. Others came. A mujahidin said, 'They are ashamed.' He handled his former foes gently, leading them to the bench, holding their hands and then leading them back, letting them lean on him when they could not walk.

One of them came out of the timber shack. He sat down and faced the pen of journalists. But before he was led away to where some of the prisoners, too badly injured to move, lay, he raised his hand weakly and flashed a victory sign. They pushed him forward, and he disappeared inside the hut.

The End of the Battle, Jalalabad, 19 December, 2001

They say the war is over, the last stand of the al-Qaeda in Afghanistan is over, but from where I am sitting, it doesn't look that way.

They say some al-Qaeda fighters are still roaming the mountainous region, but that the organised chain of command has been destroyed, and that they have been pushed back to the Pakistani border. They say that the rotting corpses litter the gorges, the caves, the gullies. From an original number of nearly 1,000 fighters, commanders say that only handfuls remain on the snowy peaks of the White Mountains.

But who has seen these bodies?

The mujahidin, who say the they 'didn't need the Americans anyway', say it's all over. 'The war, I think is finished,' said Haji Atiquallah, a spokesman for Zahir. 'Al-Qaeda have no food or ammunition.'

Since the beginning of the bombing campaign more than two weeks ago, fifty al-Qaeda prisoners have been captured. A lot more of them are dead. 'This makes us happy and sad,' says Hazret Ali. 'Sad because we wanted to capture them all alive; and happy because we have gotten terrorists out of our country.'

The mujahidin jeer. But it seems such a pale victory. Overnight, the war planes still fly, shaking the earth. Hazret Ali grimly says to me, 'Yes, the planes are still there. They hit one of my positions last night.'

On the ground, the war does not seem over. In Kabul the next week, the Foreign Minister, Abdullah Abdullah admits there are still pockets of terrorists. And through the smuggler routes that border Pakistan, villagers say that al-Qaeda are still moving across. If they had run, there were three ways they could have done it. Via the Khyber Pass, which winds down the mountains from the town of Khogiani, to the Torkhum border. Another route is via the switchback, which cuts into the Afghan town of Azrow, then to Parachinar in Pakistan. Finally, they might have escaped through the mountains, which is the shortest route. They could go straight into Pakistan through the mountain footpaths.

There is no sign of bin Laden. Some commanders say they

believe that he passed through this area weeks before and is gone. Others say he would never abandon his men and is with them, the last pockets of resistance, somewhere in the south. One mid-level al-Qaeda prisoner called Abu Abdur Rahman told reporters that Osama was with them until the twenty-eighth day of Ramadan, told them to pray, and then magically disappeared.

Later, at the airport in Peshawar, the border town of Pakistan, the representative at Pakistan International Airlines who helps me with my ticket home seems unaware he is supposed to stop bin Laden if he passes through.

'You mean, I'm supposed to call the American Embassy?' he says, surprised. 'Do you have the telephone number?'

The battle of Tora Bora is over. But it was an ending without closure. Where were all the bodies that proved al-Qaeda were gone? Where is Osama bin Laden? And why, more importantly, was it so chilling when one of the al-Qaeda prisoners flashed the victory sign as he was led away that day when I watched them humiliated, paraded around in front of the press, like animals?

There's really only one thing that matters about Tora Bora. It will be more than four years since I stood there, cold, agitated, watching those B52s. And they still haven't found Osama.

America

Before the Fall:
Two Rivers, New Jersey

11 September, 2002

Until 11 September, 2001, the biggest disaster that could take place in the Two Rivers area of Monmouth County, New Jersey was a hurricane. Signs designating Coastal Evacuation Routes dot the main roads. Most families keep supplies of flashlights and extra batteries for the times when the Atlantic Ocean batters back the sea walls. But those things, we now know, do nothing against a terrorist attack.

The Two Rivers communities – composed of several hamlets with names like Red Bank, Fair Haven and Rumson – are nestled between the Navesink and the Shrewsbury Rivers, an affluent peninsula twenty-five miles south of the tip of Manhattan Island. Middletown leads into Red Bank which leads into Fair Haven which leads into Rumson and Little Silver, perfect little matchbox villages. They are bordered by the loping green farms in Colts' Neck, which breed thoroughbred race horses, and long golden beaches of the New Jersey shore.

This is a rich place. Houses are either grand and imposing

with columns and towers and their own ponds and bridges, like something out of *The Great Gatsby*, or small, pastel-coloured, Victorian and quaint. Manicured lawns are emerald green and lush. Window boxes burst with lavender and pink petunias. While Red Bank does have a mixed community with Black and Hispanic families in certain neighbourhoods, Fair Haven and Rumson are white-bred and WASP-y. There's lots of blond hair, blue eyes and perfectly straight teeth. It's Ralph Lauren country.

Most of the inhabitants are wealthy. They commute to New York City either by ferry or train to work as investment bankers and Wall Street traders; on the weekends they go crabbing by the Navesink River, sailing at exclusive beach clubs that line the shore, or antique shopping in Red Bank. It's suburban, but sophisticated. Red Bank, with its film festivals, cafés and shops selling Prada, was voted the hippest town in New Jersey.

In Rumson – home to generations of WASPs, Bruce Springsteen and Jon Bon Jovi – there is a Bikram Yoga Centre as well as a pharmacy that sells La Prairie cosmetics next to copies of French *Vogue*, *Harpers and Queen* and *Tatler*. With more young families moving in from Manhattan, it has become a suburban version of Notting Hill.

In 1981, my parents, tired of the metropolitan rat race of the New York area, moved here. They found the pace of life tranquil and my father loved the sea. Their neighbours brought plates of home-made cookies and at Christmas time, children would gather to sing carols. My family had spent their summer holidays in the area since the 1940s, when my parents married; my four brothers and sister and I spent August days body surfing in the Atlantic and eating strawberry ice-cream sodas at Nagle's Drugstore in Ocean Grove, swinging our bare, sandy feet from stools at the counter.

There was a Norman Rockwell quality to the place. The first time I saw Frank Capra's magical film, *It's A Wonderful Life*, depicting life in an idyllic small town, I shouted to my mother, 'It's Red Bank!' If this area were a human being, it would be a beautiful teenager who had no thoughts other than cruising around in a convertible listening to the Beach Boys.

All of that magic, that innocence, changed forever on September 11. 158 people from Monmouth County died in the World Trade Center, the highest figure in New Jersey. They mostly came from the Two Rivers area. The majority came from Middletown, but Fair Haven, Rumson, Red Bank – all bedroom communities of Manhattan – took terrible blows.

Now, there are not just Coastal Evacuation Road signs. One year on, nearly every house in the Twin Rivers area has an American flag hanging outside. Every morning at 7 a.m., my mother's local radio station, which gives the ocean temperature and the times of low and high tide, plays Kate Smith belting out, '*God Bless America, land that I love. Stand beside her, and guide her . . .*' Store windows have huge signs that say: God Bless America and the Victims and their Families.

No one has to ask who the victims are; everyone knows. Everyone in this area, whether they were connected to the victims or not, has changed forever. Here in Two Rivers, we're on the flight path from Newark and JFK airports, and in the past, no one looked up at the sky when they passed. But one of the fatal Twin Towers flights took off from Newark Airport. And now, you watch people. When a plane passes, they all look up silently, wondering, craning their necks and staring into the sky, waiting for something to happen.

*   *   *

My sister, Judy, was working in the Sugar Plum Cottage, an up-market children's shop in Fair Haven that sells imported French and Italian clothes, when she heard the news of two planes crashing into the Twin Towers. She calls Fair Haven, which lies adjacent to Red Bank, 'Mayberry RFD', referring to an American television show from the 1960s which depicted a small town of corny, close-knit people who banded together in times of tragedy.

Fair Haven is only 1.6 square miles and has a population of 5,600, and my sister is one of the most recognisable people there because she talks to everyone, and everyone talks to her. She is a member of the Fair Haven Garden Club, which meets once a month in an old church and has lunches with crustless sandwiches and tea served on silver trays. When she takes her morning walk on the river from her elegant colonial-style house where she has lived for a dozen years, everyone she passes nods, beams good morning and asks about her daughter and how she gets such beautiful window-boxes.

She knows most of the policemen, the firemen, the waitresses at the Red Bank Diner, the florists, the pharmacist, the manicurist. But everyone in Fair Haven knows each other. When we sit at Edie's luncheonette, where Bruce Springsteen has breakfast most mornings, she talks to the owner, the waitress, the lady at the next table.

Like everyone on September 11, my sister remembers how the Two Rivers community reacted. 'Shock, horrifying panic,' she says. 'There were rumours flying around that our water would be contaminated, that there would be another attack. People were paralysed with fear.' There were radio reports for people to stay home, not to use the highway. But she did – she can't remember why – and one image haunts her: at a designated time when everyone was meant to stand outside their cars and have a moment of silence, she saw a Black American family silently waving a huge American flag in the autumn breeze.

But the shock in Fair Haven morphed quickly into action. Neighbours began mobilising in an almost military fashion, collecting clothes, food, water, flashlights, supplies. People queued for hours at the local Red Cross in Shrewsbury to give blood. The ferry lines evacuated people from New York for free and immediately began taking supplies across for the volunteer workers at Ground Zero. An Albanian immigrant, Zoya Bitic, who runs a Red Bank boutique, began sewing a dress made from an American flag which she displayed in her window. Two young brothers, Billy and Alex Perkins, set up a lemonade stand and raised $150 for families of the victims, two of whom lived on their street.

The chief of police, Richard Towler – who is a descendent of the original Black American community who settled Fair Haven hundreds of years ago – wasn't surprised at how people responded. 'It's a caring place,' he says. 'People look out for each other.'

Towler describes Fair Haven, which has one of the lowest crime rates in the state, as a place where there are no locked doors or cars, where neighbours set up 'block parties' on hot summer nights, where kids roam free without fear of abduction or harm. Still, the attack on the WTC sent a shockwave through the peaceful town. People were stunned and horrified. 'But they clung to each other,' Towler says.

Some of them did more than that. Garrett Bess, a thirty-five-year-old advertising executive, was sitting in his office in midtown Manhattan when the planes hit. His phone lines went down. He sent an email to his brother in California to try to get through to his wife and two small daughters in Fair Haven and tell them he was still alive. Then he grabbed his briefcase and began running – not walking – downtown towards the ferry which drops passengers in Atlantic Highlands, not far from Fair Haven.

His one concern was to get out of New York and back to his family. 'It was like an old horror movie from the 1950s – Godzilla,' he says. 'People were running the opposite way, shrieking, covered in dust and bits of rubble.'

That day, the Seastreak Ferry evacuated more than 4,000 people from Manhattan to Atlantic Highlands, and Bess was one of them. He made it on board, and as the ferry passed by the burning towers, he remembers bellowing at the other passengers, who were twittering with nervous energy: 'Could everyone shut up and have respect for people still inside those buildings?' The ferry went silent as they passed. Bess saw the flames, the hole in the sky, people jumping out of windows.

When the ferry docked, in New Jersey, Bess and the others were hosed down and decontaminated. The parking lot was full of the usual Audis, Mercedes, BMWs and Lexus, but that day, many of them were not picked up. After a few days, when it was clear their owners were never coming back to get them, local people put bouquets of flowers on them. 'And that,' says Eileen Moon, the editor of the *Two Rivers Times*, the award-winning local newspaper, 'was one of the saddest things to see.' To commemorate the tragedy, Moon ran an entire front page with the W.H. Auden poem, *September 1, 1939*:

> *I sit in one of the dives*
> *On Fifty-Second Street*
> *Uncertain and afraid*
> *As the clever hopes expire*

Of a low dishonest decade;
Waves of anger and fear
Circulate over the bright
And darkened lands of the earth,
Obsessing our private lives
The unmentionable odour of death
Offends the September night . . .

Moon worked flat out those days, writing profiles of the dead and trying to get alongside the volunteers. But for Moon, the clearest memory of that time is the smell. She woke on the night of September 11 'to an evil cloud. It took me a while to recognise it. Bodies, chemicals, a horrible, acrid smell.'

For Bess, the clearest memory was the sudden realisation that the guys he saw every day for years on the ferry were not going to be there next week. That – and how when he saw his family waiting for him at the marina in New Jersey, he burst into tears for the first time.

At home, he and his wife Dawn, a dance teacher, watched their neighbour pacing up and down on her front porch, waiting for her husband. He never came home. It was awful, Bess recalled, and he wanted to help her. 'What can I do?' he thought. 'What am I best doing? What are my skills?' It took the former student leader about ten minutes to work out. He picked up the phone and began organising a memorial service for the entire town to take place two days later.

On Friday, 14 September, in Fair Haven Fields, more than 1,500 people gathered to hear Bess and various clergy and community leaders speak. Bess had gone out and bought 1,500 candles at the local Acme, along with plastic cups which he stayed up at night cutting to make holders so people would not get wax on their hands. Then he picked up the phone and called Bruce Springsteen, whose children Dawn had taught. Springsteen is a resident here, and while people love him, they also respect his privacy. People protect him.

Bearing this in mind, Bess got Bruce's answer machine in Rumson and chose his words carefully. He told Springsteen about the service, adding, 'It would mean a lot to the community if you were there.' On Friday night, speaking to the weeping crowd, all holding candles, Bess said, 'I don't know about the rest of you, but I couldn't sit at home and watch TV. We should not endure this tragedy alone.' Behind a tree, he spied Springsteen, his wife, Patty, and their two children.

The next few days, Bess organised goods – clothes, shoes, socks – that he had collected from local residents and stowed on his front porch, to be taken to Ground Zero. He transported the piles back and forth to the ferry. A few days later, Bess bumped into Springsteen on the ferry, wearing a baseball cap and denim jacket. The singer recognised Bess from the memorial service and hugged him. 'Oh man,' The Boss said, 'Thank you for that. I needed it, the town needed it. Thank you.'

'I wasn't feeling so good. Guys I rode the boat with weren't coming home. And that hug made me feel so good,' says Bess. 'Not because it was Bruce. Just because I felt comfort.'

Down the street, Laura Jewell, a marketing executive who had discovered Fair Haven by literally driving into it, and fell in love with it, was also organising a fund-raising activity. Jewell – who worked on the seventy-second floor of the WTC in the 1980s – lost two of her neighbours, and she found she could not concentrate on work or even her two beloved dogs; she wanted to do something. 'The world stood still, but around here, you couldn't stand still,' she says. 'Husbands did not come home. Sons and daughters did not come home.'

So Jewell convinced all her neighbours and local businesses to clean out their attics and garages. She staged an elaborate car-boot sale and a silent auction. She sold sailboats and tickets to restaurants. She raised $20,000 for the victims' families.

Post 9/11, it was almost as though people who had nodded to each other before suddenly reached out and grabbed one another, in desperation, in grief. Eileen Moon explains what happened in the community over the next few weeks as something close to miraculous. 'People here are wealthy and can be arrogant,' she says. 'But there was a sense, for a few weeks, of our collective humanity. It was palatable. Churches were packed. Here, we were insulated from disaster. To have something like that happen on a blue sky morning – it struck at our hearts.

Sandy Feigen, a seventeen-year-old student at Rumson Fair Haven High School, describes it like this: 'I never thought of us as being in a war zone,' she says. 'But for a while, it was like that. So everyone stuck together.'

In Red Bank, the hub of the communities and the birthplace of the musician Count Basie and the writer Edmund Wilson, the cafés and waterfront bars went silent on September 11. From the window of his office, Stanley Sickels, the fire marshal and town administrator, could see the black smoke from the towers rising above the Navesink.

A fire specialist who knew the WTC well – he had taught classes on fire prevention and evacuation there – he immediately went to Ground Zero, where he was given the task of securing the area for the 15,000 volunteers. There's a photograph of the towers in his office now, next to his fire hat and the photographs of his kids. When he talks about the day, or the friends he lost, Sickels – a big man who coaches football in his spare time – suddenly looks small and vulnerable.

Everyone was dazed, but everyone, like Sickels, pitched in. 'It was a little bit like what I imagine London was like during the Blitz,' says Eileen Moon. Red Bank's mayor, Ed McKenna, lost eight friends that day. In response, he formed an ad hoc group, Alliance for Neighbours, which did everything from driving kids to school to fixing broken windows and raising money for school fees.

Their biggest success, however, was a concert featuring Springsteen and Bon Jovi, both of whom donated their time, which took place at Count Basie Theatre; the group raised $1.5million for the victims' families. Geraldo Rivera, the infamous 'shock' journalist for Fox News who owns the *Two River Times* and who lived across the river in Locust, donated the week's advertising rates and doubled it with his own money.

More importantly, Ed McKenna said, the group was always there for the families. 'Some women had never written a cheque before their husbands disappeared,' he said. 'Some women didn't know that they had to keep paying car payments. But whatever was asked for, people helped.'

Eileen Moon was surprised at the 'speed in which this community became a unit. When you see disparate humans rowing in the same direction, it was so inspiring. Estate agents, petrol stations, 7–11s with glass jars raising money, piles of things going across the river . . . ordinary people doing extraordinary things.'

Some of those extraordinary things were just simple acts of kindness. One wife of a victim looked out of her window one day. It was autumn, and one of the great East Coast rituals in the autumn is raking the leaves of the great oaks and sycamores that change colour vibrantly and then drop. It's one of those chores we grew up doing as children, after dinner: raking huge piles of leaves, bagging them and leaving them for the trashman.

The widow's leaves were cleared. Someone, a neighbour, she never knew, had done it quietly without telling her.

'I think Osama bin Laden's plan backfired,' says Sandy Feigan. 'He tried to ruin America, to knock us off our pedestal. Instead, it brought us closer together.'

For Garrett Bess, September 11 was 'cathartic'. He admits his life underwent a great change from the moment he stood on the ferry seeing the towers burning. 'It was a reality check,' he says. He suddenly lost interest in the rat race, in working just to make money. In December, he lost his job as part of a post-9/11 fallout and, instead of rushing back into the market, decided to take some time out. During those months, he stayed at home with his daughters. He realised how much he missed them while he worked in New York, getting on the boat early, coming home late.

Bess decided he would not return full-time to New York even if it meant a pay cut: two days a week he works from home, the rest of the time he divides between consultancy jobs and voice-over auditions, something he has long wanted to pursue. And six months after 9/11, encouraged by neighbours and friends, he decided to run for town councilman on the Republican Party ticket. He won.

'I had a wake-up call,' he says. 'Life is short. That day showed me how easily you could be snuffed out. My whole viewpoint now is – what can I do to help?'

Eileen Moon, shifting through her pile of stories on 9/11,

grows emotional as she recalls the afternoons she spent on the ferry going to Ground Zero. 'It changed everyone's lives,' she says sombrely. There's more anxiety here now. Al-Qaeda cells have been traced to northern New Jersey and several anthrax scares hit the area in the wake of 9/11, which left everyone tense and anxious. 'For a while, we were opening mail with rubber gloves,' Moon says.

At Red Bank Catholic Charities, which has been running support groups and therapy sessions for victims' families, there is a sense of time passing, but the feeling is that the anniversary will be a painful time. Grief is compounded by post-traumatic stress, which is constantly reinforced by the images of the Twin Towers. 'Watching TV is painful,' says Maureen Fitzsimmons, the programme director. 'Even seeing people in the supermarket is painful.' She calls the post- 9/11 period 'the new normal', meaning: 'We are no longer the secure people we thought we are. What's normal about dealing with anthrax, chemical weapons, planes crashing into buildings and killing your loved ones?'

Fitzsimmons smiles ironically. 'We're a little bit like an adolescent country that has begun to mature. We lost our invincibility. We're vulnerable. We need each other.'

Each person I spoke with talked of the lessons of 9/11 and what was gleaned from that monstrous day. Nearly all of them said that they had shifted their priorities. Money and the accumulation of wealth went out the window. Family and spirituality were on the rise. Monsignor Lowry from St James Church in Red Bank, who spent eight days sleeping at Ground Zero, says, 'Everyone stepped back and smelled the roses. The greatest gift is right in front of us. Family is priority. And we're all in this together.'

Sandy Feigen is engrossed in her field hockey team and getting into university next year, but she also thinks a lot about the state of the world. She says she never leaves the house now without telling her mother that she loves her. 'I am a different person now,' admits the teenager. 'Last year at this time, it never crossed my mind we would be attacked. For me and my friends, it's a rude awakening.'

Eileen Moon, who believes most people in the area are still anxious, is more blunt. 'I think people learned their lives depended on each other,' she says. 'You may be in a situation where you may have to save each others' lives.' But good came out of it, she is quick to add. Scholarships were started, action was taken.

On a late summer's afternoon, after sitting with Monsignor Lowry at the rectory at St James, I walked through Riverside Park Gardens, overlooking the Navesink in Red Bank, with my mother. Usually it is a place where there are concerts on hot summer nights, but the entrance had been turned into an impromtu 9/11 memorial by the grieving residents. 'Even God was shedding tears that day,' remarks Monsignor Lowry.

Hours after the planes crashed, people started gathering at the park and leaving messages for victims. 'I have no idea why,' Mayor Ed McKenna admits. But the tribute wall has become part of the collective healing.

I was not the only person reading the testimonies and touching the photographs of the victims. There were some trendy teenagers; a family in shorts and preppy Lacoste T-shirts; and a Japanese mother and son, tourists from Tokyo. *Vanity Fair* magazine had devoted eight pages and a major story to the Two Rivers area. The grand doyenne of American journalists, Gail Sheehy, had spent many months speak-

ing to victims and their families, and the American network
CBS had made a documentary on the same topic. The Two
Rivers area had become horribly famous, not for the beaches
or the view of the sailboats moving slowly across the river,
but because of the tragedy.

My mother and I read poems, letters, tributes to lives, and
looked at T-shirts, skis, bottles of sand and children's draw-
ings which were nestled in the lavender bushes. RIP MR
MILANO. JOE GRILLO YOUR GENTLE HEART WILL GO ON
AND ON. JACK MCCARTHY, NAVY SEAL, FATHER AND PORT
AUTHORITY ENGINEER. BETH QUIGLEY, MISSING, 104TH
FLOOR WORLD TRADE CENTER. CONTACT HER PARENTS.
GREGG REIDY, 25 YEAR OLD, MIDDLETOWN RESIDENT.
NEW YORK POLICE DEPARTMENT, WE WILL NEVER FORGET
OUR BROTHERS, 9/11.

'I don't think I can read anymore,' announced my mother.
'It's too sad.' We walked instead to the edge of the marina
where the boats skimmed by: catamarans and expensive
sailboats. A handsome couple walked by eating ice-cream
cones. Red Bank looked the same: beautiful, sleepy, rich. On
the surface, anyway.

But it has changed. As for me, a first-generation Italian
American with a British passport who never really felt
American, coming back to Two Rivers had a deep impact.
On September 11, I was far from here, in Paris and walking
down the street when a friend called: 'This is not George
Orwell. Two planes have crashed into the Twin Towers.' I
rushed to the American Embassy to see the French – notor-
ious American haters – placing flowers and signs that read '6
Juin 1944 – merci'. Weeping women touched my shoulder
and said, 'We are all Americans today.'

A few days later, in church with my boyfriend and his

family in a small village in the Alps where his family has lived for hundreds of years, a bent-over old man turned to me. 'Are you from the village?' he enquired politely. 'I don't recognise you.'

'No,' I said. 'I am American.' It shocked me, saying that. It was the first time I think I have called myself an American in more than fifteen years, since I moved to Britain. I never could identify with all those American bankers in London; the glamorous New York fashion editors or Californians I met in pilates class. When I left America in 1985; I just *left*. I wanted to connect with my European side, with my roots, and I assumed I would live out my days in my adopted country.

But after I said these words to the old man, I burst into tears. He did not seem surprised. He took my hand. He said when he watched the pictures of the towers in flames, he had wept. '*Nous sommes avec vous*,' he said. I cried all day, and most of the next week. I could not watch television news and, when I went to Afghanistan a few days later, I felt it was *my* country now, at war. I had never been patriotic before, I had always hated American foreign policy. But September 11 changed me too.

Later, I realised that what had upset me more than anything was my deep, and probably repressed, homesickness. I wanted to be at home when those planes struck. But what I really wanted was a home that no longer existed – the place where I had swung my sandy, suntanned baby feet from a drugstore bench; when people flew flags because it was the Fourth of July, not because they had been attacked by terrorists; the parades I used to march in as a Brownie and a Girl Scout, or singing 'God Bless America' in school before lunch. What I wanted was something that no longer existed – the time before the fall, before 9/11.

When Eileen Moon told me what 9/11 meant to her, I felt myself getting as emotional as I did in that church with the old man. She said it was 'a reconnection with the ideals of what this nation is about – equality, a sense of aspiration to act for the highest good. To offer an opportunity to anyone who's willing to invest in those ideals.'

Then she told me that the thing that expressed it the most for her was something she had heard; she could not remember where. 'We do not live in America,' she said quietly, sitting on the front porch of the old Victorian house, painted blue, that houses her office. 'America lives in us.'

Westbrook, Maine: Fallen Heroes

August, 2004

The day in April when Ryann Roukey found out her husband Larry had been blown apart by an explosion in Iraq was a late spring day, grey and drizzly with rain, but otherwise a day like any other. She left work at Central Maine and Power, where she works as an administrative assistant, picked up her two-year-old son, Nicholas, from daycare and dropped him at home with her teenage daughter, Sonya, so she could shop for dinner. Everything was normal.

'Just an ordinary day,' she remembers.

She was in a good mood. The day before, she had spoken to Larry, a thirty-three-year-old postal worker who had shipped out to Iraq on 5 March 2004 and was based at a camp outside Baghdad. He told her he was leaving the next day, 'to go on a mission'. He couldn't say what, but he told his wife she could see the diary he was keeping when he got back home. He had been in Iraq for less than six weeks.

Then Ryann held the phone out to Nicholas, who told his father he loved him. 'You guys sound good,' Larry said cheerfully, when Ryann got back on. She thought Larry seemed happier having spoken to their son. 'His spirits lifted,' she said. She hung up feeling that everything was going to be just fine.

There was a van in the driveway with government plates when she got home, which should have signalled that something was wrong. 'But never, ever did I consider the worst,' she says. Then Sonya met her at the door with a grim face. 'What's wrong?' Ryann asked, as Sonya took the shopping bags from her mother and motioned to the men sitting on the sofa. Ryann walked slowly inside the pretty house on the pretty street in the pretty town she had shared with Larry for years, suddenly feeling dread. 'It felt like I was in the movies,' she said.

The men were military chaplains. They told Ryann there had been an accident involving Larry. 'And at that moment, my whole life changed in a matter of seconds.' Sonya says Ryann began to cry and walk round and round in circles, in a complete panic, as the men explained that Larry – an Army Reservist with the 3rd Battalion 304th Regiment – had died with another soldier from Pennsylvania in an explosion at a suspected chemical weapons factory. He was working for the Iraq Survey Group who report to the CIA. The explosion was (and still is) under investigation.

None of this made any sense to Ryann, a muscular, well-built blonde who always wears a bracelet engraved with I LOVE YOU, a present from Larry. She is the kind of person who figured life would just go on as it always had: she and Larry and their two kids. She first spotted Larry ten years ago, when he was working as a bouncer at a bar called The Bahama Beach Club, and confidently told her girlfriend, 'I'm gonna marry that guy.' They were just two average middle-class kids in love. The worst thing that could happen to them was the long separation when Larry went off to Reserve duty. It just never occurred to Ryann that Larry was never going to call home again on Sunday mornings at 7.30 a.m. like he always did. And that he would be coming home in a coffin draped with the American flag.

At about the same time that Ryann was getting the news that Larry was dead, Betsy Coffin, who lives a little south of Westbrook, down Highway I-95 in Kennebunk – summer residence of the former President George Bush – was still trying to work out exactly what had happened when her husband Chris, a fifty-one-year-old former park ranger and police officer, died in Iraq nearly one year before. Chris was also a Reservist, and after his death received the unfortunate sobriquet of being one of the oldest casualties in the war.

It didn't make Betsy feel any better knowing that Chris had tried to retire from the Reserves before he went to Iraq, but a stop order from the government prohibited it. When he left for the Gulf, Betsy had a bad feeling. So did Chris, but he was a good soldier – he came from a long line of military and had joined the Reserves way back in 1971 – so he swallowed it and went. 'He had an awful feeling he was not coming back,' Betsy says.

The couple were deeply committed to each other – they had just renewed their wedding vows – and had no children. But each separation was getting harder. Chris had spent nine months in Kosovo before going to Iraq, where he celebrated his fiftieth birthday, and Betsy recalls how tough the last night was before he left for the Gulf. They went out for a walk on the beach and looked at the stars. Chris pointed to a star in the sky and told Betsy that they both would be looking at the same star, just from different places; he was trying to make her feel better.

But the bad feeling did not go away. The night that Chris died, 1 July, 2003, Betsy had trouble falling asleep. She knew Chris was leading a convoy down Route 8, between Baghdad and Kuwait, one of the most dangerous routes in Iraq. He told her he would call when he got to Kuwait, and she knew that he would keep his word. But something felt wrong. She tossed and turned and finally she got up and wandered into the living room where she pulled out some old photo albums, including pictures of her wedding to Chris in Colorado.

The irony was that she had not looked at them for ages. Much later, she found out that at the same time she was smiling down at those pictures, Chris was dying in his Humvee.

The military chaplain came the next day. Betsy knew what he was there for. 'I just knew,' she says, her voice cracking. One year after his death, Betsy is still reeling with pain.

All over Maine, there are pockets of sadness. Maine is a big state, with miles of pine-scented forests, glacier lakes and a rocky coastline which stretches up to Canada. It is rugged and remote and not the easiest place to live, unless you are the Bushes or the Rockefellers coming just for the summer. Only 1.2 million people live year-round in Maine, most of them concentrated in the south. The north is stony: a place to grow potatoes, where rates of alcoholism and incest are high. Cabin fever is a very real thing here. Snow can fall in April.

It's a beautiful, hard place and, as a result, Mainers are a special breed: strong, proud, with a droll sense of humour. Most communities are tight-knit and solid, with roots that go back to the days of the French Canadian fur trappers. Everyone knows everyone. People go to high school together and then take their kids to Little League games together, go fishing or hunting together. In a sense, it is the essence of small-town America.

'Mainers have always been strongly patriotic,' says Emma Dumont from Westbrook, whose family have been in the military since the Revolutionary War. Her son has served in Panama, Desert Storm, Bosnia and now Iraq, and Emma is in charge of organising neighbours to send packages to all the Westbrook boys in Iraq. Things like playing cards, packets of Dunkin' Donuts coffee, fly strips, baby wipes, books and CDs. Emma is staunchly behind the war because she is staunchly behind those fighting there – hometown boys, kids she and everybody knows. 'Mainers believe in freedom,' she adds, in a long, drawn-out accent from Down East, which is what locals call the mid-coast of Maine.

But even patriotism wanes under deep pain. The war drags on and on in Iraq, with American casualties getting higher and higher – 900 by the end of July 2004. Every morning, over coffee and blueberry pancakes, people hear more stories of atrocities. The yellow ribbons, so lovingly tied in nearly every small town when the boys left for war more than eighteen months ago, are beginning to look faded.

No one likes to admit it, but there is an awful sense of déjà vu: everyone remembers Vietnam, and Vietnam kicked small-town America in the guts because it deprived them of the kid who delivered the morning newspaper, the kid behind the grocery counter, the kid who hit the home run at the local baseball game. Now small-town America has gone to war because nearly half the soldiers fighting in Iraq and Afghanistan – Bush's 'War Against Terror' – are either National Guardsmen or Reserve soldiers. These are civilian soldiers, citizen soldiers, essentially home-town militias. Most of them sign up expecting to fight ice storms or hurricanes, or possibly build fences near the border of Mexico or Canada – not to fight insurgents in Fallujah.

The war is hurting Maine. For a state with a relatively small population, there were, at its highest point, 1,100 Maine National Guard or Reservists serving in Iraq, and that does not include the number of people serving in the regular forces. Only Iowa has sent more National Guardsmen.

It is clear that something needs to be revamped, as most of these civilian soldiers cannot possibly have the experience of full-time soldiers. The current Guard and Reserve system was designed in the chaos following the Vietnam War. Neither President Lyndon Johnson nor President Richard Nixon called up Reservists in great numbers, fearing even more opposition at home to their policies. The new design meant that when America went to war again with a volunteer force, hometown America would also go with them. For twenty-five years, these men put out fires and battled hurricanes, and the system was never really tested.

Since 9/11, all that has changed. Hundreds of thousands of them are deployed in combat now, and their tours of duties are radically extended. Guard and Reserve members make up approximately forty per cent of the forces in Iraq and Afghanistan today. And the Pentagon has recently said that figure will rise to fifty per cent.

This reliance on National Guardsmen and Reserve soldiers also means that the casualties are older – in this war, the average is twenty-seven years old. The average age in Vietnam was twenty; the average age in Korea was twenty-two. In small-town America, most people are married with a family by the age of twenty-seven. According to the *Portland Press Herald*, the most influential newspaper in Maine, 'The trend is having a profound impact on families, communities and domestic views about war.' Larry Roukey, dead at thirty-three with two kids and a wife, fits neatly into this profile of the older soldier.

'The problem is that Guardsmen have families,' says Lavinia Gelineau, a twenty-four-year-old widow. Her husband, Chris, twenty-three and a student, was killed in Mosul in April. When I called, Chris' personal possessions had just arrived and Lavinia was unpacking his boots and books in tears.

There are also questions about how prepared these men are to go to war. Larry Roukey had been well trained – he served in active duty in the army for three years and then served two years in the National Guard. He re-enlisted in the Reserves following the 9/11 attacks and was promoted to sergeant in January, 2002. And his family insist that he wanted to be in action; he wanted to serve his country.

But it's not like that for everyone. Many have not been as trained or well-equipped as active duty members of the military – National Guardsmen usually train one weekend a month then get a crash course before they go to Iraq. As a result, there have been problems.

The military police brigade accused of abusing Iraqi prisoners at Abu Ghraib, for example, were Reservists. Privately, military commanders in Washington and in combat have said that a number of Reservists arrive for duty ill-prepared and lacking specific combat skills. What is often cited is that while they may certainly be brave or fit, they lack a 'warrior ethos', which cannot be instilled in a few short weeks before they hit hostile turf in Iraq or Afghanistan.

When I stopped by a National Guard recruiting office in downtown Portland, however, I was assured by several officers that Guardsmen were sometimes better trained than active duty soldiers. They scoffed at the notion of the warrior ethos. But one soldier privately told me that so many soldiers were needed in Iraq that 'people have to be rotated so that everyone gets experience in the field'. This perhaps explains why people like Chris Coffin were chosen, aged fifty-one, to lead a convoy down one of the most dangerous roads in Iraq; or why Larry Roukey, the father of two, was killed in a mysterious explosion. I could not help but think that sounded too much like cannon fodder.

Sadder still is that most of the men who join the National Guard do it because they need the extra cash or the educational benefits. Before 9/11, many signed up pretty much knowing they would never have to serve in combat. The youngest soldier killed from Maine was twenty-three-year-old Specialist Christopher Gelineau. He joined the Guards when he was seventeen so he could pay for his education and get a business degree from University of Southern Maine. He met his Romanian-born wife, Lavinia, when both of them were cleaning dormitories during the summer to earn extra money.

'We weren't like other kids,' she says softly. 'We really had to work to go to school.' Lavinia has been outspoken and honest in her condemnation of the war and the fact that Chris was perhaps not as prepared as he could have been before he left – he worked on computers in an administrative role. Lavinia says that before Chris left, she was investigating ways to borrow money so he could pay back his National Guard student loans and not have to go. As a result, she had had a hard time over the past few months. Lavinia is not a Mainer, and people have attacked her as being unpatriotic, as being an outsider – a 'European' – or simply being 'angry'.

Nine men with ties to Maine have so far died. They are called Fallen Heroes, and they are a cast of characters who make up American small-town life, or come straight from a Frank Capra movie: the local barber, the postman, the kid who scored the prize touchdown, the delivery boy, a new father whose own mother had been killed when he was small, a Park Ranger.

'This touches every family in Maine,' the editor of the *Bangor Daily News*, Mark Woodward, wrote. 'These people are drawn from every community, from every walk of life.'

Dylan Thomas once wrote that 'after the first death, there is no other'. Major Jay Aubin was one of America's first soldiers to die, as well as Maine's first soldier to die, and most people in Skowhegan got a terrible shock because he was well-known: he played football and delivered groceries from the local market. He was the only kid in the history of the town named 'Student of the Year'. The helicopter he was flying went down on 21 March, 2003, in the earliest days of the war, amid a sandstorm and black smoke from burning oil wells. Two other American and eight British troops were also killed in the crash.

'They chalked it up to what they call "the fog of war," ' his mother, Nancy Chamberlain, said grimly.

For one year after her thirty-six-year-old son's death, Chamberlain wore a photograph of him in the place over her heart. When a year came and went, she took it off and replaced it with a small pin of a hummingbird. Because her son loved to fly.

I wanted to understand the motivation behind America's hometown militias now making up nearly half the forces in Iraq, so I went to where they come from. Westbrook, Maine, is an old paper-mill town on the banks of the Presumpscott River. Company Bravo, a National Guardsmen company, are based here, but all have shipped out to Iraq. One balmy summer night, as fireflies lit up the sky and the river glowed golden, the local fire chief gave me directions to their head-quarters, across from the high school on Stroudwater Street.

'But you won't find anyone there,' he says, pointing out the route. 'They've all gone to the war.' When I arrive, the place is closed like a drum, but there are yellow ribbons tied to the fence and a sign that reads 'Call 1–800 GO GUARD', and the American flag is flying at half-mast – Ronnie Reagan had died a few days before. And, of course, the flag was flying low for Larry Roukey, the hometown Fallen Hero.

It was dinner time on an early summer evening, and behind the front windows I could see families sitting down for their meals. Westbrook, like many towns in Maine, was originally settled by French Canadians, and even though it has ex-panded over the years – the population is now 15,000 – it is still a tight-knit and largely working-class society. Most community life centres around St Hyacinth's Catholic Church, and if you go to Guido's Diner on Main Street in the morning for a blueberry muffin and coffee around 8.30 a.m., you will hear everything you need to know about Westbrook.

Which means that everyone felt Larry Roukey's death. When the news got out, people who did not even know him rushed in to help his widow, either by bringing food, helping with the masses of bureaucratic paperwork, or planting a 'victory garden' in her front yard. The headline in the local paper, the *American Journal*, was FALLEN WESTBROOK SOL-DIER 'GIANT OF A MAN'. You can take the temperature of the emotional state of Westbrook by reading recent headlines of the *Journal*. The main stories used to be about tax reforms or parents expressing concern over class sizes. Now they include

WESTBROOK FAMILY COPING WITH LOSS OF HUSBAND AND FATHER, or HOMECOMING ON HOLD: MOTHER WANTS TO SEE SON, or SGT MICHAEL LIBBY INJURED IN IRAQ. Westbrook, like America, has changed.

'When Larry Roukey died,' the *Journal*'s editor, Brendan Moran, says, 'there was a palpable sense of the war coming here. With someone local dying, Westbrook was grieving. It was solemn. You could feel it.'

Whether or not people support the war in Iraq or George W. Bush (the town is largely Democrat), Moran explains that everyone supports their troops. 'No one wants to make the mistake of what happened to soldiers in Vietnam, coming home and being mistreated,' he says. There are even some Iraqi dissidents living in the town, who run the local liquor store; even they support the war.

I first arrived in Larry Roukey's hometown on Flag Day. I didn't know it. But as I drove through town, the air smelled of freshly cut lawns and a Little League baseball game was in heated progress on Warren Field. A couple of teenagers were hanging out, hiding cans of beer under their T-shirts. There was a ceremony sponsored by Veterans of Foreign Wars in a park by the river. There, a dozen old soldiers gathered solemnly – veterans of Korea, World War II, Vietnam. Some of them leaned on canes and one wore a baseball cap.

Old Glory – as the American flag is known – was held by a Vietnam veteran, Paul Boivin, and someone else read the lyrics to the Johnny Cash song, 'Ragged Old Flag'.

> Is this the first time you've been to our little town?
> You see, we're proud of our ragged little flag.
> She went where she was sent by Uncle Sam . . .

A woman sang 'God Bless America' and then everyone recited the Pledge of Allegiance with their left hand on their heart. Some of the soldiers had tears in their eyes, and I found myself growing as emotional as them, perhaps because all of these men had fought such incredible battles and there were only half a dozen people to honour them standing under the elm tree with me.

Afterwards, the men showed me the monument which lists the names of all the Westbrook residents who have served, and died, in foreign wars. For thirty-five US dollars, a veteran's name can be inscribed in a brick.

Then the men begin to tell their war stories. This is the saddest part. It's a few days after the sixtieth anniversary of D-Day and there's a lot of nostalgia floating around America, a lot of comparisons between what happened in 1944 and what is happening today in Iraq. World War II was fought by people the American broadcaster Tom Brokaw called 'the Greatest Generation'. To them, fighting against the Nazis was a just war, a 'good war'. They tell me how they enlisted to go and fight evil, to liberate Europe, when they were still teenagers, straight from working in the local mill. Iraq, in contrast, appears to baffle them.

'I can't see why we're there,' says Colonel Phillip Spiller, who got the Silver Star for bravery in World War II and was a former mayor of Westbrook. He's got a son in Iraq, so he chooses words carefully. 'Iraq is like Vietnam – we can't tell the enemy. I support the soldiers there, but I think we're going to lose.'

One man, Laurent Chretien, fought in the Battle of the Bulge. Another, Raymond Reitze, spent twenty-six months in a German POW camp called Stalag 2B and weighed ninety-six pounds when he was finally liberated. There are men standing on the field with me who fought bloody battles in the Pacific, and merchant seamen who spent World War II in submarines.

'We were doing something that really mattered,' Ray Reitze tells me the next day over a blueberry pancake breakfast at Guido's Diner. Ray can only eat half of his, because after the prison camp two thirds of his stomach was removed, but he's still got some feisty views.

Like nearly everyone I spoke to in Westbrook, Ray supports the troops – he had two sons in Vietnam and a grandson, Scott McKinley, who was a marine in Iraq – but he's ambivalent about the cause of the war. He's now eighty-four and he's frail, but he wants to talk about the difference between fighting in Europe in 1944 and fighting in Iraq in 2004. At the small, neat home outside of Westbrook, where he lives alone, Ray shows me the telegram that his wife received when he went missing in action. He told me how he was beaten and tortured and watched his friends die in the prison camp.

War and imprisonment scarred him terribly. His walls are full of mementoes of the Stars and Stripes, of photographs of him as a young soldier before he was captured. It seems like a part of his life was left back in Stalag B in 1943. He of all people knows how horrible war really is, so when I ask him about it, he takes my hand and says with tears in his eyes, 'You don't know what freedom is until you lose it.' On Iraq and the death of young people like Larry Roukey, he just nods and says hollowly, 'I really don't know why we are there.'

I spent a couple days in Westbrook to see how the community responded to Larry's death. Larry came from a big extended family, half-Italian, half-Irish, with roots deep in the area. He grew up in the bordering town of South Portland, and his kid sister, Dotty, was a well-known high school athlete and most people knew the Roukey name. After school, Larry worked at a chain of sandwich shops, Amato's, and was best friends with the owner's son, Jeff Reali. Of Larry's death, Reali tells me solidly, 'He was thirty-three. He should have been home with his kids.'

When Larry died, everyone felt like they had lost a friend, or at least someone they knew well. He became a kind of Everyman: a figure of a hometown boy who had done what he was told and paid a terrible price for it. When his body arrived at Portland Airport (the airport, ironically, where the 9/11 bombers first entered the United States), the staff on the ground saluted him.

At his full military funeral down at St Joseph's Church in Portland – where Roukey married Ryann eight years ago – 600 people, including the governor, came to pay tribute. People lined up on Stevens Avenue and the schoolchildren were let out early so they could wave flags as Larry's coffin passed.

'It was almost as though the entire state came together for the death of one soldier,' says Ryann Roukey, recalling the pageantry. Dotty Roukey read the eulogy and recalled how her brother had commandeered her doll's house as a child to use as his GI Joe fortress. Soldiering went way back in the Roukey clan. His father had served in Korea, his grandfather in World War II. Larry died serving his country, was the emphasis.

Dotty Roukey, a pretty, freckled redhead who lost both her parents and now had to bury her only sibling, is stoic when I meet her for a beer in a downtown Portland hotel bar.

'He wanted to go to Iraq,' she says, picking at a plate of pretzels. 'After 9/11, he felt that now was the time to defend his country.' In fact, Dotty points out that Larry re-enlisted after 9/11. 'He told me that if ever there was a time to help his country, it was now.' But I can see the sorrow behind Dotty's bravado; she lost her only brother in the desert a long way from home.

As for Ryann, she says that soldiers do their duty, but she now has to raise a little boy alone. When Ryann met Larry, he was already in the National Guard, but later joined the Army Reserves. She was prepared that she was going to be the wife of a soldier, if only a civilian soldier. In the several times I spoke to Ryann, I never heard a trace of anger or regret.

'I'm a firm believer that Larry was in Iraq because of 9/11,' she told me firmly. 'I have NEVER felt this was not our war.' She pauses, playing with the I LOVE YOU bracelet. 'I know Larry was there for a reason.'

Larry's colleague at the post office, Jimmy Page, echoes this too, as he shows me around the post office which has set up a tribute to Larry, a window with a photograph of him in his uniform and a sign that says: WE SHALL NEVER FORGET.

'When he re-enlisted after 9/11, he felt he had to do it,' Jimmy says. 'He had a calling.'

The only thing that does make Ryann angry is the fact that Nicholas will grow up without a father. Watching TV one day, the child caught part of Ronnie Reagan's elaborate funeral. He suddenly turned to his mother and said, 'Daddy's not coming back.'

'That,' Ryann says later, trying to supervise her own kids and her sister's – as well as some neighbourhood kids – for a backyard barbecue, 'hurt the most.'

*   *   *

I spoke to other fathers from Westbrook whose sons were in Iraq and I spoke to people over lunch – lobster rolls, the local speciality – at Olivia's Diner on Brown Street. I spoke to shopkeepers and people walking their dogs. People genuinely felt Larry's death, but everyone supported him. No one said, 'George Bush got us into this war, and it's a mess!' as I expected. Oddly enough, the only vocal opponent to the war in Iraq was Larry's grandmother, Mitzi Rumo – always called Nan – who is eighty-four.

Mitzi is a strong, handsome woman whose roots go far back in Maine. 'When I was growing up, everyone helped everyone and if you needed anything, you went to your neighbours.' She's a devout Irish Catholic who wears the medallion of Our Lady around her neck and goes to mass every day at St Joseph's, where Larry was married and where his funeral mass was celebrated.

After 8 a.m. mass, she always goes out to breakfast with friends, and I meet her at the Dunkin' Donuts in Westbrook early one morning. Nan says she raised Larry when he was little, and she is furious with the White House for taking him away from her.

'I believe Bush went into Iraq with a vendetta and he didn't need to go there,' she says firmly, clutching her paper coffee-cup. Then her eyes fill with tears. 'He was such a good, good boy!' she says. 'He was my pride and joy!' It's a simple statement, nothing unusual, but hearing her say it is heart-breaking. I cannot imagine a mother, or a grandmother, sending her son off to war. Nan reminds me gently that it is not the natural order of things to have a grandson die before you.

And although she is fit and healthy, there is such a veil of sadness around Nan at the loss of her pride and joy, that when she drives off in her car, emblazoned with a yellow ribbon and bumper stickers supporting our troops, I almost feel that sadness lift.

What happens when someone dies in a desert far, far away from the rocky coast of Maine? At first, everyone feels it, everyone helps. People fixed Betsy Coffin's car for free, and the local accountant refused to take money to fill in her tax forms. The engraver of Chris Gelineau's headstone refused to take a cheque from his widow, Lavinia. People put a flagpole up in Ryann Roukey's front yard, and soon it will have a light that stays on all the time, in memory of Larry. There were parades all over Maine for the Fallen Heroes.

Then, even if the widow has a lot of community support, she is eventually left alone with the terrible knowledge that her beloved is not coming back. To cope, Lavinia Gelineau and Betsy Coffin both keep their husbands' voices on their telephone answer machines. Both describe the terrible void they feel, and Lavinia sends me an email with a quote from Emily Dickinson; 'Not knowing when the dawn will come, I open every door.'

Betsy Coffin, who keeps her email sign-on, 'Betsy and Chris Coffin', is on a slightly different quest; she wants the truth from the US Government. She was never really satisfied with the story the army gave her – that Chris' Humvee swerved off the road to avoid an oncoming vehicle on the road to Kuwait – so she began to dig around to find out what happened, to demand answers from high-level army officials, to prod all of her army contacts.

'I became an annoyance,' she admits grimly. She waited eight months to find out what happened, and then she began to do her own investigation. She loved Chris too much to just let him go without knowing how he died, who he was with, and if he was in pain at the last minute. After Chris left, she kept finding notes he had hidden all over the house; 'Dearest Bets – Right this minute, I'm thinking of you, and smiling.' He also left a prayer for her.

> May the Lord hold me and thee in his care
> While we are apart from one another
> Until we are together once more.
> So rest easy, my love, until we are together again.

This is why she wanted to know how he died – they were too close for her to live with a lie. And the more she dug, the more she learned of his last moments: that it probably was not an accident, but an ambush; that a crowd of Iraqis surrounded the vehicles and a soldier had to fire his gun to keep them at bay; that one of the soldiers there later told Betsy that 'it was worse than Somalia', and that Chris' watch and wedding ring – something he treasured – were stolen. This pains Betsy the most.

There are other things that haunt Betsy. Chris called Betsy every day on the cell phone that she bought when he left for Iraq, and he was the only person she gave the number to. The night before he died, she waited and waited for his call to come from Kuwait to say he had arrived safely. It never came. Betsy says she 'waited and waited and after three days, I turned it off.'

She still doesn't have the heart to turn it back on.

In the aftermath of death, there is a deathly quiet. After the military funerals, the flags flying low, the yellow ribbons, the neighbours bearing endless casserole dishes for supper, there is an awful calm.

The last night I drive through Westbrook, seeing Everytown USA: there is the McDonald's and there is the local grammar school and there are all the backyard barbecues and fathers grilling hot dogs and mothers passing out bowls of potato salad. With the death of Larry Roukey, Westbrook is forever scarred. One more brick in the memorial in the park by the river, and now Iraq has come to hometown America.

A few days after the anniversary of Chris Coffin's death, Betsy Coffin sent me an email. She was back at work in a local hospital after staying with family for Chris' one-year anniversary, but the pain wasn't getting any better. When I spoke to her, she sounded strong but wounded. Chris had been her life and her love, and she still wore her engagement, wedding and three-diamond ring – which Chris had given her and which symbolised the past, present and future.

But that ring now was also cruel reminder. The present was not great; the future seemed bleak; and as for the past, Betsy was haunted by the fact that both she and Chris had an eerie feeling all along about him going away. Fear. But she wanted to clarify something about that, about their fear.

Dear Janine,

. . . Chris was really concerned that something would happen and he wouldn't make it home but he wasn't concerned for himself, he was afraid of what it would do to me and the pain I would experience. He told me his other great fear was that something would happen to one of his soldiers and he wouldn't bring them all home. He didn't want to have to face a husband or wife, or mother or father and tell them he wasn't able to bring their loved one home. This was so typical of Chris, always worrying about others.

I spoke to him almost every night while he was deployed and since it's been over a year you'd think I'd be used to not hearing his voice on the line but still I miss him so . . .
Take care,
Betsy

Israel

The Long Wall

November, 2003

In 1973, Winston S. Churchill III, grandson of the British wartime prime minister, asked Ariel Sharon how Israel would deal with the Palestinians.

Sharon, then a brigade commander on the southern front during the Yom Kippur War, replied in a jaunty fashion. 'We'll make a pastrami sandwich out of them,' he said. 'We'll insert a strip of Jewish settlements in between the Palestinians and then another strip of Jewish settlements right across the West Bank, so that in twenty-five years' time neither the United Nations nor the United States, nobody, will be able to tear it apart.'

Thirty years on and Ariel Sharon is seventy-five years old and Prime Minister of Israel. All over his country, you see that sad pastrami sandwich, the most recent addition to which is his latest brainchild, the security fence. The use of the word fence – with its connotation of impermanence – could be seen as misleading, because while in some areas the barrier is indeed a metal fence – which one can peer through and see the stony hills of the Holy Land – in other places you see ugly, grey concrete slabs rising eight metres from the ground, waiting to be erected into a far more permanent structure.

Driving north from Jerusalem along Highway 6, in some places you see walls topped with barbed-wire coils, like ugly snakes, while in other spots there are observation towers with nervous soldiers pacing inside, or World War I-style shallow trenches. Many Israelis say they need this wall, that it is necessary to contain the infiltrators who cross into Israel and detonate themselves in market places or on buses. They say it is the best tool for fighting terror. But for Palestinians, the wall is merely another attempt to grab more of their land and their dignity, and a psychological bombshell. Whatever their views, most ordinary Israelis see the cost – $1 million per kilometre – as ludicrous.

Fourteen years after the Berlin Wall came down, another apartheid-style wall is swiftly going up. As of November 2003, there were 145 kilometres completed, and when it is finished, the wall is expected to run to 720 kilometres, to extend the length of the West Bank. That is, if the country does not go into economic meltdown first. With unemployment running high – and despite warnings that the project might bust the state budget – the Finance Ministry recently allocated nearly $400 million from the 2004 budget to the upkeep, maintenance and the debt incurred by the first section of the fence. And there's still a lot more to build.

The deep rift between Palestinians and Israelis – which many analysts and politicians I spoke to believe is at its lowest point since the first Gulf war, if not since 1948 – seems symbolised by this steadily growing inanimate object. Recently, senior members of the Israeli Army gathered to protest against

Sharon's crackdown, believing that the more oppressive the prime minister is in his efforts to contain the three-year Palestinian intifada, the more rebelliously the Palestinians will respond. This means the army's job will become more difficult and more teenage soldiers will come back from Gaza or the West Bank in body bags.

'We were against this, we did not want it,' one Israeli Defence Force officer said privately of the wall. 'We felt it would only do us harm, and that guarding it would be impossible.' But there were plenty of others who applauded the wall – lobby groups such as the Security Barrier for Israel, or the Jewish (and some non-Jewish) immigrants from Russia, America and Ethiopia who live in the 111 settlements scattered across the West Bank. Settlements which were supposed to be halted in 1993, according to the Oslo agreement, but which have continued to rise up, year after year.

Even the name of this great divide itself causes argument. The Israelis call it a security fence; the Palestinians call it an apartheid wall, or sometimes a 'barrier of death'.

Simply by driving through the centre of Jerusalem, or by entering a shopping mall on Saturday evenings after the Jewish sabbath finishes, you understand immediately why the Israelis crave security in these dark times. The sense of collective paranoia and fear – that a suicide bomber could strike at any minute – is overwhelming. In that respect, the terrorists have done their job properly. And no matter how many fences or walls or checkpoints go up, you still have the sense that one or two suicide bombers will slip through, by force of sheer will and determination.

But for Palestinians, most of whom feel they are being punished collectively for the wrongdoings of a few, the issue is that the wall cuts deep into their land, crippling communities. And despite the fact that the wall contradicts international law – unilateral separation violates the Fourth Geneva Convention which also protects people against collective punishment – they feel powerless to stop it.

Perhaps most damaging, however, are the psychological implications of being fenced in and cut off from the wider world. 'It feels like the Warsaw Ghetto,' said one resident of Tulkarm, a city shadowed by walls and fences.

It is an image that makes many Israelis flinch. For moderate Israelis – who crave peace and who understand that by 2010 there will be more Palestinians than Jews living in the West Bank, Israel and Gaza put together – the wall is not only a physical obstacle, but also a symbolic obstacle to the peace process itself. Yossi Beilen, the former Israeli Justice Minister under Ehud Barak and the architect of the Geneva Peace Accords – an alternative peace treaty, formulated outside the government, which is rapidly gathering support from ordinary Palestinians and Israelis – looked startled when I asked him about the wall. Then he said calmly, 'It is childish, stupid, expensive and idiotic.' Finally, he added, 'It won't help anything. It might worsen the situation.'

For some, Beilen's prediction has already come true. In many areas, the wall has destroyed decades-old ties between Israeli and Palestinian communities. In places where once you would find Palestinian farmers drinking coffee with Jewish settlers who had come to their villages to buy food or petrol, now there is only seething anger.

The main objection – besides the moral one that it undermines peace – is that the wall doesn't follow the Green Line, Israel's internationally recognised pre-1967 border. Instead, it snakes into the West Bank, annexing more Palestinian land, at times by as much as four miles. And the bitterness left over from 1948, when most Palestinians fled their land, has produced a new generation who will fiercely guard their lands until death.

'Because this small bit of land is all we have left,' explains Nabil, a young journalist.

There are other economic considerations. In places such as Qualqilya, which is referred to as the 'bread basket of the West Bank' because of its fertile soil, it is believed that a string of wells could end up on the Israeli side. The Palestinian mayor of Qualqilya has gone as far as to say that the wall will deprive residents of 'thirty-two per cent of their water resources'. Mustapha Barghouti, a community leader from Ramallah, goes further, saying that, 'One third of Palestinian agriculture has been destroyed because of the wall.'

All of this naturally fuels more resentment, and makes groups such as Hamas and Islamic Jihad more popular because, in their advocacy of violent struggle, they offer the desperate an alternative to helplessness.

'How do you kill a dream of peace?' asks Ra'eda Ta'ha, whose father was an infamous Palestinian activist (or terrorist, depending on who you are talking to) who was killed when he hijacked a plane from Tel Aviv to Belgium in 1972. We are sitting eating a calm lunch in Ramallah, plates of cold salad and fish and fried potatoes, when the mention of the wall suddenly infuriates her. The slight young woman seems to grow in stature, leaning forward in her chair and raising her voice.

'Building that wall is killing the dream. After it started going up, people who before were calm became furious. Then we want to do something, to react. Because we really have nothing left to lose now. When you are humiliated every day, you must have a form of expression.'

A report prepared last summer by the international donor community noted that, during the first phase of the wall's construction, around 12,000 Palestinians in fifteen villages will find themselves on the Western, Israel-facing side of the fence. That means they will be physically separated from the rest of the West Bank, and potentially cut off from their farmlands, workplaces and schools. In some communities, such as Abu Dis, a suburb of Jerusalem, the wall cuts straight through the town's high street, pushing half the town into the West Bank and the other half into the municipality of Jerusalem.

It creates a weird, schizophrenic atmosphere, making it almost impossible for Palestinians to go about their daily lives. Picking up children from school involves passing them over a wall, which is coated with either Hebrew graffiti – THE JEWISH NATION ALIVE! – or Palestinian graffiti – small Nazi symbols or the date that Fatah, Yasser Arafat's political party, was born. A business transaction involves finding a crack in the wall – a 'talking crack', as it is known – and shouting over the din. A trip to the market requires begging a border policeman to let you pass.

Further up the hill in Abu Dis, the view is heartbreakingly beautiful because it is exactly the same as it was 2,000 years ago. But where once, on a clear, cloudless day, you could hear the call of the muezzin all the way from the Dome of the Rock in Jerusalem's Old City, now all you hear is the whirr and crush of bulldozers.

Walid Ayyad, whose family owned the Cliff Hotel, which stood for decades and was largely used by pilgrims and students, is standing calmly watching Jewish workers tear down the place to make way for a new bypass. A professor of international relations and Middle Eastern politics, Ayyad is articulate and calm, even though the building only started two days ago.

'If you are angry, you can't think rationally,' he says. 'My aim right now is to minimise the bad. To stop them from taking all of my land.' He says that when he was first approached by Israeli officials and offered money, he refused.

'Because it would mean I was selling my land, and that is something I will never do,' he says.

So he hired an attorney and is trying not to think it will be a useless endeavour. 'When you take it easy, you get things,' he says in a Zen-like voice, staring out over the stony hills. It must be devastating to watch the hotel his grandfather built in 1918 being torn apart. But he does not flinch. Although he later says quietly, 'I do think it would have been easier for them to build bridges rather than walls.'

These days, the West Bank feels like a wasteland. Whereas towns such as Hebron or Ramallah once had their own vibrancy, with commerce between the Palestinian and Israeli communities flourishing, now there is a terrible sense of isolation. Life often comes to a complete halt because the bigger towns and cities are cut off from each other and are usually only accessible by a series of 'bypasses' which are open to Jewish settlers but closed to Palestinians.

Then there are the Israeli Army checkpoints to navigate and the bleakness of the wall itself. In al-Jerushya, a small village on the outskirts of Tulkarm, the Abu Omar family can see their land – olive groves that have been their source of income for generations – from their back garden, but they can only point to it, across the high metal fence. 'Even the animals can't go there,' says Myriam Omar, seventy-five, the grandmother and matriarch of the family.

Technically, the family's house is now on the West Bank side of the fence, while their land is trapped on the Israeli side. 'No olive harvest for us this year,' says Myriam glumly. She describes the night the Israelis came to her small village. 'They shouted in bullhorns to us that there was a curfew,' she says. 'We all stayed in our houses.' When they came out, many of their olive trees had been cut down.

'Then they said sorry, we made a mistake, those were the wrong ones to cut down. But it was too late.'

Then the fence went up and the family could not go and collect the olives for harvest. Instead, the Israelis gave them maps of the land that was now in Israeli hands, and on that map was Myriam's family's land. With special permission, one or two members of the family can sometimes walk ten kilometres down back roads to reach the land and work for a few hours. 'But it has destroyed the village,' Myriam says.

'People are scared, more than anything,' adds Yusuf Jallad, a thirty-year-old clerk in the Municipality of Tulkarm, who brought me to meet the Omar family. 'Not just that this is the olive harvest time and they have no work or money. But the fact that peace is really gone. We're back to pre-Oslo days.'

His friend Jamal, also a clerk, talks more about the economic deprivation and also the interruption to their lives. 'We can't even go to Jenin, the next largest town, any more,' he says. 'Unless we use secret roads.'

To reach his own house, Jamal now has to walk thirty kilometres out of his way. He does not own a car. The problem, he says, is the soldiers along the way who make him feel utterly powerless. 'They can tear up your papers. They can stop you from going to your home for the night.' I ask Yusuf later how the wall has really affected his life. He thinks about the question for a while.

'The suffering is not easily translated,' he says. 'Because the physical suffering is really minimal. It's the psychological point of being behind a wall. You feel as though you are in a cage.'

He says the wall makes him worry all the time. Not just about money, but about his family; about getting his children to school because they have to cross the fence; about getting to hospitals if there is an emergency; about his wife.

But mostly he worries about the future, which he says is totally obscured by the physical reality of the thick, grey slabs of concrete.

Arafat's Last Ride

November, 2003

Not far from Yasser Arafat's embattled compound at the edge of the West Bank town of Ramallah is some graffiti scrawled in a childish hand. 'My name is Samia,' it reads. 'I am excellent at geography. But I can't find Palestine on a map.'

Neither, these days, can Yasser Arafat. Boycotted by the US and Israel for his failure to curb terrorism, ageing rapidly, confined to his crumbling muqata'a (compound) by Israeli forces, and confronted with scathing criticism of his administration from Palestinians, Arafat grows increasingly isolated from the streets. Outside, a bloody intifada that is nearly four years old continues to rage.

Occasionally, the seventy-four-year-old leader's popularity does rise, but this usually happens after the Israelis issue a dictum to either exile or assassinate him. Aside from those moments, the future for Abu Amar, as the Palestinians affectionately call him, is grim.

Like the muqata'a itself, which is nearly all bulldozed and blown up by Israelis during various incursions, Arafat is battered and weary. His state-in-waiting still does not have a fully developed political system, and the peace process is halted while the violence grows. A recent report issued by the Palestinian Legistlative Council, written by one of his former spokesmen, calls for the resignation of the current government and for elections. The future does not look bright for a man once thought of as untouchable, whose plane crashed in the Libyan desert and who managed to walk away unscathed.

The question is how long Arafat's iron clutch over the 3.5 million Palestinians in the West Bank and Gaza can continue. And who, if anyone, can take his place. In the meantime, there are his people, most of whom lead terrible lives, but who still cling to him, more out of familiarity than out of trust.

Outside the muqata'a, a few tired-looking soldiers stand constant guard, raising and dropping the Palestinian flag and chain-smoking cigarettes. Nearby, a dusty refugee, a Palestinian whose family were exiled to Jordan in 1948 after the Israeli War of Independence, stands with a hand-lettered sign: MR PRESIDENT I HAVE WALKED FROM JORDAN TO SEE YOU.

The man has been waiting for days. He says he is here because he and his family want to come home. They want their house, which is now technically on Israeli land, back. They still have the key. The guards don't bother him, and the refugee still has enough belief in Arafat to think the Old Man – as he is known to his close cronies – will suddenly appear and, after more than fifty years, liberate his village.

'He still believes in Arafat,' says one of the guards proudly.

But the dusty Jordanian refugee is becoming one of the very few. Even within his Fatah movement, there has been open criticism and calls for Arafat to step down. And from outside, even some of his former staunch supporters have lost patience. Last month, in a report to the United Nations Security Council, Special Envoy Terje Larsen openly criticised Arafat. King Abudullah of Jordan suggested that Arafat 'needs to have a long look in the mirror to be able to see whether his position is helping the Palestinian cause or not'.

But most people agree – Arafat is so deeply entrenched in the Palestinian mentality, so much a part of the framework of society and the folklore, that the emergence of a new leadership, however dynamic, will be gradual.

First, before looking at Arafat, one must understand what it really feels like to be a Palestinian. To attempt to understand one small fraction of the humiliation ordinary Palestinians endure daily in the face of Israeli military closures, it is necessary to sit for several hours waiting to cross a checkpoint from the West Bank into Israel.

You cannot drive for a few miles without running into one: there are approximately 482 checkpoints which divide the West Bank into 300 clusters and Gaza into four, separating families from each other, workers from businesses, students from school, the sick from medical treatment. Most Palestinians can never leave their villages.

The Israelis control the roads, sea, sky and air and say the military crackdown is imperative: a response to a wave of suicide attacks over the past four years. But the fierceness of the closures – which the Palestinians regard as collective punishment – combined with the 'security fence' being built by the Israelis across the West Bank have spurned a new type of deadly apartheid. Whereas once there seemed to be some form of peace on horizon, now the repression, combined with the relentless wave of attacks on Israeli citizens, has driven an impermeable wedge between the two people.

'The military closures have created an economic and humanitarian crisis,' says Mustapha Barghouti, a community leader from Ramallah, who is often cited as a potential post-Arafat figure by moderate Palestinians. 'Actually, I don't think the political situation has been this bad since 1948, or that people have been so divided.'

The checkpoints are a metaphor for the division. The Palestinians calmly submit to the interrogation and searches, but underneath there is boiling rage. A rage that has prompted the Israeli commentator Gideon Levi to call the checkpoints 'the assembly line of suicide bombers'. Even hard-line army chiefs recently argued that Ariel Sharon must alter his strategy to contain the intifada – they fear the army will take the blame for the wave of suicide attacks on Israel.

This is what it is really like. Depending on their mood, Israeli teenage soldiers in mirrored sunglasses – many of them new immigrants to Israel from Ethiopia or Russia – decide the fate of whether or not a man with polio can cross to Jerusalem to get medical treatment. Or whether or not a pregnant woman can get to Hadassah Hospital inside the Green Line. Or whether or not a lawyer is allowed entry to visit with his clients. The soldiers are there to weed out potential suicide bombers, but the end result is that innocent people simply trying to live their lives suffer.

In Hebron, the Palestinian residents – about 120,000 – rarely leave their blockaded town. In Nablus, the West Bank city that got singled out for particular brutality along with Jenin during Sharon's April 2002 military incursion, Operation Defensive Shield, the checkpoint is even more cruel. There, a row of Palestinians on foot – students, teachers, doctors – stand under the blazing sun, cordoned off from waiting cars. The wait – depending on whether the soldiers have finished their cigarettes or their lunch break – can go on for hours. One elderly man stood with his sheep on a lead.

'This sheep,' he shouted to me, 'will get through the checkpoint before me.'

In September 2000, the collective frustration that the peace process was not moving, combined with a provocative visit by then opposition leader Ariel Sharon to the Al-Haram Al-Sharif – one of the three holiest sites for Muslims in the world – gave birth to the second Palestinian intifada. Within days, scores of Palestinians were dead. Within weeks, hundreds. The average now, nearly four years on, is that three Palestinians die each day. As they were beaten back by Israeli forces who had use of Apache helicopters and armoured APCs, the Palestinians turned to the most effective weapon they had: a simple explosive belt and a waiting list of young wannabe suicide bombers willing to die for the cause of liberation.

'Because death has got to be better than life in a refugee camp,' one told me.

Briefly, Yasser Arafat enjoyed his popularity boom that accompanied the new uprising. He rode the wave, not starting the intifada, but neither did he stop it. Very soon it was clear he had no control over it. Or, for that matter, of the new breed of militants rising from the refugee camps and crowded cities, who would stomp out whatever was left of the peace process. In the Gaza Strip – from which Israel intends to withdraw unilaterally within a year – the power vaccum created by Arafat's confinement and the lack of jobs and services has allowed both Hamas and men like Mohammed Dahlan, Arafat's forty-two-year-old former security chief and an American favourite, to flourish and grow.

Neither of them are friends of the Old Man.

Flashback to October, 1993. The handshake on the White House lawn. A taciturn Yitzhak Rabin, a tentative Yasser Arafat, a grinning Bill Clinton. The following year, Rabin and Arafat would receive the Nobel Peace Prize. Clinton's domestic problems would be overshadowed by his role as a peacemaker in the Middle East.

But the reality behind the Oslo Peace Accords, which led to the handshake, were more complicated. Arafat had gambled by backing the accords, which many Palestinians regarded as a sell-out on crucial issues, most notably the right to return for Palestinian refugees displaced after the 1948 war. Splinter groups like Hamas and Islamic Jihad – which had minuscule support before Oslo – refused to back the peace process and became popular opposition groups.

It did not help that back in the West Bank, many of Arafat's political appointees to the newly founded Palestinian National Authority (confusingly referred to as either the PA or the PNA) – which was meant to administer to the needs of the Palestinians in the occupied territories – were mostly his Fatah Party cronies from Tunis. This emphasised the already widening gap between 'insiders' – the new generation who had grown up in the territories and were struggling against the occupation from within – and 'outsiders' – those who had worked in exile.

The embryonic PA emerged out of an occupation structure, and it has grave shortcomings. It consists of an elected legislative council, a cabinet and largely ineffectual ministries. It was crippled from the start by the limitations of the occupation, and later by corruption. Even some of Arafat's closest advisors at the time, men like Abdullah al-Hourani, a former PLO Executive Council member, tried to warn him that the structure was essentially useless.

'But Arafat was too interested in these salutes, these garbage removal ministries, these symbolic things,' sighs al Hourani, who now works in Gaza as a political analyst. 'No one could tell him otherwise.'

As a result, the PA essentially became a one-party system. Hamas and Jihad were left outside to seethe and regroup. It was therefore only a matter of time before corruption flourished, as the millions of dollars of donor money poured in and quickly went into the pockets of a very chosen few. The PA defended itself, saying it was operating as best it could, given the restrictions.

'It's not a perfect democracy, and I'm sorry we did not complete that under occupation,' counters Michael Terazi, a Harvard-educated lawyer who is part of the PLO negotiations team. 'We are not Kuwait that had a war fought to liberate us. We are not Kosovo that had NATO fight to reverse ethnic cleansing. We have to negotiate for what we deserve.'

It also did not help that the Palestinian people are governed, confusingly, by two parallel political structures – the PA for those inside the territories, and the PLO, which looks after the needs of the diaspora. The duality can only contribute to the ineffectiveness.

But the whole system is so confusing. Here is one example, a microcosm of the chaos that is Palestinian politics. One clear Saturday morning in Ramallah – which is the Palestinian equivilant of Washington D.C. – the Palestinian Legislative Council (which is essentially the elected Palestinian parliament), was meant to convene. It was an important meeting, to vote on potential candidates to replace Abu Ala (Ahmed Qureia), the newly installed prime minister.

The position of prime minister is another bone of contention. It was created by amending the law last year, after pressure by America and Israel to have an alternative leader to Arafat. The first prime minster was Arafat's number two in the PLO, Mahmoud Abbas (Abu Mazen), who was installed in May 2003 and left last September, with much bitterness and frustration. 'Arafat just did not want anyone else around with the slightest hint of power,' said one insider.

After Abu Mazen came Ahmed Qurei, or Abu Ala, the former speaker of the PLC. Abu Ala, a charismatic and highly intelligent man, was doomed from the start. Like Abu Mazen, he seems to spend most of his time locked in battle with Arafat over 'security issues' and hanging on to his emergency government by his fingernails. In the past few weeks, he has submitted his resignation, which was refused by Arafat, and glumly gone back to his position.

Given all this confusion, the PLC meeting I am watching in Ramallah quickly disintegrates into a farce. First there is the news that the representatives from Gaza can't make it to Ramallah because they can't get through the checkpoints. Then a large screen is lit up so the Gazans can at least participate via video link-up. But as the meeting begins and quickly descends into shouting chaos, the screen remains blank, focusing on an empty room somewhere in Gaza. The delegates there, it seems, were not informed of the correct time. Everyone shouts, smokes cigarettes and leaves.

Outside is a plump and well-dressed Sa'eb Erekat, the Palestinian cabinet minister and one of the few Palestinians around who still believes in 'the spirit of Oslo', of which he was a negotiator. He now holds the position of Chief Negotiator between Israelis and Palestinians, and while some Palestinians sneer that he is an 'Oslo addict', Erekat is a popular figure, and he's using the opportunity to give interviews to foreign TV crews and distribute maps of the security fence, or 'apartheid wall' as the Palestinians call it.

But the other delegates, disgusted at the failed meeting, are leaving.

'We were supposed to have a vote. How can we have a vote if no one shows up?' one shouts.

The problem, some civic leaders say, is that Arafat does not want votes, does not want harmony. As long as there is chaos and disorder, he is in control.

'It's a one-party government. He doesn't want to share leadership with anyone else,' says Mustapha Barghouti. 'The other groups are outside the circle, there isn't room for them.'

'He is used to being the only one,' echoes Abdullah al-Hourani. 'When he saw Abu Mazen moving in the international community circles and growing as a representative of the Palestinians, getting support from people, it made him angry. He put obstacles in front of him.'

Other observers believe that Arafat deliberately creates pockets of power amongst his own rivals and possible future successors – individuals like Mohammed Dahlan, or Jibril Rajoub, former director of the PSS in the West Bank; or Abu Mazan and Abu Ala.

'He's creating all these rival power bases so that after he goes, they will fight each other and there will be total chaos,' says Abu Sattar Kassam, an outspoken Nablus opposition leader who was gunned down on the street in 1994 after writing an anti-Arafat book. He believes the men were sent by Arafat, yet the attack still did not deter him. Abu Sattar

Kassam continues to publish pamplets and speak – some would say – far too openly about the leader and his corrupt habits.

The solution to the potential civil war scenario, and to this minefield of political error, should be elections, but most people here burst out laughing when this is mentioned. No one believes Arafat and Sharon – each for their own reason – will allow them.

'Arafat's been avoiding our call for the past year for a unified leadership, unified strategy, unified message, unity between groups,' says Mustapha Barghouti. And Ahmed Hisham points out that elections are logistically impossible under the military closures.

'How can we conduct elections while Israeli tanks and checkpoints dominate the territories?' he asks. 'How can people move freely, how can we move ballot boxes?'

So for the moment, Arafat remains firmly rooted in his broken-down palace, surrounded by a handful of guards, and a Palestinian flag that keeps going up and down, every day.

Aside from the division between Palestinians in the territories and in the diaspora, there are also the divisions between the West Bank and Gaza. Gaza, less than two hours' drive from Jerusalem, has always been like entering hell: a place of heat, dust, squalor, infinite poverty and searing anger. It is believed that fifty-five per cent of people there are on the poverty line and sixty-five per cent are unemployed., Many of the young, bright people in their twenties and thirties who speak three or four languages and read the *New York Times* and *Le Monde* online have never left Gaza, never even been to Jerusalem, because they are not allowed to enter.

The only way to vent anger is by leaning on a car horn in a traffic jam, and so the streets are full of the cacophony of ancient cars. I am not surprised Israel intends to withdraw from this awful place within a year: who would want it? Gaza does not hold the same religious and historic memories that the West Bank does, and it certainly has no economic value.

One million Palestinians squashed into a narrow strip of land about seventy miles long. Given this claustrophobia, it is not suprising that Gaza was the birthplace of the first intifada in December 1987, and is now the breeding ground for Hamas, who are responsible for most of the 104 suicide bombings over the past three years.

In 1994, Yasser Arafat, returning from exile in Tunis, drove through the streets of Gaza and announced that Gaza would soon resemble Singapore. Ten years on, I drive through the narrow streets crowded with donkey carts and thick with unleaded petrol fumes, with rank sewage spilling onto the sidewalks, and wonder what happened to his Asian dream. Like most of those Oslo visions, they seem to have been traded for unabashed violence.

And it is a vicious circle – the stronger the occupation grows, the stronger the popularity of Hamas and Islamic Jihad. 'We reject the word violence,' Khaled al-Batash, a political leader from Islamic Jihad tells me, when we meet at a dusty hotel overlooking the Mediterranean. 'We see it as fighting an occupation. Were Churchill and de Gaulle re- garded as violent people? When the occupation ends, the violence will end.'

Many Palestinians, particularly in Gaza, echo this. It is believed that seventy per cent of Palestinians support the suicide bombers, and every other street corner in the camps displays a different poster celebrating suicide attacks. The Palestinians call then 'martyrdom operations'.

'With each suicide bomber, there is five per cent appeal added to Sharon,' says Ghassan Khatib, a former labour minister in the PA. 'And with each Israeli assassination, Hamas' popularity rises.' In a peaceful situation, he adds, there would be no way that Hamas could succeed. 'But in violence, they grow. They flourish as a result of the failed peace process.'

Every time I have been to Gaza over the past fifteen years, there has always been disaster and violence: Israeli Apache helicopter attacks killing civilians; Hamas killing young Israeli soldiers; incursions into Rafah camp resulting in the death of women and children. And every time one side hits, the other side hits back harder. It is a frustrating and horrible cycle to watch. 'For every action, we have a reaction; it's totally natural,' an al-Aksa – the armed military wing of the Fatah Party – brigade commander calmly tells me later that day, when we meet in a safe house that I pray is not being watched by Israelis.

I go to see one of the results of the 'actions'. In Ramla, near Tel Aviv, a place that was once a Palestinian village before 1948, a Jewish funeral takes place. It is for nineteen-year-old Sgt Sarit Schneor, who was shot in the Netzarim settlement in Gaza.

Sarit's friends and army colleagues are there to watch her coffin being lowered into the sun-scorched earth. They talk about how she loved her boyfriend, loved life. Her army friends, most of them teenage girls – young and pretty with long, shiny hair and skin still mottled by adolescent acne – hug and wipe away each other's tears. But no one I spoke to questions why Sarit was in Gaza, or why Sharon is sending such young people effectively to their deaths.

While there is a dissident faction of the Israeli Defense Force (IDF) who refuse to serve in the territories 'because we get tired of being the bad guy', as one young soldier put it, Sarit's friends requested Gaza, because 'it's more challenging'.

I meet Yaffo, the mother of one of Sarit's friends. The group of young friends had just finished their military training and Yaffo tells me that she was so very proud to watch them get their names called and go up on a platform to receive their papers. All of them wanted to go to Gaza, she said. All of them wanted to fight the enemy. She introduces me to Noa, her daughter, a fragile beauty with pale skin and tears running down her cheeks.

I ask Noa, grief-stricken but seemingly sensible, what she thinks of the Palestinians, does she think there can ever be peace?

Noa stares at me wordlessly for a few seconds. 'I hate them,' she says finally, and turns away.

A few days later, in a refugee camp I can not name in Gaza, I meet a young Palestinian Hamas operative a few years older than Sarit.

In another world, they might have met at a beach club or a restaurant on the edge of the Mediterranean which borders Gaza, a sea that in many places the Palestinians are not allowed to swim. They might have talked about music or film. They might have shared a Gold Star beer. They might have fallen in love.

But this is all a fantasy. Abu Mojahed will never meet young Israelis the same age as him unless he is sent to kill them. And they will never meet him, unless they are roughing him up at a checkpoint or gunning him down in the street.

He's a Hamas operative; Sarit and her friends are soldiers. Just arranging the meeting with him takes days, and patience and planning. He's wanted by the Israelis, so we have to take precautions.

We agree to meet in an abandoned house in his refugee camp. The go-between who arranged the meeting closes all the windows, shutting out the mournful sound of the muezzin, the call to prayer from the nearby mosque. Finally Abu Mojahed enters, rushing into the room and scanning it as though he is already looking for a getaway.

My first thought is how incredible young Abu Mojahed is, with his fair skin that is barely able to grow the prerequisite Osama-style beard and his large stick out ears like Alfred E. Neumann. Added to the boyish effect is the American baseball cap he has perched on his head.

I suddenly think that Abu Mojahed, one of eight children who grew up in a refugee camp, will probably never grow old to marry or have children.

'When I was a kid,' he tells me, 'all I saw was beatings, arresting, killings, houses getting blown up. I didn't see any love or peace.' The saddest moment is when I ask him if he would like a wife and children. Abu Mojahed's pale face lights up.

'I would love that,' he says. Then his face drops. 'But imagine I am walking down the street with my kid. There is Israeli shelling. It kills my kid, maybe my wife. That's what happens to so many people here. Why should I choose that life?'

Instead, he's got his eyes on paradise. He wants to be a suicide bomber, and has applied many times, but the powers at Hamas need him elsewhere, to attack settlers and soldiers. His expertise is laying mines and booby traps, firing rockets and arranging ambushes with soldiers. He knows that one of these days his number will be up and the Israelis will either kill or capture him, but he doesn't care.

'So they kill me,' he shrugs. 'So I go to paradise.' He looks out towards the closed window, barricaded from the camp below. 'Either way I win.'

The day before, I met Abu Qusay, a military commander from the al-Aksa Brigade. Despite the popularity of Islamic Jihad and Hamas in Gaza, Fatah still rules here, garnishing the support of roughly thirty-six per cent of the Gaza population as opposed to thirty per cent for Hamas. It is still Arafat's show, even in the closed world of Gaza.

Abu Qusay was clean-shaven and wore a neatly ironed checked shirt, but again, we met in a safe house, on the twelfth floor in an empty apartment. I knew we were going to the right place because another man rode the elevator with us, carrying his dry-cleaning under one arm and a Kalashnikov under the other.

Since this intifada began, the al-Aksa Brigade has claimed responsibility for many of the suicide bombing attacks. While Arafat has said, 'Yes, I am against terrorism,' members of al-Aksa say they pay close attention to what he says. 'If he tells us to call a cease-fire, we call a cease-fire,' said one al-Aksa leader in Jenin. The members, who are believed to be around 450, are allegedly paid out of the PA budget, but the mandate is officially for them to 'encourage peace' – not to reward them for attacks. It is difficult, however, to see where they draw the line.

Abu Qusay is a typical member of al-Aksa, born out of frustration and rebellion and repression. One of nine children, he grew up in Shati, one of the most crowded and poverty ridden refugee camps in Gaza. A true child of the first intifada, he played by throwing stones at Israeli tanks and spent seven years in an Israeli prison for a reason he will not be clear about. He was released after Oslo, but as he watched the peace process disintegrate it appeared to him that the only solution was a military one.

He said the al-Aksa Brigade was created because there was no other alternative. 'There was, and is, no political horizon,' he said, chain-smoking. 'Resistance is the only means.'

We walk to an empty room while he puts on his al-Aksa face mask to be photographed. Through the murky glass window, there is Gaza City, sprawled out in front of us, dirty and desperate. Abu Qusay is preparing for a mission, but he will not say what. It is a few days after the Apache attack.

'If there is action,' he says, picking up his gun, 'you can be sure, there will be reaction. We are all – Palestinians and Israelis – in a dark tunnel that Sharon has created.'

There is stillness most days inside the muqata'a while Arafat fights off his enemies – the Israelis who threaten to deport or execute him; his own political rivals – but also, it is rumoured, grave illness. The past few weeks of late summer have been total chaos: the seizing of the Gaza police chief and some French aid workers; the off-again, on-again resignation of Abu Ala; and a report from the Palestinian Legislative Council written by five legislators, including Arafat's former spokesman, blaming the Palestinian leadership for failing to make decisions. Arafat is seventy-five years old. He's been fighting a long time. He must be exhausted.

In the past four years, Arafat has been outside the muqata'a only once or twice, and has made few television appearances, which leads people to talk. Last winter, all of

Ramallah was talking about Arafat and his mysterious ill-ness. While his doctor says he is suffering from simple stomach flu, others hint at something graver. That inevitably leads to the conversation of who will take over when the Old Man goes.

For many, it is hard to imagine life without him, as he has become the poster child of Palestinian resistance. 'Remember, he did bring the Palestinians back from the brink of extinc-tion,' says Michael Terazi. 'He may not be the right man for the job, but he did do that.'

Which is part of the great Arafat myth – survival. He has survived expulsions from Beirut and attacks in Tunis. In 1992 when his plane ran out of fuel and crashed in the Libyan desert, his pilot and others were killed, but Arafat emerged relatively unscathed. He has managed to ward off political coups and assassination threats. He's survived the corruption charges. He's still alive and living in two rooms at the muqata'a in confinement with his fax machine and his gun, even if the Israelis call for his exile and his own people call for him to step down.

But others argue that Arafat can not be replaced. 'Even if most Palestinians on the street believe that they are in one valley and the government is in another, Arafat is still much loved,' argues Ahmed Hisham. 'The confinement has turned him into a hero.'

But that still does not mean he can do the job. The pop psychology theory is that Sharon and Arafat are co-depen-dents and that the intifada has served each other's needs: Sharon is seen as the great general, Mr Security, intent on protecting his battered country; Arafat gained back the street cred he lost by signing Oslo and also by being isolated by the Americans and Israelis. The British writer Robert Fisk has gone so far as to describe them as 'Sharon the merciless, Arafat the corrupt: nothing meaningful to offer each other'.

But eventually, both Sharon and Arafat will go, and in Arafat's case, it may be sooner simply due to physical deterioration. As for who will take his place, it is a question his advisors say they never ask. 'Power sharing does not come into his world,' says one.

Still, there are some leaders who offer an alternative to the violence. For a time after Oslo, many people regarded Hanan Ashrawi, the softly spoken scholar of Middle English, the former dean of Bir Zeit University and a member of the PLC as the kinder, gentler face of Palestinians.

For a time, Ashrawi was a beacon of hope: someone both the Americans and Israelis could negotiate with, someone the Palestinans admired. But Ashrawi resigned from her post as Minister of Higher Education in 1998 after two years, and although Arafat frequently tries to lure her back into a ministerial role, she refuses. She does not, she says, see 'a commitment to change'.

On why she resigned, she chooses words carefully. 'I wanted credible people in my government,' she says slowly, 'and I did not get it.' We are sitting in her Ramallah office and the TV is blaring news of an attack in Gaza.

'I believe this is the most crucial and dangerous period we are facing,' she says softly, gesturing to the TV. She suggests that the solution to the problem may lie in something as drastic as asking the UN for protection. 'We should say the Palestinian Authority can no longer function,' she adds. 'We are paying the price of an authority incapable of meeting people's needs.'

There are other names floating around. Marwan Barghouti, the powerful grass-roots leader who is said to be the force behind the intifada. But Barghouti was convicted of murder in the Israeli courts in May, and might not get out of prison before he is an old man. Then there is Mohammed Dahlan, who has openly criticised Arafat of corruption, incompetence and selfishness, and who is clearly having his moment right now, taking advantage of Arafat's weakness. There is Sari Nusseibeh from the revered Jerusalem family.

Or perhaps, as Hanan Ashrawi adds, after Arafat, there will be lots of people. 'They will all have to stand together,' she says. But she does not sound convinced. The other alternative, as many point out to me, is the fear of civil war if Hamas and Jihad remain outside the leadership.

But for many of the ordinary Palestinians I spoke to, there is a sense that they are beyond politics. A 107-year-old man I met in Deheishe refugee camp near Bethlehem expressed it the clearest. The man was so old that he remembered the Ottoman Empire, World War I, the Arab uprising. He recalled days in 1916 as easily as he recalled the day in 1948 he was expelled from his village, not far from this camp. Yet when asked about leadership, he shrugged: 'I think it's God and only God who can help us,' he said, 'and not Arafat.'

And yet, there is some sign of dialogue between the few Palestinians and Israelis who have not given up hope, and who are working on channels outside their governments. Yossi Beilen, the former justice minister, and the former Palestinian Minister of Information and Culture, Yasser Abed Rabo, met secretly in abandoned Jerusalem parking lots to try to resurrect a peace process, the result of which became the unofficial treaty, the Geneva Accord. Sari Nusseibeh returned from meetings at the UN with Ari Ayalon, the former head of the Shin Bet, the Israeli security services, where they produced a grass-roots statement of principles for a two-state solution.

Some people, like Saeb Eraket have not entirely lost faith. He says he believes it is an 'historic inevitability' that Palestinians and Israelis will someday live together in peace.

But certainly not in this generation, certainly not with Sharon and Arafat in power. The view from the ground, from the squalid camps and the graffiti-riddled walls of encircled West Bank towns tells another story. For the moment, the Israelis live with the terrible black paranoia of waiting for the next attack, one that they will never be able to repel.

And all the Palestinians have is a Berlin-style wall which is quickly rising up in the middle of what is left of their historic homeland; a leader who can not leave his tank-scarred compound; and every day, fresh blood on the street.

NOTE: *Yasser Arafat died on 11 November, 2004 in Clamart, France. He was seventy-five years old. He was succeeded as chairman of the PLO by Mahmoud Abbas, aka Abu Mazen. In January, 2005, Abu Mazen also convincingly won the election for President of the Palestinian Authority.*

TWO: FORGOTTEN WARS

The Fall of Grozny

February, 2000

The darkened room is full of wounded Chechen fighters who retreated from Grozny last night over a minefield. There's the smell of blood, heavy and warm; sticky puddles of it all over the floor. Fresh amputees mumbling or screaming in pain, lying on dirty cots. They were tricked. The story goes that a Chechen commander bribed a Russian commander with $10,000 to let his men escape Grozny unharmed. But the Russian gave them a route over a minefield.

It's a terrible story. As soon as the fighters realised they were walking on mines, it was too late to retreat. Some of the older ones, braver ones, went forward, calling out to their friends, 'See you in paradise.' Others stepped on the remains of the bodies of their colleagues, bits of leg or arm or torso, to shield themselves from whatever mines lay below. The ones that survived arrived here, in this suburb called Alkan Khala, in their winter white uniforms covered in blood. They dragged the stiffened, frozen dead behind them by the arms or legs. Some were crying or tossing their guns on to the cold earth. Anger, sorrow, fear.

It is so hard to admit defeat. The commanders lied to me; they told me Grozny had not fallen. But the soldiers told me the truth. 'If we got out of the town, it means we're going to do something more effective,' one of the commanders kept repeating. He said he and his men were headed to the mountains. Another commander said, 'This is winter. What can we do in the winter? Just wait and see what we do in the spring.'

A third commander looked at me suspiciously. He says that the Chechens no longer need Grozny. They are regrouping and considering tactics. 'What does Grozny mean now? Empty walls? Empty buildings?' he says. 'There are more beautiful cities for us to take. Even Moscow. We have enough trained guys. We have enough will to fight.'

At the first aid centre, the doctor operates by generator, which flicks on and off. There are dozens of amputations to be done, without many painkillers or much anaesthetic. When I walk by, I see the flickering light, I see more blood coating the floor, but I can't stay long to hear the screaming. In a small room, a lone doctor in bedroom slippers performs an amputation with minimal anaesthetic. The patient lying on the wooden table squirms. But that's all. He just squirms.

A sobbing woman wanders from room to room, looking for her brother. 'Where is he? Please tell me where he is.' She finds her young soldier brother shortly afterwards, dead and covered with a white sheet on a stretcher in the corridor.

The fighters who are somehow not wounded, many of whom have been inside the city since October, wander through the first aid centre, helping the injured. Dirty syringes and ancient drips litter the floor; bloodstained stretchers are propped against walls. One soldier tries to stitch a wounded friend's bloody feet with a needle and thread while the man faints from pain.

'Come on, buddy,' he says, slapping him lightly.

All the time the bombardment continues. Dje, a twenty-six-year-old woman fighter, says the past few weeks inside were a living hell. 'The Russians are dropping every kind of bomb imaginable,' she says. 'Cluster bombs, deep-penetrating bombs that wipe out the basements, even chemical bombs. The only thing they aren't dropping are nuclear weapons.'

Dju is more honest about the city falling. She says she received the order from her commander to gather her things and leave Grozny through the Russian defence ring. At one point, along a sixty-yard corridor, the Russians were so close, she says, they could practically see each other. 'But they don't like to fight us man to man. They have artillery and planes – we have fighters.'

The greatest pain was losing her comrades, crossing that minefield, knowing so many were going to step on the wrong piece of earth. She says she is worried about her friends she left behind in Grozny. She says there are still several thousand Chechen fighters inside the city centre, as well as 40,000 civilians, mainly ethnic Russians, the elderly, women and children, who cannot get out even if there were a way.

I leave the first aid centre and walk to a shelter. There are two shelters in the village, one for women, one for men. Inside the women's shelter, there's a crib set up for babies, and a stove. 'We're organised,' says an older woman. 'We have to be.' There are jars of pickled vegetables, which they offer me. I refuse. A younger girl tells me the bombardment – the aerial bombs coming down every so often, the tank rounds more frequently, the mortars – are not the real problem.

'No, the real problem is in the morning when the Russians will enter this village and clean it,' she says matter-of-factly.

'What do you mean – clean?' I ask.

'They throw grenades in the shelters and in the houses of the people,' she says. 'The fighters will be gone by then, but we have nowhere to go.'

By late afternoon, as the light dims and the deep Caucasus cold sets in, I go back to the hospital. Chechnya is totally isolated: there are no foreign aid workers here, one doctor, no UN and, aside from me, a German photographer and a French reporter, no journalists. The place could get blown off the map and no one would know.

'Or the Russians can kill you and who will ever witness this?' says one soldier.

At the field hospital, the soles of my heavy boots are full of blood. The bottom of my jeans are lined with a thin stripe of red. The mattresses where the young fighters – all in their twenties – lie are also soaked red; the doctor is now on his fourth amputation. On the second floor, in a small room at the end, a twenty-six-year-old fighter named Muslim lies in a corner with half a foot covered in a bloody rag. He has been defending the capital since August and came out last night.

'I stepped on one of those mines that injure but don't kill,' he says. 'It was a gift from the Almighty.'

The man in the next bed was not so lucky. He was blinded by a 'frog' mine, which springs into the air before exploding. The place where his eyes once were has swollen like grapefruit. His face is purple with bruises and he mutters incoherently as his comrades try to soothe him. Then a famous commander comes into the room. We all stand up. The commander stands by the blind man's bed for a long time with a look of terrible regret on his face.

'To go into the centre of Grozny now is suicide,' one soldier says. 'There is nothing left there, nothing! We defended it until it was time to leave.'

Later the famous commander shouts at me, wanting to know why the West has done nothing but stand by and watch the disintegration of Chechnya.

'Our first war was for independence,' he says. 'When we fought for independence, they called us bandits. Now, when we fight for Islam, they will call us terrorists.'

'I don't know,' I say, embarrassed, staring down at my bloody boots.

The wounded soldiers, in their agony, call out Allahu Akbar – God is Great – to each other. But Yeva, a young lawyer, says the war is not really about religion; it is about freedom. 'Can't anybody help us? Don't we warrant any mercy from the world?'

Later, I walk through the frozen night. My breath comes out in puffs. Mousa, a soldier who is with me says, 'I wish you could see Chechnya in the spring! The wildflowers are so beautiful.'

Now the stars are beautiful, and the red light of the tracer rounds. I don't sleep at all at night; I sit up eating a bowl of beans and telling jokes with the youngest soldiers. There is nothing else we can do. At dawn, they get orders and leave. They are walking along the railway tracks to the mountains and they ask me to come, but I know the Russian helicopter gunships that have been bombing us all night will follow them and kill most of them.

'I'll stay,' I say.

'But you will die when the Russians find you,' says one.

The light is grey. The soldiers take the dead with them. The villagers are going too, dressed in their familiar refugee clothes – layer upon layer of coats and dresses and scarves and hats. They pull sleighs of supplies. They've decided to walk through Russian lines, through the tanks. They say they will dress me up like a Chechen and when the Russian soldiers speak to me, they will pretend I am mute. I don't speak Chechen.

I am too frightened to eat. One old woman gives me pickled corn and bread, shaking her head as a mortar crashes in the distance and a machine-gun rattles. 'Hear that?' she says nonchalantly. 'This is the music we live by.'

Somehow, I get out. I drive through the Russian front lines, through the tanks with a Chechen and a baby on my lap. As we drive forward, I see the tanks entering the village. To clean it, to punish it.

Another village, a few days later

The bombing began shortly after lunch. I was talking quietly to a Chechen man. The crack of the bomb, very close, stunned us. Then he stood up. 'Bunker! Bunker!' he screamed.

We stumbled into our shoes and grabbed warm clothes. It only takes half a minute from the moment your brain registers danger until the time you arrive in a safer place, but that time stretches like hours. I remembered enough to know I had left my documents in my rucksack back in the house. 'My passport,' I said.

'Fuck your passport,' he said. 'The house is about to get bombed.'

But my greatest fear is not having my papers. 'Please, I have to go,' I say weakly, moving to get up. He pushed me towards the bunker. A kid ran into the house at lightning speed and returned with my bag, some blankets and a kerosene lamp. Inside the bunker – a ten-foot hole in the garden – women with their heads wrapped in heavy scarves were already cowering with fear.

Three other women climbed down the rickety wooden ladder, passing a fat two-year-old boy. He appeared too shocked to cry, but the twenty-two-year-old girl holding him, her nerves frayed from the shelling, began to scream for her aunt to come down. There was another loud explosion.

'Why us? Why us?' cried one of the old women.

'Because 1 February is a holiday, and the soldiers get paid, so they get drunk and like to kill people,' one man explained calmly.

It was silent for a moment. I took the kid on my lap as his cousin buried her head in her hands. Then the women began to pray, their voices drowned out by new explosions. We sat together in the dank cold for an hour or so and waited. Finally, a villager came and shouted down into the darkness: 'They hit the house two doors away. Four kids dead coming home from school. One woman, her whole back is pierced by a rocket . . .'

I thought of the children I had seen that morning, walking on the snowy unpaved road to school with plastic rucksacks on their backs. School had recently opened. They had seemed so excited and so normal as they walked along holding hands and throwing snowballs at the horse and cart riding by.

Inside the bunker, we sat. I tried to get up, to stretch my legs. I needed air. 'Do you want to die, like those kids?' one of the women hissed. I sat down. The helicopters circled over for the rest of the day and then, as night fell and the curfew began, so did the shelling. Every time we tried to climb out of the bunker, we heard the whirl of propellers close by and ran back in. The Russians had decided to give the village a thrashing. 'Every time you think you are safe,' Magamir, a twenty-seven-year-old fighter from the first Chechen war, said, 'they fuck you.'

This place is nine miles from Grozny. It's been occupied by Russian troops since 11 November. It's a terrible place, synonymous with tragedy. It is thought to be the most-destroyed village in Chechnya and even though it has already been taken by Russians, for some reason it is still being punished.

When we get out we walk, crunching our boots in the soft white snow. A group of villagers has gathered in front of the bombed house, watching the flames lick around the structure before the beams collapsed. There's a former fighter called Said, screaming in English, 'You see what they do to us? Do you see?'

We take a quick tour of the village before heading back to the house. Nearly every house has been gutted by fire, bombing or looting. Nearly every family has lost someone: one old man, Zia, lost sixty relatives in a 1995 'massacre'. His old face drips with tears.

The night before, as we huddled around listening to Radio Liberty, a villager arrived to say that some locals had shot down one of the helicopters that was tormenting them, and the Russians were furious. Another arrived to say five houses were on fire on the next street from rocket grenades.

Finally, more good news: another villager arrived to say the Ingush-Chechen border was sealed and no one was going in or out. We were trapped. Nothing to do but to continue with our thin and tasteless soup and listen to the shelling. The twenty-one-year-old who cooked for us shook as she poured tea. She ladled out the soup but she had none herself.

'Eat, darling, eat,' her aunt said. But the girl pushed her long hair back and shook her head.

'I have lost all appetite since the shelling began,' she said.

The House of the Blind, Grozny

Only thirty residents remain at Grozny's shattered House of the Blind, where once there were 400. They cannot see the smashed ruins of the city all around them. But they know the worst is not over. They made it through the bombing but now they have emerged from the darkness underground to an empty future.

'We just wait to see if someone comes to talk to us,' says Lyubov Zilipayeva, a fifty-three-year-old ethnic Russian who sits toying with a paper clip, a dirty woollen hat pulled low over her sightless blue eyes.

'To be honest with you, I don't expect anything to happen in the next year or two,' says Nurdi Belershemenkhov, a Chechen who lost his sight in a car crash when he was twenty-eight. His tinted sunglasses are held on his head by a dirty shoelace and he has a bad cough from weeks of living underground.

'Life teaches you not to expect good things. I've been waiting my whole life for good things to happen. I guess now they won't.'

His friend, Palenedin Dameployav, is wearing a Russian fur hat, no shoelaces in his cracked leather shoes, and he carries a white cane. Palenedin and his twin brother were blinded by glaucoma at the age of three. Before the wars he worked in a state-run radio factory and was a ham radio operator.

'I used to talk to people in Alaska,' he says proudly. 'I could take apart and put together any radio.' All that ended when Russian troops took away his radios in 1995, fearing the Chechen rebels would get their hands on them.

'They took my guitar and my bedding too,' he says. This time he managed to squirrel away a few bits and pieces – 'parts of a telegraph machine that I was building. It was almost finished when the war started.'

Palenedin lives on the fifth floor of this gutted building. Iron bed frames dangle from balconies, and you can still smell the smoke. Despite the fact that white flags flew over it before the war, and it is the only institute for the blind in Chechnya, it was totally and brutally bombed.

When Palenedin got out of the basement last week, he first went to find his flat, climbing up the five floors with no walls and no banisters. For a sighted person, it is a perilous journey – one could easily fall on the rubble and plunge down five storeys. For a blind man picking his way through brick and shredded wood, it is all but impossible.

'All of their touch marks – the doorsteps and the exits that they used to know to manoeuvre their way around – are gone,' says Marina Sergeyeva, thirty-four, the librarian.

Her library, with its statues of Pushkin, Chekhov, Turgenev and Mayakovsky, is now, thanks to the Russian bombers, a piled heap of the braille books and books on tape that she worked so hard to acquire. 'We didn't have much before,' she says, picking up a braille book. 'Now we have even less.'

On 1 February, their basement was rocked by deep-penetration bombs. A door blew off the hinges, injuring one man; the others panicked, trying to make their way to the exits. 'It was awful, people stepping on each other,' says Fatima, a nurse, who was hit by shrapnel in her chest.

Everyone ran out but one woman, Gali, another nurse who is married to one of the blind men. Her body remained under the rubble for seven days. The blind went down to help to retrieve it. Then her husband laid it under the stove in the basement and wept by it every night, whispering 'Sleep, my Gali, sleep.'

Lyubov Zilipayova, who worked in the radio factory alongside Palenedin and Naudi, says that the Chechen fighters inspected the House of the Blind and thought the basement a perfect shelter, 'but they realised the danger they would put us into, so they went away'.

For everyone else in Grozny, it's not over yet. There are rumours that all civilians will be evacuated from Grozny so the Russians can raze the city to the ground.

'The fighting still isn't over, I know it,' says Palenedin, standing in the food line, with Naudi hanging on his arm, to collect a bowl of buckwheat. 'Before the war, all of us worked. I know it's impossible now.'

The blind are joined in the line by the same filthy group of civilians every day – the same four children, the same crazy woman from Ukraine, the elegant woman with the fur-lined boots.

'Oh there you are, you're still alive,' one neighbour greets another.

She stares at him coldly. 'Of course I am, you didn't bury me yet,' she says.

St Valentine's Day, Grozny, 14 February, 2000

The Russians have wiped Grozny off the map. It is uninhabitable, even for the packs of hungry wild dogs. Hussein,
one pro-Moscow Chechen working as a volunteer grave
digger, tells me the dogs are tearing apart the bodies of
the unburied throughout the city.

'The dogs are eating the corpses,' he says.

I wander through the city in a trance. It is difficult to find a
building not gouged by bombs or reduced to a pile of bricks.
Apartment buildings with no rooves are booby-trapped and
mined. There is no water, electricity, heating or telephones.

When this war started, there were about 400,000 people
living in Chechnya's capital. But Grozny now has only a
small, ragged band of civilians: the brave, the stupid, the old,
the ill. The ones who could not run away. They are the living
dead, emerging from hiding places. They shuffle out of their
cellars, clutching plastic soda bottles to fill with water. Some
wear white armbands to distinguish them from fighters.
Most are women; some are so old they are nearly bent
double.

When the military curfew descends at 6 p.m., nearly
everyone goes back to the cellars, but those caught outside
tell stories of drunken Russian Interior Ministry troops
looting, shooting randomly into cellars, taking women away.

The first unconfirmed reports of rape are filtering through.
Alpatu, forty, says she left Samashki, in western Chechnya,
on 1 February with three women friends, aged thirty-nine,
twenty-three and forty.

They arrived at the first Russian checkpoint in Grozny and
produced their passports. Alpatu was lucky – she was last in
the queue. The others were marched off and not heard from

again. 'They were soldiers from Dagestan and North Osse-
tia,' she says. 'I've tried to find my friends. What is strange is
we haven't found the bodies.'

The rape stories are not limited to one side. Another
woman, an ethnic Russian, comes forward weeping, clutching a photograph of a beautiful teenager; her fifteen-year-old
daughter.

'Chechen fighters came on 15 November,' she says slowly.
'They burst into the room, wearing black masks and carrying
Kalashnikovs. They said, "We need her", that was all.' She
has searched three months in vain for the girl. 'Nothing,' she
says, rubbing her red eyes. 'She just seemed to disappear.'

The Russian emergency services have set up four 'feeding
points', which include hot showers in an attempt to prevent
an epidemic, as well as a full surgical hospital. But in the
Staropromyslovsky district, once heavily populated and less
damaged than other city areas, there were fewer than 200
people gathered. They wait silently for three hours in the
freezing cold, shuffling their feet for warmth, for a bowl of
buckwheat kasha, a cup of sugared tea and a loaf of dark
bread.

More are creeping to the hospital, complaining of shrapnel
wounds, infections, illnesses or tuberculosis.

Near Minutka Square, Lyobov Yasinsaya, forty-two, a
Ukrainian doctor who has lived in Grozny for years, keeps
screaming. She just opens her mouth and screams and
screams. It's terrible to witness. She says she could not leave
the city because her elderly mother and her four children
were unable to travel. She came out of the cellar ten days ago.

'We had to steal to get food and we often had no water.
Now the war is over, I have been standing here for two
weeks, and no one will help me!'

She is covered with dirt and grime, her face hidden behind weeks of unwashed soot. She stares at her hands, cracked and raw. 'I'm an educated person, I hate going around like this, but I have descended into the condition of a monkey.'

There's an old lady next to her called Dzhanat Aktulayeva. She's sixty-two and says she has gone through two wars, as well as deportation in 1944 to Kazakhstan. Her son was killed in the 1994 war and she raises his three children on her small pension.

'We've been tortured,' she says. 'Life in Grozny has been hell on earth.'

I stay longer, a few more weeks. One night, on the crackling satellite phone, someone tells me the Russian secret service are looking for me. I'm in the country illegally, and my reports are being translated and broadcast on the evening news.

'You have to leave,' he says. 'If they catch up, they will kill you and make it look like an accident. A land mine. A random explosion.'

I get to Moscow and stay in a grand hotel, shaking as I hand over my passport. I double-lock my door and move the heavy wooden table in front of it. I run a bath. Total and utter paranoia. Frozen to the bone and filthy. When I lower myself into the water, it quickly turns brown.

I get on a flight and go back to London, but I am numbed by the cold of Chechnya, by the weeks of writing down stories and testimonies in my small notebooks. I put the notebooks in a black box and vow not to look at them again, for a decade or two. One night, walking down St James, I see a famous film director coming out of a fancy restaurant. He has read my reports. He stops and shakes my hand. By chance, he is with the director of the Royal Society for the Blind.

Then the image comes back to me: the tinted sunglasses; the white flag; Palenedin's radios. I ask him to help me, help them. He gives me some numbers, all of which prove fruitless. I try some charities in Moscow. Red tape and unhelpful Russian shrews. Eventually, I give up.

I never go back to Grozny. In September, 2001, trying to get to Afghanistan, I take a flight to Moscow. The passport official sniggers when my name comes up on the computer. He calls the airport police. They frogmarch me off to a dark room and leave me there. My cell phone does not work. They will not let me use their phone. They laugh at me and no one speaks English. I feel tears stinging my throat, hot and senseless. I am afraid.

Eventually, they put me back on a plane to London.

'Don't come back here,' says the burly guard, shoving a beefy hand on my back.

'What did I do?' I shout. 'I have a visa! I'm allowed to come to this country!'

He looks at me with icy hatred. He says one word and then pushes me onto the plane.

Chechnya.

Evil Things Happened Here: Samashki, Chechnya

February, 2000

Taissa had just laid her two-year-old nephew, Turpo, down to sleep on a cot, covered him with a pile of rugs and put a green fleece hat on his head in an attempt to keep out the cold. She was washing the dishes with water that she had drawn from the well that morning, and she wanted to go outside before the 4.30 Russian-command curfew began.

But as soon as she heard the first crack of the rocket, then the aftershock that rattled the windows of her house, she ran outside and began screaming for her aunt Mata and her older sister Raisa. She didn't even bother to put on her shoes, despite the rain and mud outside. She just ran to the bomb shelter in her slippers and thick socks, her long blonde hair swinging behind her, tears running down her cheeks.

Taissa spent her twenty-first birthday in a bomb shelter, and she is sick of being frightened, being cold, being poor and being stuck underground sitting with the old village ladies, praying that the next bomb doesn't fall any closer. What she really wants is to be back in Siberia studying cosmetology, learning how to give a French manicure and going out to discos at night.

Now, her social life consists of a battery-operated radio that plays bad Russian pop songs or occasionally something Western such as Cher's stupid song, 'Believe'. When that happens, she leaps to her feet and dances wildly, watching her moves in the cracked mirror that hangs on the wall.

The rest of her daily life passes with the monotony of Chinese water torture. When she is not dreaming of her other life, she is working – cooking for her family, trying to be creative with limited ingredients – or sitting in the dark in the evenings listening to Radio Liberty, the US-sponsored station, getting depressing information about the Chechens losing the war. Sometimes the Russians, who occupy the village, enter on foot, and then she and the family go down to the cold underground bunker and hide, or run to warn other neighbours. 'Last night they came and stole our dishes,' she says. So her task for the day was to find new ones to use. 'Every day it's something,' she says.

At times, Taissa feels more angry than scared. 'Why me? Why don't I have a normal life like any other twenty-one-year-old? They stole our youth, our best friends, our happiness.' But at other moments, when the Russian helicopters fly closer and closer, leaving a trail of bullets outside the shelter where we hide, she squeezes herself tight into a ball and screams like an animal. It is a primal sound, but she can't help herself: it is not natural to be trapped underground for hours on end, in an old root cellar surrounded by neighbours guessing how many people have just been killed. 'The worst thing is to feel that you lost your power,' she says miserably.

Samashki, this village eighteen miles west of Grozny, is a cursed place. At first glance, it seems almost normal for a

Chechen village that has been under Russian occupation since November. The people go about their business with a scared, frightened look, walking the wide, almost medieval unpaved streets where old men in long felt coats and astrakhan hats ride on pony-driven carts. The market is meagre, selling a few stale Bounty bars and acid-flavoured orange soda from Russia; the grim Soviet-style buildings that house the local schools and the clinic open and close randomly depending on how much pressure the Russians put on the civilians. It appears to function, in a dysfunctional kind of way. Then you look closer. Almost every building is burnt, gutted, driven through with rockets, shells, bullets. And the people walking through the streets have a glazed, almost crazed look in their eyes, the result of severe post-traumatic stress.

'Most villages in Chechnya have suffered,' says Valya, an ethnic Russian who married a Chechen man and has lived here since 1969. 'But this place . . . evil things have happened here. Why are the Russians attacking the Chechens? They are good people, and what is the sense of this war? My grandchildren sleep with their eyes open now.'

There is nothing strategic, historic or symbolic about Samashki, yet since the first Russo–Chechen war, which lasted from 1994–1996, it has been constantly targeted, with brutalities aimed more against civilians than against soldiers. Part of it has been an intimidation campaign launched by the Russians during the first war, to try to teach civilians a 'lesson' about what happens to a village if they are partial to fighters. It is a vicious way to treat innocent people who are merely trying to survive: it has become more a war against civilians than a war against fighters.

'As My Lai did in Vietnam, Samashki came to symbolise

the senseless horror of war that was aimed as much at the civilian population as the rebels,' wrote Thomas de Waal and Carlotta Gall in their book, *Chechnya: A Small, Victorious War*. According to Mark Lattimer from Amnesty International, 'The village of Samashki has become a terrible exemplar of the Russian forces' inhumanity in Chechnya – in both Chechen wars it has repeatedly been subjected to deliberate or indiscriminate attacks on civilians.'

'Our village was a normal place,' shrugs Taissa's uncle, Mousa, who is called back from putting out a fire down the road (the result of a rocket attack) to give the chronology of the town. 'Now it is the most destroyed town in Chechnya.' Its name is so symbolic with destruction that a Russian human-rights group, Monument, wrote an entire book about it called *By All Available Means: The Russian Federation Ministry of Internal Affairs Operation in the Village of Samashki*. The detailed report not only gives startling evidence of what happened inside this village, but also provides lists of the dead and lists of the houses, buildings, schools and dwellings that were destroyed.

We could reprint an entire account of what led up to the wasting of Samashki, but the simplest starting point is April, 1995, when the Russian command ordered Special Forces troops to flush out fighters. After a brutal artillery bombardment, during which most of the population cowered underground, a specially trained unit entered the village on foot, with tanks and armoured personnel carriers following behind. Basically, it was a time of terror; the soldiers laid waste to anything they could find.

'For two days, they conducted zachistka, or cleansing operations, here, which means they pretty much killed everything that moved,' explains Mousa. 'Not just killing men of fighting age, but old women, children, animals. They locked civilians in cellars and threw in grenades.' The Russians performed house-to-house searches, shooting civilians point-blank in the streets or in front of their homes. By the time the 'operation' was finished, more than 100 – all but four of them civilians – were murdered and 100 men were taken away to 'filtration' camps.

The testimonies from the survivors of the assault are chilling. 'They opened bunkers, poured in petrol and burned people alive,' says one old man, Zia, who lost sixty members of his family. 'They lynched one child under a tree and put a sign underneath him which said, 'The Russian Bear has awoken.'

'We thought they were on drugs,' explains Mousa. 'We found syringes later. That would be the only way to explain it. War is war, but how can you burn living people?' And, indeed – although Russian officials deny it – drugs are common among the Russian armed forces. On 13 April, days after the massacre, journalists (who, along with the Red Cross and Médecins Sans Frontières, were denied access to Samashki during the operation) were finally allowed inside the destroyed village. Those who gained access to Samashki reported finding syringes and ampoules containing Promodol, an anti-shock tranquilliser, and Dimedrol, a powerful narcotic. Both are issued to Russian soldiers in their first aid kits. Russian pharmacists later said that the drug cocktail combined with alcohol (vodka is generally consumed in large quantities by soldiers) could result in extremely aggressive behaviour. This, combined with the survivors' testimonies, gives a twisted, even more sinister account of the terrible story.

The Russians still insist Samashki was not innocently

targeted, that it was a place that harboured Chechen soldiers. But the villagers deny this and say that they ordered all fighters out in an attempt to keep the war from coming to their doorstep. According to one of the village elders, dozens of fighters who were hiding in the nearby woods were all told to leave in March, 1995, so that the village would not be at risk.

That summer, the villagers tried to repair their houses for the winter and to store fruit in their cellars. They had barely recovered from the trauma of April when a second assault on the village came nearly a year later, in March, 1996. While a small unit of Chechen fighters staved off an attack with hunting rifles and knives, the Russians pounded the place for ten days. 'It was savage,' recalls Mousa. The Russians used aerial bombardment and fuel air bombs known as 'vacuum bombs', which explode above ground killing everything in a wide range. Virtually every dwelling suffered some kind of damage, or was levelled. People who survived the attack crawled out of their bunkers amazed to see that others had lived through it.

When the first war ended, many of the people who had fled from Samashki began to return home, shocked at what they found. 'So many were dead, or their houses were just black holes,' says Mousa. 'Others found all their animals gone. Women who had fled found their men had been taken away to camps.' Then, in October, 1999, just as people were beginning to believe that they might be sending their children back to school, or getting enough money for food to last through the winter, it started again: this time, a new war. Human Rights Watch, the independent monitoring group, says an attack started on 15 October, with the heaviest assaults taking place about ten days later.

'Dozens of Samashki civilians were injured or killed,' they say in a statement which also quotes one resident, Hava Avturkhanova, whose daughter was injured during the attack, who claims that 'ninety-five per cent of Samashki's dwellings were aflame' by 27 October, and that many residents were killed or wounded.

After that, the sensible fled, taking what was left and going to Ingushetia, preferring the life of a refugee to the life of a terrified citizen who doesn't know when the next shell is coming. The ones who stayed on, such as Taissa's family, did so either because they could not afford to run away, or because they stubbornly refused to leave their village.

As a result, the Samashki residents who have stayed are a shattered but resilient lot, living out their tortured days in a haunted ghost town. There is the frail but dignified doctor, Abdul Wahid, who every day puts on his yellowed shirt and faded tie and a battered overcoat and walks to his 'clinic' – a few rooms in a former kindergarten. 'We can't heal, we can only give injections,' he says wistfully. There is no ambulance – it was shelled in October and stands blackened and burnt, a testimony to the brutality of war, in the middle of the road.

The drugs at Dr Wahid's clinic are outdated, and the Russians have taken his instruments, even the clinic's table and chairs. But Dr Wahid, who was deported along with most of the Chechen population to Kazakhstan in 1944, is strangely untouched by bitterness or frustration at the inability to perform his work.

'When they took us away on that cargo train in 1944,' he recalls, 'everyone was saying, "Where are they taking us?" We thought they were going to throw us into the sea or kill us in some faraway place.' But he was determined to survive and that instinct has allowed him to stay alive this long. As a child, it took him two years to learn the new language, Kazakh, so that he could go to school, and he struggled through medical school in a foreign tongue. But the experience, if anything, has made him stoical. He appears to accept his grim lot in life, trying to treat tuberculosis and heart disease with a few aspirin, vitamin B that expired in 1998, and outdated Novocain.

But the frustration of trying to patch up the remains of bloodied, mutilated children must wear him down. He shrugs. 'I continue. I try not to complain,' he says, adding that the clinic opens every day at 8.15 a.m., and they begin to light the kitchen stove and warm the place, just so people know that they are there. 'We can't really do anything, and for the very sick – people with cancer – there is nothing,' he says. 'But still, they know we are here. That in itself is a comfort.'

Down the road, the school is closed today following a rocket attack in which children were killed the day before. The school's teacher, Sara Mogammedovna, a stern but cheerful forty-two-year-old, has educated an entire generation of Samashki children. 'I have been here for twenty years,' she says, 'And from an educational point of view, this war has kicked us back twenty years.' She used to love to teach her children Russian literature: the beautiful stories of Chekhov, the poetry of Pushkin, the novels of Tolstoy. 'We used to think it was the light of Russia.' Now, she says, she can't bear to speak the language. 'They annihilated our souls,' she says. 'I can't speak about their heroes any more.'

Standing outside her closed school – by order of the Russian command – she points at the bullet holes that scar the building. 'At last count, I lost 100 of my children,' she says, adding that during the first war, when the Russians entered Samashki during 'cleansing operations', they would walk by groups of children and shoot at them.

'We don't teach children history,' Sara continues. 'The children teach us. I sleep in the same bed with my ten-year-old. He says, "When I am thirteen or fourteen, just let me go and kill one Russian."' She sighs. 'The children of Samashki saw when they opened the doors of those cellars where people were burnt alive. How can I educate them after that?'

Down the road, as twilight arrives, Mashoud, the seventy-year-old village elder, sits with two other men watching the winter sun go down over Samashki. In the fading light, the elderly man has the painful look of defeat etched on his strong features. Elected by a 'tamoot' – a group of men – it is Mashoud, as head of the Samashki Administration, who makes the journey every day to the edge of the village to negotiate with the Russian command. He negotiates with them for 'issues about daily life' – for food, for electricity, for curfew rights – and in return is expected to keep the Chechen fighters out of the village, a difficult role for him to play. On the one hand, he is a Chechen, with patriotic feelings. On the other, he has watched his people suffer enough and wants to avoid any confrontation he can.

'When Samashki fell on 11 November (last year), I asked the fighters to leave,' he says. 'I begged them, because this village has seen enough bloodshed. I said, please, I am afraid for my people.' He then wrote a letter to the Russian government, swearing that no 'wahabi' (Muslim extremists) or fighters remained inside, 'so please leave this place in peace'.

It was not to happen. Since November, whether or not there have been fighters inside, the village has sustained attacks from the Russians. And although the official line from Moscow is that the war is now over, 50,000 Russian troops remain in the Chechen region.

Sometimes their attacks are in the form of house-to-house cleansing operations; sometimes it is artillery; sometimes it is rockets from helicopters. On the day that Taissa cooked me lunch, the house next door was rocketed: four school children were killed; a housewife was severely injured; and a row of houses on the street were damaged and burnt. There had not been an attack for weeks and the people were beginning to feel a false sense of security, lounging outside their houses, milling around in the wan winter sunlight. Then, out of nowhere, came the terrible crack of a bombardment.

'Just when you think you are safe,' said Mousa, 'they fuck you.'

The irony is that Samashki, like many Chechen villages, is home to ethnic Russian families. Valya, a sixty-two-year-old Russian grandmother, lives with her family in one room down a muddy alley next to a field that was once for cows. For lunch, she is making a pot of rice with boiled milk. It is the same meal the family will have for supper. It is the same meal they have eaten all week.

Her house is destroyed. Only one room functions, and she has taken care to keep it warm and neat, with blankets where the family sleeps neatly rolled up on sofas during the day. Her son-in-law, a teacher in Samashki, was killed in a bombing, and now her daughter and their two children are living with Valya and her husband. Another son died during a bombing raid, she says, from 'fear'.

Originally born in Ukraine, Valya met her Chechen husband in Kazakhstan after World War II. In the thirty-one years that she has lived in Samashki, as a Russian in a

Chechen village, she says she was never treated with any kind of discrimination. 'They were good people. They accepted me as one of them.' Now, with her own countrymen destroying her village and her family, she is no longer proud to be Russian. 'I am ashamed. People say, "Look what your brothers are doing!" But the Russians aren't my brothers any more – the Chechens are. We are suffering in this war together.'

The days I spent in Samashki passed listlessly. They begin early – the women rise at six and boil water for tea, or begin to make the bread. Everyone tries to carry on the life they might have lived before, but it is difficult when the economy of a village – as well as its soul – has been ground down. The days were spent ducking in and out of bomb shelters, depending on the intensity of the shelling. Nights were spent huddled around a radio, with occasional knocks at the door in which everyone sat up looking terrified: warnings of house-to-house searches came frequently. A neighbour would enter and say excitedly, 'The Russians are in the western part of the village.' Then everyone would frantically gather their things and move to another house. Sometimes there would be whispered messages about certain fighters who needed to be fed and housed as they passed through town en route to the mountains, and instructions about where they were hiding.

At six in the morning, the old woman in the house where we had been moved to hide rose early and began to bake a pancake, a Chechen speciality, served with curd cheese and plum jam. She had promised to make it, and she was determined, shelling or no shelling, to make it for her guests. But as the tea was boiling and the house was just beginning to warm with the heat of the oven, an old villager burst into the house and said that he counted sixty-two tanks at dawn driving down the main road, but that the Russian commander claimed to be lost on his way to another village. 'They're back! They're back!' he shouted.

Everyone tried to calm him. But it didn't help the tension in the village; more people were trying to find their way out of the place, convinced that it could not stand a fourth attack and that this time they would not be lucky. When I ventured out to find the village elder to ask his opinion, I was told that he had fled that morning, for Ingushetia. 'It's not safe any more,' his friend said. 'Everyone should go.'

We left Taissa, Turpo, Mousa and everyone else at midday. They were going to stay on. We said goodbye with sadness; we knew we would probably never see each other again. By the time we got to Ingushetia, walking over the border, we heard the news from passing refugees that Samashki was already under heavy attack.

Divine Injustice: Northern Nigeria

June, 2002

Peter Ajayi sits quietly at an outdoor restaurant, showing a photograph of his three youngest children wearing blue and yellow choir robes. It is a suffocating morning in Kano, northern Nigeria, a city which has operated under sharia, or Islamic law, since 1999. Since then Kano, and surrounding towns in other states, has exploded into religious violence between the majority Muslims, who support the new law, and the few Christians who are attempting to live under it. Since the establishment of sharia, thousands of people have been killed in clashes and hundreds of churches have been burnt down.

Life for the Christians – who are unfairly seen as pro-American, pro-West – is becoming intolerable. 'We don't have a political voice,' says Dr Gabriel Oja, pastor of the First Baptist Church in Kano. His parish has been reduced by forty per cent since sharia was established, either by people leaving or being killed. 'There is no single Christian in government in Kano. Not even a councilman.'

Peter Ajayi's three children – Shola, fourteen, Dupe, eleven, and Moji, eight – are part of that equation. They were children who went to church every day and wanted to grow up to be doctors and accountants. They were ambitious, their father says proudly. But they will never grow up and never go to university because on 14 October, 2001, while Peter was away on business, Muslim fundamentalists arrived at the Ajayis' bungalow.

In the previous few days, there had been anti-Christian riots in Kano in response to the US-led bombing of Afghanistan. The riots left hundreds dead. Muslims were attacking Christians with knives, swords and fire. Peter's wife, Christiane, had spoken to her husband that morning and reassured him that she and the children were safe. Now she assumed he had come home early and she answered the door without thinking.

The men at the door looked at Christiane calmly and said, 'We have been sent to kill you because you are Christians.' They then doused the house, and her, with petrol and set the fuel alight. While Christiane went up in flames, the three children, along with a visiting cousin, were trapped in their rooms. They screamed for their mother, but she was trapped in the kitchen trying to extinguish the fire and could not reach them. In the end, Christiane threw herself out of a window. The children perished.

Peter, wet-eyed, spreads out more pictures on the plastic table: the children at school, at home, playing, singing. The little one had a beautiful soprano voice, he says. They went to church every day; their mother was the choir leader. 'They were innocent children. The men who did it saw my wife's face . . .' He misses everything about them: their smell, their voices, their jokes and their tears.

Then he takes out another set. His wife (now in America

and still traumatised by the event) recovering from third-degree burns in a Lagos hospital. More than one year on, her legs are still raw and purple. Her face looks like a mask.

But there is one photograph that Peter has not seen. It is a photo kept locked in the safe of the church he attends, guarded by Dr Oja. It is a photo of four tiny roasted bodies lying next to one another, trying to protect each other from the flames that were engulfing them. Bones poke through the scorched skin. The limbs are twisted at unnatural angles.

The shock of it would be too much for Peter, who has to continue living in Kano, where Christians are under more and more pressure from radical Muslims to leave. Oddly, he bears no malice towards his Muslim neighbours, whom he has lived alongside for twenty-five years. He has no bitterness, no hatred in his heart. 'I just miss them so much,' he says of his children. 'I cannot forget them. I think about them all the time.'

Islam was established in Nigeria around 900 years ago, as a result of trans-Sahara trading caravans and holy wars. Muslims now account for around forty-five per cent of the population and mostly live in the north, with the Christians living mostly in the south. There has long been tension between the two groups, but in the northern regions where the Christians are in the minority, the atmosphere is steadily deteriorating. As Dr Oja says wearily, 'People are growing more and more intolerant.'

Sharia law, in its purest form, is meant to curb corruption and ensure justice. But when the law arrived in Nigeria – admittedly one of the most corrupt countries in Africa – there were political motives, as northern politicians used sharia to garner millions of Muslim votes in the region. The people, who live in villages without electricity, without clean drinking water, without even polio vaccinations for their babies, accepted it because they believed it would end the chaos of their miserable lives. 'There was pressure to implement sharia law because conventional Nigerian law had not worked,' says one Nigerian attorney.

As Islamic commentator Dr Akbar Ahmed explains: 'In the ideal, sharia provides justice and compassion in society. However, the reality today is – from Nigeria to Pakistan – that ordinary people can expect little justice and no compassion. This is particularly true where women are concerned because of ignorance and prejudice.

'Most Muslim nations have not clarified the legal codes which were set up when they achieved independence half a century ago. The sharia, tribal custom, and central government laws inspired by Western sources, overlap, clash, and are juxtaposed. A priority for Muslim leaders must be to bring the different sources of law into consonance with the demands of life in the twenty-first century.'

Since sharia – which is also implemented in Saudi Arabia, Sudan, Turkey, Pakistan and Libya – began to be implemented in Nigeria in 1999, there have been three amputations, four people have been sentenced to stoning, and eleven children await amputation for petty theft: some for stealing a cow, some for stealing a shirt. All this, despite the fact that the constitution of the Nigerian Federal Government prohibits cruel punishments such as stoning or amputation.

In Nigeria, human rights groups and lawyers attempting to defend the victims say that sharia only applies to the poor, those without a voice, who silently accept that they must suffer for Allah. 'There has never been a rich person sentenced to stoning,' says one aid worker. 'Yet there are judges who have sentenced others to death, while their own girl-friends have become pregnant. There are rich men whose daughters have got pregnant. Nothing happens to them. It is only the poor who suffer.'

And so people live with sharia hanging over their heads. But perhaps what is most chilling is the meekness of the victims, their willingness to accept their fate. When you meet Amina Lawal, for instance, the thirty-one-year-old mother of three who has made headlines all over the world since she was sentenced to be buried up to her neck and stoned to death by 2004 or whenever she finishes weaning her ten-month-old daughter, she smiles gently and talks about Al-lah's will, Allah's way, Allah's path. Her faith is real, yet her meekness is hard to fathom given the sentence hanging over her: how could she not worry about the fate of her daughter, or the agonising death that she may undergo?

'This is divine law, we are slaves of Allah,' Judge Labaran Mohammed told me, at the Upper Sharia Court in Gusau, Zamfara state. 'There are no options, no debate about it.'

Bizarrely, these medieval and barbaric practices take place in the same country that was to host the Miss World contest until the deaths of more than 200 rioters caused it to move to London. When I was there, preparations were still under way, and it was impossible to ignore the strange and horrible irony in the red carpets rolled out for the contestants. Some had boycotted the event, but others said they were showing their solidarity by attending. Although quite how strutting around in high heels and full make-up will help the fate of ignorant village women condemned to death is baffling.

The women arrived from London in Abuja, the Nigerian capital, the same evening that Amina Lawal arrived from her small northern village to meet me. The 'Queens', as the

Nigerian press dubbed the contestants, are predictably beautiful, young and thin. Amina is also beautiful, but her prospects are somewhat less alluring. The Queens wore very little, despite the fact that it was the strict holy month of Ramadan here, and the widespread disquiet felt at their presence by many senior Muslims which was to erupt into such violence.

Hajiya Laila Dogonyaro, the chairperson of the governing board of the National Council on Women's Development, condemned the pageant, saying, 'No religion could ever tolerate the show of nudity and anything that could lead to the abuse of women's rights' – which is at the very least hypocritical, given that the Nigerian government has done nothing to protect women under sharia law.

The Abuja Hilton, where the Queens were spending their first night, was awash with young girls in miniskirts, tight jeans, belly-baring tops, skirts slit up to the thigh and platform shoes. Ten minutes away from the chaos of the girls, the dancers and the traditional Nigerian music that was pounding out in the lobby, Amina waited for me in the house of her lawyer, Hauwa Ibrahim. Wrapped up in a green hajib, she was barefoot and nursing her baby, Wasila, who is scrawny and has scared eyes.

Amina's face is wide, clear and devoid of fear. She has tiny feet and hands and seems lost in the hajib, which she pulls tight around her. While she has been made a symbol of the suffering of women under sharia and used by the press as an unwilling spokesperson on the Miss World subject – she was cajoled by Italian aid workers into saying that she wanted the Queens to come to give her solidarity – in fact, Hauwa Ibrahim says Amina knew nothing about the Miss World contest. This is hardly surprising, bearing in mind that Amina lives in a village with no electricity. Having now been made aware of this bizarre contest, she says that she would watch it 'out of curiosity' if she was in a place that had a television set.

Speaking in Hausa, Amina talks about her life, which has been predictably miserable. 'Life was having just enough food to eat.' Unschooled, she was born into a large family and married off to a man before she began menstruating – 'I grew to love him,' she says – later giving birth to two children while still a teenager. He left her, she married and divorced again, and she went back to live with her father and his four wives. Life with her family was hard. She was befriended by a man, Yahaya, who one day took her on his motorbike to meet his relatives. But he stopped in a field and raped her. From that one encounter, she fell pregnant with Wasila.

When Amina's pregnancy became obvious, the hizbah – the religious vigilante police – took her to prison. Yahaya denied the rape and was cleared because under sharia a man can only be prosecuted if four people swear that they saw him having sex with the woman. Amina was sentenced to death by stoning in March, 2002. Her first appeal, in August, was rejected. Hauwa Ibrahim is waiting for another and says she will go all the way to the Nigerian Supreme Court if she has to, to prevent the death.

Amina seems so preoccupied with her baby that she shrugs off her sentence. Is she frightened? 'God will take care of me,' she says. And her baby, who will take care of her? She rolls her eyes heavenward. 'God.' She bears no hatred, no anger towards the man who raped her or towards the judges who sentenced her. But she does say she is angry at the law. 'Yes, I'm angry,' she says, holding the baby against her cheek. 'But I leave everything to God.' If she wins her appeal, she says she just wants to get married again. Under sharia, it is the only way a woman can be protected.

Sharia was implemented as full-scale criminal law in Zamfara state in 1999 and quickly spread to eleven other states in the north. Its birthplace was Gusau – the state capital, and now one of the strangest places on earth – where Governor Sani used it as a political platform. He launched it in a fiery speech at Akilu Square, a dusty patch of ground where children – boy children – now play football.

A remote, dusty 'capital' perched high near the Niger and Benin state border, Gusau resembles Saudi Arabia more than Nigeria. Women are clothed head to toe in hajibs. Signs in Arabic – which few people read as Hausa is spoken widely in the north – spell out inscriptions from the Koran, or demand vigilance. Bus stops designate that women can, or cannot, wait there. Posters dot shops and houses, calling out for sharia: 'I support sharia. The constitution of true believers. It saves, cares, protects, judges.'

At night, the town goes dead black – there is no electricity – and the hizbah, consisting entirely of volunteers, cruise the streets in blood-red uniforms. They use vans borrowed from the Nigerian Boy Scouts and look for sinners who will be picked up and packed off to sharia court in the morning.

In the morning heat, we go to one of the many sharia courts scattered across Gusau. It is virtually a shack in a dirt yard, with goats and chickens and cows in the front. A young father, Ibrahim Namadi, was caught stealing a cheap gold-plated necklace to feed his family. It was his first crime. He is sweating and close to tears, waiting for his sentence. A crowd gathers, open-mouthed, waiting to hear the judge, who wears a blue silk kaftan, white snakeskin shoes and a blue turban.

Ibrahim Namadi gets forty lashes, and not amputation,

because the state did not provide for him, and he was forced to steal. His face shows no emotion as he is led outside to a bench, where he lies while a man with a whip stands over him. Someone begins to count as the whip falls. The 'counter' holds a tape recorder, the product of which will be played on local radio – a warning to anyone else thinking of lifting a cheap necklace to feed their children. Ibrahim is writhing on the bench as the whip falls, trying to protect himself. He moans and makes animal-like noises. The crowd is silent, fascinated. It is terrible to watch. Afterwards, the judge lets me talk to the victim, who is clearly in shock. His eyes are wet, he is sweating and a rank smell comes from him: fear. Under the eyes of the beaming judge, he tells me that he 'will never commit a crime again'.

There is little sign of life, or joy, in Gusau. There is more a pervading sense of fear, or more importantly, of an indigenous culture being crushed and another one being imposed. Now, under sharia law, people live joylessly, almost as though they are waiting for the blow to come down.

In June, 2000, Buba Bello became the first man to undergo amputation in Nigeria. Now forty-three, he wears a bright pink kaftan specially sewn to hide the stump on his right hand. Urged on by his 'patron' – the chief of the anti-corruption unit in Gusau and one of the men responsible for chopping off his hand – Buba tells of a life of crime from the time he was a teenager. He says that he was almost relieved when he received the sentence for amputation, because it meant his life of crime was over.

The operation was painless. He was given a general anaesthetic and woke up with a neatly sewn stump. That in itself makes it more chilling for me – that a doctor, trained to save lives, took the time and effort to anaesthetise a patient and then hack off his perfectly healthy hand. But Buba is oddly cheerful. 'The state provides for me now,' he says. They also gave him an all-expenses paid trip to Mecca, so now he bears the title of al-Haji, one who has made the Haj. He's got a new, young wife. And he will certainly never steal again, one of the anti-corruption officials says menacingly. However, a local official later tells me that Buba was picked out to be an example because sharia was newly installed, and someone had to show the people that the government was serious. Afterwards, to show they were also merciful, they sent him on the trip to Mecca.

When night falls in Gusau, the people come out on the street for Iftar, the traditional breaking of the Ramadan fast. They eat under the orange lights of the lanterns which dot the central square. Around 11 p.m., the hizbah begin gathering, some in red uniforms. 'Originally, when they first started up, people were really afraid of them,' says Mohammed Dosara, a local journalist. 'Now people have got used to their presence.'

There is one place in Gusau where the hizbah cannot go. On the edge of town, inside a federal army base, local people have constructed their own Sin City. The soldiers – who come from all over the country and are not all Muslims – would have had a revolt if beer had been banned on their base, so local people took advantage of this protection and used it as a way to have their own 'safe haven' from the hizbah.

The contrast from the centre of Gusau to here – a distance of maybe five miles – is extraordinary. Corrugated iron shacks have been turned into bars, complete with red lights fired from a generator. There are discos and even a makeshift cinema, showing a forbidden action video to an open-mouthed crowd. There are prostitutes, there is roasted dog-meat, there is hut after hut full of people laughing, watching Jennifer Lopez shimmy around in a bikini on a beach on MTV, and there is lots of alcohol.

But the place does not stay open all night long, and eventually people have to go back to their homes, trying to avoid the hizbah who wait to clamp down on the sinners who are often so drunk they fall by the side of the road. Is it worth it? The courthouse, the lashings, maybe prison? One man who sits drinking a huge bottle of Star beer in a flashing red-light disco says that it is. 'For a few hours here, everyone forgets about sharia,' he says.

In New Gawu, a village off a dirt track three hours' drive from Abuja, where the Miss World Queens slept soundly, two people are condemned to death by stoning because they fell in love. They are both awaiting their appeal. One of them is Fatima Umaru, thirty-one, who gave birth to a daughter from this union, a little girl who later died. Fatima is now under house arrest in the village, ill with abdominal troubles and heavily pregnant by her fourth husband. The other is her former lover, Amadu Ibrahim, the most handsome man in the village, who is married to a teenager. He is the first man to be sentenced to death by stoning.

The tragedy of his and Fatima's case is that they were lovers and conceived a child before sharia law was introduced to their state, Niger. It was Fatima's father, in fact, who turned them in – he wanted his daughter to get compensation from Amadu, who is dirt-poor. But his plan backfired. An original five-year prison sentence was passed on the lovers, which was later overturned to death by stoning.

I visit Fatima's parents in their hut. It is brutally hot and a crowd of barefoot and naked children gather. Fatima's mother, Rakiya, says she is not happy that her daughter has brought this kind of shame on the family. 'I taught my daughter to be a good Muslim,' she says, sitting on the ground shelling peanuts which will be their lunch. 'I taught her to say her prayers. Now people in the village are not happy.'

Fatima's father, Usman Omar, who clearly feels guilty that he started the ball rolling in the first place, says the last time he saw his daughter, a few weeks previously, she could not stop crying.

A short distance away is Fatima's lover's house. Amadu, who is a firewood stacker, takes us to a field behind the village mosque, where he tells me that he loved Fatima, who had been his neighbour for many years. They first fell in love, he says, on a rainy afternoon when they were trapped in a market stall escaping the bad weather. 'She started it!' he says. Afterwards, they were inseparable. They used to go for secret walks in the bush outside of the village. But when Fatima became pregnant, Amadu would not marry her. 'She was too old,' he says. 'She's older than my first wife.'

Instead, Fatima married someone else, her third husband. But when he found out about the child, he left her. Then her baby died. Then the religious police came. Fatima married again, while still under investigation, and got pregnant again. Now she sits in another village, away from her family – who scorn her – and her former lover. She is due to give birth in the next few weeks.

'I last saw her when they took us both out of prison after sixty-six days,' Amadu says. He does not seem bothered that she married again. 'I looked at her. She looked at me. We didn't say anything.' He pauses. 'I still love her!' he exclaims. 'Even with all of this.'

We leave the village with its African-style Shakespearean

cast of characters: a pair of star-crossed lovers; Fatima's four husbands; her father who tried to use her situation to make money; her bitter mother. 'In these poor places, sex is the only way of having fun,' says Felix Onuah, a local journalist. 'A law preventing it will never work. You can't break the fabric of village life just because you decide to change the law.'

The Nigerian federal government says it will never allow Amina, or others, to be stoned. In the wake of the Miss World controversy, a deputy minister in the Foreign Ministry issued a statement reassuring the contestants that it could not happen. But lawyers say that the federal government has never intervened before. It has never challenged sharia hard enough. It was not there when the twelve state governments fell to sharia, or when these authorities chopped off hands or flogged people for lying. It was not there when women were stopped from riding the same buses as men, or ordered to wear head-to-toe coverings. Hauwa Ibrahim says a woman from the government's Women's Ministry once came to a sharia court session. 'She just didn't understand at all,' says Ibrahim. Nothing came of her attendance.

Hauwa Ibrahim was born and raised a Muslim, but she refuses to talk about religion. The thirty-five-year-old lawyer, who is married to an Italian, takes on cases like those of Fatima and Amadu, Amina, and others without pay. Her first sharia case was in 1999 when she fought in vain to stop a woman being lashed 100 times for lying. Hauwa has a soft, round face. She loves her country, but she also fears for its future, particularly in the wake of September 11, after which the Muslim and Christian gulf seems ever wider. We stand outside her house talking about Amina. The sun is sinking; it is growing close to Iftar. Nearby, a mosque begins the scratchy recording of the muezzin's call to prayer.

'People in Europe tell me Amina will never be stoned,' I say. Hauwa looks at me. She does not agree. 'Until the law is tackled, the cases will keep coming,' she says. 'There are a lot of fundamentalist fanatics who have lost their minds. They can do anything.'

Sindi Medar-Gould from Baobab, a women's human rights group, says emphatically, 'We will not let them carry out Amina's stoning,' and vows that her organisation, and others, will fight to the end to free the victims. 'Sharia was meant to end corruption and bring order to the chaos,' she says. 'But the reality is slowly beginning to dawn on women, many of whom do not understand the law.'

Hauwa Ibrahim believes that someone, eventually, will have to be stoned to death, as an example that Islamic justice will be served. It might be Amina, it might not. The Miss World controversy brought the world's attention to the plight of these people, but as Hauwa Ibrahim wearily pointed out, 'The moment the Miss World glamour goes, we will still be here.'

The Battle of Algiers

June, 1998

The afternoon that I flew into Algiers, thick storm clouds lined the sky and the plane shook violently like a child's toy. It appeared to be an omen. The day before I left, the Berber protest singer Matoub Lounes had been assassinated by Islamic fundamentalists and there were angry demonstrations on the streets of Paris and Algiers. On the plane, passengers discussed his death with dull resignation, as though the singer was a symbol for all of the horror in Algeria. When I landed at the airport, I heard the eerie sound of yo-yo, the women ululating. Not for the first time in my life, I felt that I was in a very foreign and very strange place.

My bodyguards met me at the airport. I had four, assigned by the government for my protection. Sometimes there were seven, sometimes there were three, but they were always present, in an annoying but reassuring way. Since January 1992, when the military interrupted the country's first democratic parliamentary elections, Algeria has been locked in a conflict between the government and the 'terrorist' groups – a catchword for Islamic rebels. It is estimated that 80,000 people have been massacred since then, most of them civilians. In the first two weeks of October alone, 215 people were killed, and according to American intelligence sources, that included 83 killed by government forces in a major sweep of the Ain Defla provinces.

The ways these people die are not pleasant: entire villages have been burned at night, women and babies decapitated, young girls' throats slit (a popular method of killing known as the 'Algerian smile'), old men burnt alive. When I read through back issues of newspapers, the killings are relentless: during the holy month of Ramadan this year 1,100 people were killed; the week before I arrived, rebels slashed the throats of fourteen people; two weeks before that, a bomb in a marketplace killed seven; the day before that five policemen were killed and sixteen people died in another market bombing; in April forty people were killed in an overnight attack.

This is a drum roll because I am trying to make a point. Every day, people die: 100 a week, it is estimated. Nine on a beautiful autumn day in a small hamlet; thirteen on the day I sat writing this story when a bomb exploded in an Algiers shop. I think of Matoub Lounes, who once sang: 'The grave awaits us all, whether it is today or tomorrow.' In Algeria, the grave is always premature.

Now, approaching another new year, and one year away from the millennium, things are getting worse, not better. While Kosovo, Iraq and Central America have driven the story off the pages of the newspapers, the situation in Algeria steadily deteriorates. In September, the Algerian president, General Liamine Zeroual, announced he was leaving office mid-term and called for early presidential elections in February (they have now been moved to April). Zeroual was due to serve until 2000 and his hasty exit was seen by the

Algerian media as an act of cowardice, of a captain aban-
doning a very leaky ship. For most ordinary Algerians,
however, that announcement had deeper repercussions: it
meant that the country would slip further and further into
chaos. As of mid-November, no political party had nomi-
nated a candidate or said it would nominate one, and no
electable politicians had given any clear indication of their
intentions. 'I am afraid,' a young Algerian journalist told me,
'that all this uncertainty, all this transition will bring about
even more killings.'

When you ask who is responsible for the killings, people
shrug their shoulders and roll their eyes to the heavens. The
government blames the Muslim extremists, yet there is a
theory that the government, whose job it is to ensure the
safety of ordinary Algerians, is now conniving in their
murder to inflate the threat to itself and justify its repressive
and undemocratic policies. There are many unanswered
questions. Why, for instance, do many of the massacres take
place a stone's throw away from the military and security
barracks? Why, when villages are being razed and women
and children are screaming for help, does the army do
nothing to help them?

Initially the victims of the killings were intellectuals, women, foreigners, young girls who dared to attend school –
those deemed to have been tainted with Western decadence.

When journalists became too outspoken, they were killed –
seventy have been murdered in what the World Press Review
calls 'one of the most brutal campaigns at silencing the press
since the dirty war in Argentina in the 1970s'. Most of the
Algerian journalists live in a heavily protected government
compound near the seaside. Four newspapers which ran a
series of unprecedented attacks on presidential adviser Gen-

eral Mohamed Betchine and Justice Minister Mohamed Adami were 'squeezed' financially by the government, forcing them to suspend printing. *El Watan*, Algeria's most important independent newspaper, resumed printing this month after a month-long closure. *La Nation*, run by the award-winning journalist Salima Ghezali, remains closed.

But the majority of people killed or victimised are not journalists; they are not even literate, they have no voices. On a sweltering hot summer day, I drove – along with ten bodyguards plus army protection – into a part of the Algerian countryside known as the Triangle of Death. The town we stopped at, Hammam Maloune, was small and insignificant, with small dwellings carved into the side of a mountain. That day, there was a feast and local farmers had walked to the town with their goods: jars of honey, embroidered fabric, pieces of silver jewellery. Outside, there was the sound of music – the flute, the tabla drum – but there was no sense of celebration. On one stand, next to a table of aromatic spices, was a white poster with scores of black and white photographs of people. Ordinary people, some very young, some old, some with bulging frightened eyes, some with no expression. Who are these people? I asked. There was an uncomfortable silence. 'Victims of terrorism,' I was told. After some prodding, I got a figure for the number of people killed in Hammam Maloune: eighty-seven since 1992.

The mayor of the town did not tell me what everyone else told me about Hammam Maloune – that it was renowned as a place rife with fundamentalists where many indiscriminate killings took place. I had come to meet an old woman, in her mid-eighties, who looked after her eighteen grandchildren because all of her children had been murdered. But when I tried to find her small house down a narrow, dusty pathway,

I was told that she had 'gone to a wedding'. So I will wait, I said, preparing to sit out the afternoon. 'Oh no, no!' the mayor said, excitedly, and lapsed into Arabic with my bodyguards, who began shaking their heads violently. After a few minutes, it was decided that I would meet someone else. Obviously, the powers that be did not want me to meet the old woman.

Instead, I went to another house, a small windowless compound with mud floors. A sixteen-month-old baby called Sara with hennaed feet and earrings crawled on the floor and one of the bodyguards – the toughest looking one, the one with the Kalashnikov – lay down his gun and picked her up, cooing with delight. Mint tea was brought out; we appeared to be waiting for someone. It was the house of Nora Aissat, who is eighteen and whose father was killed last summer by fundamentalists. 'Why him?' I asked. 'Why anyone?' she answered quietly. 'He was on a bus, on his way to town . . . there were twenty people on the bus, and they chose eight to kill. One was my father.' Her face tightens. 'I hated the fundamentalists before he was killed. Now I hate them more.'

And then Fatiha Kabas walked in the room. I stood up, because she had a kind of grace that made you want to stand up, but she shyly took my hand and motioned for me to sit. Then she stared at the floor. She looked frightened, delicate, much younger than thirty-five-years old. I thought she was beautiful, until she began to talk and her face changed. I do not think I have ever seen anyone so sad, so beaten by life as her. She looked damaged.

In the haunting Italian-Algerian film, *The Battle of Algiers*, which depicts the tragic history of the Algerian resistance against France from the mid-1950s until its independence in 1962, the women play a central role. It is the women who rally the men, plant bombs, nurse the wounded and keep the revolution moving ahead. It is a depiction of women during wartime rarely seen, and it shows the extraordinary courage of the Algerian women in particular. In a sense, this is what I expected when I arranged to meet Fatiha; instead, I met an ordinary woman who had been broken by war. Resistance and conflict meant nothing to her; she was a simple person, a seamstress, she said, whose life had been destroyed simply because she was in the wrong place at the wrong time.

Fatiha had lived in her village all of her life except when she took jobs in other villages. One summer day three years ago she was on the local bus going to another village to look for material for an upholstery job. She took a seat in the back of the bus. She was dreaming, nodding off, when the bus stopped. This is what she remembers: 'There were ten men. They had long beards and kohl around their eyes, they were dressed like Afghan fighters. They stopped the bus and got on; they looked around and saw there were four girls on the bus. They made us get out. We stood in front of it and then they let the other girls go and they took me. I was dressed correctly that day – nothing provocative. I wore a scarf around my head, a long skirt, a little but not much make-up. I had on a jacket to cover my arms. They took me with them. The bus went off. I was alone.'

As she tells the story, Fatiha's posture changes. She drops her head to her chest, ashamed, as thought it is her fault: for being beautiful; for being taken by the fundamentalists. She speaks slowly, in French, sometimes in Arabic. Her eyes well up with tears and one of the bodyguards gives her a crumpled Kleenex. He nods for her to continue.

'First they beat me. They put a blindfold on me and put my hands behind my back with rope. Then they carried and dragged me along a road which I thought led up to the mountains. They kept saying: "You are not a good girl. You are a whore." ' She begins to cry.

Fatiha was raped repeatedly over the next few days. She does not know by how many men, but she believes ten. And as they were raping her, they told her they wanted 'to spread Islam, to make the country pure'. She thinks she passed out at some point, because when she woke up the men were gone. They had left the camp to pray; she could hear them calling out 'Allah Akbah! God is Great!' With a strength she did not know she had, she untied her ropes and, still blindfolded, made her way to the top of the mountain. 'I thought, if I went up, I could get down.' She was cold, in pain and in shock. She had not eaten in days. At the top of the mountain, she got the blindfold off and realised she was at a local water reservoir. She found a path to the village and ran down, crying, 'but not too loudly, because I knew if they found me again, they would kill me'.

What has happened to her since? Not much. A local doctor told Fatiha that she is suffering from 'post-traumatic stress' and that she should see a therapist. But Hammam Maloune is a long way from Algiers, and there are no therapists near the village. 'The thought of travelling to Algiers,' she says, 'is terrifying.' Anyway, she has no money and is not sure she wants to talk about what happened to her. The villagers feel sorry for her, but now that she is no longer a virgin, it is doubtful she will find a husband. 'I am the only one in the village to have been raped,' she says. The bodyguard, with the baby on his lap, looks at her sympathetically, but there is something else in his eyes – it is true, she is viewed now as damaged goods.

She lives with her older brother. She forces herself to go out sometimes. She quit her job as a seamstress because she couldn't stitch as well as she used to. For that, you need a steady hand. Yes, she feels unbearably lonely . . . but at least she didn't get pregnant. She looks away. She now works with children, as a kind of teacher. She loves children, but she knows she will never have any of her own. 'Why not?' someone asks. It is a ridiculous question. She looks up, tears streaming down her face, then leaves the room to walk home.

I first heard the story of the rape camps through Houriya Sayhi, a forty-six-year-old film-maker who won a prestigious Courage in Journalism prize in 1995 for documenting the plight of the young women who had been kidnapped and raped by Islamic extremists. When she accepted her award for another of her films, *Mother Za'ara*, which is about a brave old woman who lives on after most of her family is wiped out by fundamentalists, she gave a speech which left the audience in tears. 'I just wanted to give these people a message from Algerian women,' she said, 'that we live in a country where girls are killed for going to school.'

Since 1989, Houriya, who works for Algerian television, has been making profiles of women, in particular the rape victims. When I first heard about these victims, I was sceptical. I had never heard of 'rape camps' outside Bosnia, and when I questioned her about specific details, she grew edgy and defensive. She did not want to give details about where the camps were, for instance, or how many girls had been raped. 'It is not my job to give statistics,' she said. 'It is my job to give a voice to the victims.' She is often thwarted in her work. As a staunch Communist (she won a scholarship to university in Moscow when she was eighteen), she often finds herself excluded from the inner circles of the state television. But despite this isolation, she has refused numerous offers to go and work in Europe or America. Many other journalists – including Salima Ghezali, the recipient of last year's European parliament's Sakharov Prize for Freedom of Thought – have chosen to work partially outside Algeria. But the mere suggestion of this sends Houriya into a rage. 'I have made the decision to stay in Algeria, to fight in Algeria, even if I am frightened, even if I feel that my life is sometimes at risk,' she says, practically shouting. 'My job is to go into the field and get the pictures. Even if I work for Algerian television – and that means I am working for the government – I fight from the inside. I am always the opposition, always fighting against the regime.'

Houriya is tall for an Algerian woman, broad-shouldered, with large hands and feet. At forty-six, she is striking, with her tight jeans and small T-shirt. She gives the sense of great physical and emotional strength: later, she will tell me that as a teenager she had been a professional athlete, and the training and discipline has stayed with her throughout her life. She appears fearless and defiant: she says that when she goes to film the Islamists, she always wears jeans, even though they insult her (women, according to the strictest fundamentalists, must dress head to-toe in chadors). She continues to make provocative statements. 'Even the Algerian war,' she says, 'is told through a macho perspective. No one ever talks about the works of women. Or the work that women did here in the unions. Or the fact that women create the life here. I want my daughter, who is twenty-four now, to live in a country where a woman has equal rights as a man. And not where she will die trying to have them.'

She has frequently been targeted and physically attacked by Islamists, the first time in 1975, when leading a student demonstration. But she is, she says, of strong stock: born during the Algerian war against the French occupation, her earliest memories are of demonstrations and riots. 'I must have been about five or six, and I remember putting the Algerian flag inside my dress and walking right by the French soldiers on my way to school.'

As a teenager, she remembers wearing her brother's clothes. 'I wanted to be treated equally, like a boy,' she says. 'I could not understand why I wasn't spoken to with the same kind of respect that they are given.' Later, when she became a professional athlete, she was given 'the opportunity to be free. Sport let me become an equal. When I trained, for once, there was no difference between men and women. But when I went back to my neighbourhood, there were problems – in the Muslim world, a female professional athlete is no longer regarded as a virgin.'

Despite that, she married, had a daughter and divorced. Divorce in Algeria is a lengthy and traumatic process – not only must the woman get the permission of her husband to divorce, but if she wants to marry again, she must get the permission of her father, her brother or even her eldest son. Houriya did not marry again. Instead, she started writing for a newspaper called *Hope* and eventually began to make films. 'All of my films are like my children,' she says. 'It is the same experience as giving birth. Because it is such a battle to make them. The outside world only sees Algeria in terms of blood. I wanted to show another side. Beautiful, courageous women who are touched in their skin. Because these are the people who make history in Algeria.'

One of the women whom Houriya admires is Jasmine Belkachi, who is a near-legend in Algiers. Her story is so dramatic that she appears like someone straight out of *the Battle of Algiers*. Jasmine was fourteen years old when she carried a one-kilo bomb for the Algerian resistance, and it exploded before she reached her intended target. She lost both her legs and was imprisoned by the French for ten years, serving two before she was released in a prisoner exchange. She was the youngest of the Algerian girl combatants, and when she was released, she became a national heroine. 'I was stubborn, so stubborn when I was that age,' she says. 'The men did not want to give me the bomb. I insisted. I said if they did not give me the bomb, if they didn't let me continue to fight for Algeria, then I would take a knife, go to the city, and kill a French soldier.' She was sent to New York by Ahmed Ben Bella, then Algeria's prime minister, for medical treatment paid for by an American benefactor. She had five operations and still goes back for treatment.

Dressed in silky trousers and a low-cut blouse, she is flirtatious, sexy and outrageously outspoken. The first thing she does after bringing out the tray of coffee is ask me – in perfect English – for a copy of *Newsweek* that was published last January with Princess Diana on the cover. 'I am obsessed with Diana,' she says. What she sees happening now in her country rips her apart. 'What I miss the most are the intellectuals who are being killed off,' she says. 'We fought so hard for an independent state and now we have a country where the educated are being killed.' She pauses. 'And the others who matter, who have something to say, are leaving.'

All three of the women above are women who have helped to carve a new Algeria out of the old French-occupied country. And what of the younger generation? One sweltering afternoon, I took a trip to the beach and wandered over the black sand where clusters of teenagers lay on their stomachs reading newspapers and listening to the radio. When I stopped to chat with them, most were too frightened to talk, and certainly to talk about the disturbing times facing their country. But in a small café on the edge of the beach, I saw an especially pretty teenager in a bikini top and a pair of jeans, flirting with a group of soldiers. This girl, I thought, does not look typical.

I was right. She was eighteen and happy to vent the frustration she felt at coming of age in a country in the midst of such chaos. Her name was Hannan Boucheba, she was studying to be an accountant, and she lived with her elderly grandmother, her mother and her aunt. She longed, however, for her own place, 'my independence, my own life'. She felt stifled by the strict code in Algiers, by the fact that she could not walk down the street wearing the kind of clothes she wanted to wear (tight, skimpy) 'without everyone thinking I am a bad girl'. 'It's tough being young in Algeria,' she says. 'People expect you to be a certain way, to stay home, to wear a chador, to cook.'

Hannan does not have a boyfriend at the moment. 'I loved somebody but he went with another girl,' she says, pouting. Then she quickly adds, 'But it's OK, there are so many, many men. And there are two kinds of girls today in Algeria. Girls who don't follow the rules, who do what they want, who sleep with men if they choose, who take pleasure. Then there are girls who pray all the time and who live for paradise. The truth is, I don't really want to be married. I want a man in my heart and not in my home. I want to have my freedom. But that will never happen in this country.'

It is an extraordinarily brave statement for a young girl to make. Later she takes me to her local disco. There, she tells more of her story: she was abandoned as a child by her father; her grandmother brought her up. When at last she met her father, aged seventeen, he tried to rape her. 'He did not penetrate me, I am still a virgin,' she says. 'If a Muslim girl loses her virginity, she has nothing.'

She now has an older man, 'a kind of patron', who takes her out to dinner and buys her things. 'But he is not a lover,' she insists. She says she needs money, a visa to the US or Canada in order to escape the oppressive life that she is doomed to follow unless she leaves Algeria now. 'I have a personality of my own,' she says. 'I will die if I can't be free.'

That same day, I meet another young woman only a few years older than Hannan, but from an entirely different background. She is Assia Athmania, twenty-seven, a teacher and a fundamentalist in the Hamas party. At her third-floor flat in central Algiers, she answers the door dressed head to toe in a chador with her face covered. Assia is intelligent – she is the daughter of a lawyer and speaks excellent French, English and Arabic and has a sound knowledge of the Koran. Her job is to present the Islamic argument in a more favourable light.

We sit on the floor and drink tea. In the kitchen, her mother arranges a tray of cakes and her other sisters – all dressed in chadors – sit and listen. Assia's goal is to raise awareness of Islam through the cultural level. 'We have to open minds and open brains,' she says. 'The culture of peace and democracy is the culture to change minds. For us, religion is acting to develop humanity.'

I ask why women must wear the veil. 'We wear it to be identified as Algerian women,' she says simply, smoothing back her headpiece. 'It does not mean that by wearing it, I close myself to other people. It means that I open myself.' She says that the Hamas party – which in Algeria is not as radical as in other parts of the Arab world – believes in 'peace, change and objectivity'. It is not a religious party, she insists. It is merely there to 'offer a different solution'.

How does she feel as a young woman coming of age in the troubled times in Algeria? She flinches slightly. 'We are from the independence generation,' she says. 'Algeria has always given revolutionary lessons. It is country which had nothing and which fought against France, a country which had a lot. We have learned from these lessons of resistance.'

Does she believe that she is pursuing these 'lessons of resistance' by encouraging Islam? She shrugs. 'I have a belief in the future.' Which is more than Hannan, the young accountant I left dancing in the disco, has.

The day I left Algeria, the city was calm, but the next day a bomb would explode in a marketplace, killing thirteen people who just happened to be walking by. Wrong place, wrong time. I thought of Hannan and Salima and Houriya, and the remark that someone made to me: 'The people who are usually killed are not famous, are not important. They are people you would never know.'

At the airport, my bodyguards left me at passport control. I felt oddly naked without them. When I went through and boarded my plane, the last thing I heard was the sound of the yo-yo again, the women ululating. It is a strange, spooky, and yet ancient sound. When you hear it, you understand briefly what this country is about, and the role that women play in it. It is a strong sound. And it seems to define the kind of women who live in this haunted and dangerous place.

Brother Number One:
Freetown, Sierra Leone

May, 2000

I heard of Kurt Schork long before I met him. Central Bosnia,
early autumn, 1992. A road north of Travnik leading towards the Vlasic Mountains, a stream of Muslim refugees
crossing. A city on the verge of falling. A sense of urgency, of
panic.

There was a car crashed in the road. People trying to flee in
a hurry. They died near a bridge, thrown through the wind-
screen, necks broken. Their blank eyes stared at the grey sky
above them. They looked surprised, as though death had
caught them at the wrong moment.

An old bus passed, teeming with the youngest soldiers,
heading north. Someone had scrawled on the side of it:
VOLUNTEERS FOR JAJCE. Scared faces peered out of dirty
windows. They looked seventeen. They knew they were
going to die.

I was with a photographer. We were trying to walk to
Jajce, where the fighting had intensified. Weeks were spent
drinking coffee with soldiers, smoking cigarettes, trying to

gain their trust. The commander of Muslim Fourth Brigade laughed at our suicidal request.

'Someone else is already ahead of you,' he said. 'Reuters guy. Kurt Schork.'

Later, I heard there was a new verb coined after him: 'to schork'. Meaning to demand, shouting, storming, pushing, perhaps physically, to get through an impossible checkpoint. To find the story on the other side.

I finally met him in Sarajevo.

Sarajevo was hellish, apocalyptic. Freezing, starving, terrifying. Packs of wild dogs with ribs jutting from ripped fur roamed streets gutted by mortar holes. Blood was splattered on buildings. The dead, the drunk, the insane. Hundreds, thousands of shells a day. Resilient civilians gathered at corners, waiting for the right moment to run together across the road. Outsmarting Serb snipers on the hills ringing the city. The sadness.

Most of the reporters did stints; it was the only way to stay sane. Six weeks in, wearing our Kevlar flak jackets; three weeks out; six weeks back in. Kurt rarely took breaks, maybe once or twice a year, then he panicked about what has happening back inside. He stayed the duration of the war, running the Reuters office, initially on the fifth floor of the Holiday Inn, overlooking Sniper's Alley.

He lived a floor below, in a cold room with one bed, one neat desk with a pile of books – Rebecca West, Michael Ondaatje's *In the Skin of a Lion* – a sleeping bag and a tape recorder. There was a pile of diaries in which he recorded the day-to-day events of the siege: how many shells fell; what the weather was like; what he did that day; how many people died.

Why? I said.

Someone might want them someday, he replied.

He had a tape – from his days in Kurdistan, witnessing an execution of Iraqi soldiers by Kurdish guerrillas. He had been travelling with the Kurds for months, but he was still shocked by the cruelty. He recorded the sound of the bullets, the Iraqi prisoners begging for their lives. The cries of the executions.

In Sarajevo, he woke between 5 and 6 a.m. There was no water in the rooms, but he was clever. He fashioned a strange, makeshift shower in a corner with a plastic jug of cold water he fetched from five flights down in the basement. With Sabina or Samir or Amra, local journalists who worked in the Reuters office, he would check the morgue at Kosevo Hospital. He counted the dead, began to write their stories. He would always return to check back on people he wrote about, on the wounded that he had dropped his notebook for and rushed to take to the hospital.

He fell in love with the city and the people: their courage, their isolation. He was morally outraged. He refused to believe what the UN and the international community was saying: that they were doing all they could. He knew it was a lie.

He was older than most of the other journalists, because he did not enter the profession until he was in his forties. He looked younger than his age – forty-five when I met him in 1992 – and was solidly built, like an athlete. He looked quintessentially American: he wore khakis or baggy jeans, and a blue fleece under his flak jacket with his press card around his neck. He sat at the dining table with his fists jammed in the pockets: a protective stance. He did not smoke; he played football at university, and had gone to Oxford as a Rhodes Scholar with Bill Clinton, whom he did not like. He drove a Russian-made Lada, a battered, junky thing, until Reuters gave him an armoured Land Rover to use.

He was a vegetarian because he loved animals and wrote about the Sarajevan who fed the dogs. He quoted a man, who compared the beasts with the people involved in the ethnic conflict: 'Dogs do not recognise breeds among themselves, they only recognise behaviour.' He wrote about the four people who died on New Year's Eve, 1994 from artillery shells as peace negotiations were being pounded out for the hundredth time. He wrote about a three-year-old girl called Amina Memisevic who, when asked who Santa Claus was, replied without skipping a beat: 'He's a good man. He doesn't kill children.' He wrote about the morbid humour of the city under siege:

A man walking Sarajevo's streets at night comes upon a checkpoint where a soldier is interrogating a civilian pedestrian.

Suddenly, the soldier draws back and opens fire with his Kalashnikov, killing him instantly.

'Why did you do that?' asks the passer-by.

'Because the man didn't have permission to be out after curfew,' replies the soldier.

'But it's only nine o'clock, the curfew doesn't start until ten,' says the passer-by.

'I know where the man lives. He would never have made it home in time,' replies the soldier.

He wrote about old people dying from the cold in their beds in their own waste; about internecine fighting between Muslims and Croats in central Bosnia, about life in a

Sarajevo orphanage. One day in May, 1993, he grabbed me as I was running up the stairs of the Holiday Inn. He was stunned, grey with upset. A young couple, one Serb, one Muslim, had got married and tried to cross the Vrbana Bridge to tell their parents on the Serb-held side of Sarajevo. They never got there. A sniper got them first, and their bodies lay in the crossfire, entwined, until UN soldiers could get them out. 'It's like *Romeo and Juliet*,' he said, stricken with sadness. He sat down at his desk, furiously writing.

Two lovers lie dead on the banks of Sarajevo's Miljaka river, locked in a final embrace. For four days, they have sprawled near the Vrbana Bridge in a wasteland of shell-blasted rubble, downed tree branches and dangling power lines. So dangerous is the area no one has bothered to recover their bodies.

From then on, Bosko Brckic and Admira Ismic, both twenty-five, became known as Romeo and Juliet of Sarajevo.

Kurt had a terrible temper. Most people feared him; some did not understand his complexities. Everyone respected him. He was not a cowboy journalist and he showed open disdain for those who were, for the 'tourists' who visited the city to say they had been there, or who took unnecessary risks because they had a death wish. He had little patience; the Reuters office often echoed with his shouting. Corinne Dufka – a photographer now working for Human Rights Watch – who opened the Reuters Sarajevo bureau with him in the summer of 1992, remembers their arguments.

'He was intense and driven. My first impression was that he was inaccessible,' she says. But, she adds, she admired him. 'He had a lot of integrity, he would make people in power uncomfortable.' Their biggest fights were over how to cover a story. 'Both of us liked to live on the edge. We were both on the same wavelength. We wanted to cover the story better than anyone else.'

Sean Maguire was the third member of the 'Dream Team', as the Reuters desk referred to them. A pugnacious, intelligent Scot, he was one of the few people Schork respected. 'Sean,' he once said, 'is really *smart*.' The two went heli-skiing together during their rare breaks and travelled to some of the more dangerous locations in Bosnia together. They got on because each had nerves of steel during crisis moments and did not panic. Still they fought, particularly when Maguire decided to pursue a different, more traditional work path than Kurt and went to work on the desk in London.

'We had some amazing stand-up rows,' Maguire admits. 'He was not a team player. When I had to sub him, we would fight like crazy. But ultimately, he was a professional and proud of his work, sweating his guts out, and was always suspicious of other people not putting in the effort.'

He particularly remembers Kurt's intense anger with a French soldier after the Frenchman drove past a wounded civilian and did not stop to take him to the hospital. Emma Daly, a journalist from the *Independent*, also recalls restraining Kurt from physically laying out another UN soldier when he tried to prevent them from getting to the scene of a shelling.

'Volcanic rage could erupt', says Daly dryly. 'Especially at checkpoints if he was thwarted by authority.'

It was not an easy life, but he once told a young Serb

woman that his job was 'the closest approximation of happiness'. In the besieged city, he ate the most limited diet imaginable – eggs, pasta, bread, tea – and never complained because he said the civilians were eating worse. In Kurdistan, he lived on boiled eggs for a year. He rarely drank, but on New Year's Eve, 1992, he managed to find a bottle of champagne and chilled it all day outside his window. The only time friends saw him drunk, he said that when he died, he wanted to be buried in Lyon's Cemetery in Sarajevo. He wanted to be alongside the Bosnians, his name among the long rows of makeshift wooden graves.

He did not die in the Bosnian war, but on 24 May, 2000, Kurt Schork died in Sierra Leone, on a dusty red road leading to Rogburi Junction, along with a Spanish colleague, Miguel Gil Moreno de Mora of the AP. They were killed by who we believe were teenage RUF rebels wearing T-shirts and flip-flops, who sprayed their cars with gunfire.

He would not have mourned his own death because, I think, he would have felt he was simply doing what he did every day – his job. In 1983, before he became a journalist, he submitted an uncommissioned editorial to the now-defunct *Boston Observer*, reflecting on Ernest Hemingway's reporting in the Spanish Civil War.

Hemingway found in it [war] the waste of carnage, possibilities of dignity, honor and glory. But he was not so tough or so jaded as to confuse war with murder. And that's why his writing of the Spanish Civil War seems so startling fresh today. Even in war, even in a war tottering on chaos as it was in 1938, Hemingway insisted on moral conduct.

The intentional killing of soldiers in battle by bullet or bombs is war. The accidental killing of civilians – even journalists – in the cause of battle is war. The deliberate killing of civilians, where they live or work – is murder.

The impact of the piece is more chilling because when he wrote it, Schork had no intention of becoming a journalist nor any indication that he would go on to become, in the words of Richard Holbrooke, 'the greatest war correspondent of his generation'. He was then working in Boston as an urban planner and real estate developer. Something had touched him, had resounded deeply about the killing of civilians during war.

As Roger Cohen of the *New York Times* would later say of his friend: 'Mr Schork was driven by a desire to ensure that nobody could claim ignorance.'

Kurt had lived so many lives that unless you knew him really well – which few people, even his closest friends did – you were constantly surprised when he revealed another layer.

He was intensely private, highly intelligent, highly strung. He hated mediocrity and grew restless easily. He had fierce loyalties to those he loved, and as the oldest brother of four children, took the role of protector.

Buddies, mates, were key. Later, his friends in Sarajevo would refer to him as Brother Number One. When he graduated from high school, where he captained the football team, he went to Jameson, a small private college in North Dakota, a place where his friends also got accepted, so that they could play football together. Even then, he was intense. Geerte Linnebank, the editor-in-chief of Reuters, recalls a college friend of Kurt's telling him a story.

One night, a group sat on the second floor of their dorm, as the snow outside fell deeper and deeper. Kurt was silent, staring out of the window. After some time, another friend asked him what he was doing. He told them that in exactly half an hour, it would be safe for them all to jump out of the window. 'He had calculated the rate of snow falling, and the thickness, and established when it was possible to jump without injuring themselves,' Linnebank says. 'There was a medical student with them, and he had even worked out that the medical student went last so he could tend to the injured.'

At Jameson, a professor recognised his brilliance and encouraged him to apply to Oxford as a Rhodes Scholar. 'He was an All-American guy, smart as hell and a great athlete,' recalls Frank Keefe, who met the twenty-two-year-old Schork at Merton College on 8 October, 1969. 'He had a winning way – fifty per cent of what it takes to be a Rhodes Scholar.'

They had rooms next to each other and played rugby during their free time. But Keefe remembers feeling alienated at Oxford. It was the height of the Vietnam era and the American jocks felt isolated. 'We were intimidated by a lot of those Oxford guys,' Keefe says. 'We were living in a museum that hadn't changed in 500 years with these gangly English, instead of being part of the action at home.' One night, the two friends wandered down to an anti-war meeting. The organiser was a guy from Arkansas called William Jefferson Clinton. Walking back to Merton, the two discussed Clinton's disarming charisma. 'Everyone else in the room just kinda disappeared,' Keefe remembers Kurt saying.

At the end of his first year, Kurt married a long-time friend, Kirsty Hansen. 'If he was the All-American boy,' Keefe says, 'she was the All-American girl.' On a perfect summer day, they exchanged vows in the Romanesque church in Iffley, outside Oxford, and drank champagne in the pub before going down a punt on the Isis to the Restaurant Elizabeth. It was, Keefe would later say, a particularly glorious and innocent time.

He and Kirsty eventually split. Several years later, he married Betsy Coleman, an intern he met in Washington during his political days. They too split. As one old friend observed, 'He was a man's man, but he loved women. He had an unshakeable attraction to both.'

When he died, he had been living in Washington with Sabina Cosic. A brilliant young Sarajevan who first worked at Reuters with him from 1993, and who had received a law degree before she turned twenty-two, she went on to complete an MBA at Tulane and to work as an investment officer for the World Bank. Like Maguire, Schork was in awe of her mind. 'I don't think I've ever met anyone with a brain as quick as hers,' he said, a few nights before he died. He was amazed that she had learned the Russian language in a matter of months.

At Oxford, Schork studied English Literature and stayed for an extra third year, before moving to Joy Street on Beacon Hill in Boston. Keefe – then working in Lowell at the Regional Planning Agency – pulled his rugby buddy in to be his deputy. Schork knew nothing of urban planning, but within months became a key player in the revitalization of Lowell.

'He didn't know anything about regional planning before, but he was a natural,' Keefe says. 'He used his charm.' It was a theme that would reappear often in the next decade: his ability to adapt to any situation, and to excel. 'He could fix anything,' one editor at Reuters would later say, and Steve Pearlstein – a journalist from the *Washington Post* who first met Schork when they both worked for Congressman Mike Harrington, and who later edited his first pieces at the *Boston Observer* – would say, 'Even his first pieces were excellent. Perfectionist stuff. He wouldn't let you change a word, but you didn't have to. It was like everything. He taught himself how to ski and he became a great skier. He liked challenging himself.'

In 1978, Schork left Lowell to join the staff of Harrington's office as chief of staff. Pearlstein recalls their first meeting. 'He walked in and said, "I'm the new administrative assistant." I then realised Harrington had offered him my job. You would have thought it would have resulted in tension, but it didn't.' Pearlstein liked him, he decided, when he read Schork's first memo: he had used the word 'cohere' as a verb. He still has a photo of the two of them, leaning against a wall, listening intently to Harrington giving a speech they had written.

Later, along with Harrington and Keefe, he would form a private real estate company and rehabilitate some prime buildings in the Boston area – the Baker Chocolate Mill in Dorchester; Hawthorne Point in Gloucester – but he was primarily interested in politics. He took a leave of absence from Harrington's office to run Bill Bradlee's campaign. 'He was fascinated with politics,' recalls a friend. 'But when they weren't pure enough, he soured. He was a real idealist.'

The souring would also happen with Michael Dukakis, with whom he also worked on and off, as well as Mike Harrington and Bradlee. He was a perfectionist who demanded perfection from those around him. 'Whether it was related to women or the words he put on paper, it was all very carefully thought through,' says Tom Herman, a lawyer in Boston who knew Schork for twenty years. 'The standards he expected of others were the standards he expected of himself.' The curious thing, Herman muses, is that those kind of 'boring, didactic qualities' might create an unpleasant, narrow individual, but not in Schork. 'He loved to laugh,' says Herman.

But he tired of people and things easily. 'The theme was boredom,' says Pearlstein. 'Jobs, women, football, vegetarianism. When he left, he left completely.'

'You always had the sneaking suspicion you were boring him,' admits Sean Maguire. When that happened, he had the ability to cut himself off and simply move forward, without regret, reinventing himself. When he was disenchanted with politics, he followed another mentor to work in Manhattan at the Metropolitan Transit Authority. He knew nothing of subways and trains, but he would later say that he loved the job, although he still felt there were other things in his life to do. He wanted to write and to travel.

One day, with a journalist girlfriend, he packed his kit and moved to Hong Kong, where he wrote for the *South China Morning Post*. He was proud as hell of his work and he posted all of his stories to his younger sister, Lisa Stone, and to Tom Herman. When he came back to Boston for a visit, he sat in Herman's Beacon Hill flat and talked for hours about Sri Lanka and hanging out with the Tamil Tigers. They went out for long vegetarian Chinese dinners and he talked about riding his motorbike through a minefield to meet a Tamil commander. Herman says, 'I never saw him happier.'

In the wake of the Gulf War, he went to Kurdistan for Reuters. He stayed for one year, long after the TV cameras and reporters went home. The plight of the Kurds touched him, and he was getting his first exposure to seriously dangerous work. When he travelled with the fighters, he would sometimes have to bury his satellite phone under a tree and go back to reclaim it to file his copy. He swam across freezing rivers to reach battles. He was obsessed with telling the truth at whatever cost. He made his name with the execution of the Iraqi prisoners.

Corinne Dufka was shocked when he played her the tape on the anniversary of their deaths. It was sometime in the summer of 1992 in Sarajevo, shortly after she met him. 'Why was that so important to him?' she asks. 'Why was he honouring that day? Sometimes I think it was the injustice of the situation. True commitment . . . or was it a desire for excitement and escaping something?'

But Sean Maguire, who first encountered Kurt in Kurdistan in 1992, believed in his tenacity as a reporter. 'He was living in monastic conditions in a grim hotel. He was a vegetarian in a meat-eating country. He would think nothing of getting up at 6 a.m., driving five hours to check out some river where he heard there was a disturbance, then finding nothing, driving back and getting up the next day at 6 a.m.'

Kurt fell in love with Sarajevo, with its crippled lifeline and battered civilians, where he was sent to open the Reuters office in the early summer of 1992. He recorded the sound of mortar attacks and played them in his room as he was writing, so that he could remember the terror and thud of the impacts. He did not break for dinner and flood himself with alcohol to ease the unbearable tension of the place. Instead, he worked late in his room. Once I asked him why he didn't ask the waiters – who managed to preserve their dignity during the siege by wearing neat white shirts and black ties, and who played football inside in the empty cavernous rooms of the hotel because they could not go outside – to bring him food.

He looked stunned. 'I would never make them walk up the stairs if they didn't have to,' he said. There was no electricity; it was four long flights to his room.

'There was a kind of ascetic quality to him,' Sean Maguire says. 'Like he was better than the rest of us and didn't need alcohol to take the edge off.'

Aside from becoming the moral conscience of the press corps he also became a mentor to a host of younger journalists. Joel Brand, a twenty-two-year-old from California, arrived in Bosnia in March, 1992, on a Eurail Student Train pass. He briefly met Schork in central Bosnia, but when he arrived in the capital that summer – a particularly dangerous time after aid flights had been shot down by Serbs and several journalists killed and wounded – he called Schork from the aerodrome.

Brand had vomited on the military flight into the besieged city, because of nerves and turbulence, and he needed to get a ride into the city or the UN would force him to return on the same plane. He asked the Reuters correspondent to come and collect him.

It was a suicidal request, asking anyone to drive down Sniper's Alley in an unarmoured car. Brand knew it, but he was desperate. As he puts it, 'Kurt barely knew me. But I had no choice.' There was silence on the other end of the phone line – which miraculously worked on that day – while Schork contemplated it.

'He came to get me,' Brand says, 'in his shitty Lada. When we pulled out from the airport, he said, "Here we go. Good luck." ' When they arrived at the dark, deserted Holiday Inn, speeding in like maniacs to avoid gunfire, into the underground car park, Schork barked at the receptionist – 'Give him a room at the back' – and told Brand not to walk on the gutted side of the hotel, where there was sniping. Then he said 'see you later' and calmly walked off. If the death-defying trip had unnerved him, he did not show it.

The two grew extremely close. 'Our relationship was a blend of father-and-son and friends,' Brand says. 'He was an incredible teacher. He taught me the value of having a moral compass.' At one point, Brand remembers both of them saying that if they were killed, they would promise to be buried in Lyon's Cemetery.

Years later, when Brand also distinguished himself by living in the city for long periods without a break, and was close to breaking point, Kurt took him aside and told him to go home and find another story. 'My nerves were totally shot and he recognised I was exhausted before I did.' Brand left; Kurt stayed until the bitter end.

'When *are* you leaving?' I once said, on a visit back to Sarajevo in 1996. He had finally moved out of the Holiday Inn and was now living in a house near the orphanage on Bjelave.

'When they hang the last dog,' he replied, smiling.

I flew into Sierra Leone at the beginning of May, entering the country as everyone else was fleeing. The UN had falsely claimed the RUF rebels were closer to the city than they actually were, and the traumatised population panicked. The World Food Programme helicopter I took from Conakry, Guinea to Lungi Airport near Freetown was empty except for myself, the photographer Seamus Murphy, and a twitchy emergency worker from Médecins Sans Frontières.

Families with overstuffed bags of hastily-packed possessions waited to clamour on board our chopper to go back to Guinea. A solemn woman sat in a beach chair under a palm-thatched hut, stamping passports and checking visas. A grim government soldier with a British rifle stood menacingly behind her. Both were listening to President Kebbah's emergency warning on a tinny radio: 'Anyone who tries to harm this beautiful country,' he said in a deep voice, 'will be severely punished.'

There were hardly any journalists in Freetown, and with some nervousness, I settled into the UN compound at the Mammy Yoko Hotel and prepared for the worst. Within days, Kurt arrived. I was not surprised to see him, hands thrust into his front pockets, grilling the World Food Programme's Aya Schneerson in the lobby of the Mammy Yoko hotel. At the morning and afternoon UN briefings – frustrating, useless for information – he turned to me and whispered with vengeance, 'If David Wimhurst says one more time he can't answer the question I'm coming in with a video camera and filming him saying that.' He laughed scornfully. 'I don't want to embarrass them – but I've got no choice.'

We met up on the front line near Masiaka the next day, and he warned me about the next checkpoint, about these wild teenagers called the West Side Boys who wore T-shirts and were stoned out of their minds on ganja. The next night, at Alex's Bar, we ate a quiet dinner, rushing our food before curfew fell. He talked about the book he was writing about Bosnia; about Sabina's work at the World Bank in Washington; about the flat they had just bought and the furniture they'd purchased in Bloomingdale's. He drank a beer, and said that he now ate meat because of a health problem. Mark

Chisholm, Yannis Behrakis and Matt Biggs from Reuters joined us, and they agreed a time they would wake up the next day to work. Kurt laughed about the West Side Boys. 'Man, those guys are just like a pick-up basketball game,' he said. 'Everybody wants to play centre.' We laughed and parted; Kurt kissed me goodnight on the cheek.

It was the last time I saw him alive. I flew out the morning he died and learned he was dead when I arrived in Paris, via Mauritania. Waiting for my bags at Charles de Gaulle Airport, I switched on my cell phone and saw I had a message. It was Sky News. 'Can you call us urgently about the dead journalists?' I felt a chill down my neck. It was too early to phone them, so I rang a friend from French TV and got them to read me the wires from Freetown.

When they read out Kurt and Miguel's names, I said, 'It can't be true. Check again. It's not them.' They had been killed at the time I boarded the helicopter from Freetown to Guinea.

To me, they had always seemed immortal. I had a flash of memories, as vivid as old, weathered photographs: Kurt in the Reuters office in Sarajevo, laughing with Samir as we watched *A Fistful of Dollars* on Bosnian TV; Kurt running up the stairs to the balcony of a battered church on Sniper's Alley during Christmas Eve mass; Kurt standing up with rage at a UN briefing in which the spokesman said that Sarajevo was not technically under siege. Or walking up the steaming asphalt road in Sierra Leone and telling me to go interview a certain aid worker. 'He's worth it,' he said, cynically. 'Believe it or not.'

A few days later, in Washington, we gathered – a tribe of dazed friends, colleagues and family who had come from Bosnia, Serbia, Africa, Europe and Asia. Richard Holbrooke read at the service. Mark and Yannis held up the watch they found in his Sierra Leone room and called for reflective silence.

'He was the best,' Dada Jovanovic, a young Serb working for ABC News who met Kurt in Sarajevo, said simply. 'When you talk about physics, you talk about Einstein. When you talk about journalism, you talk about Kurt.'

Later, we took over the basement bar of the Hay-Adams hotel. Chisholm, a South African cameraman who had known Kurt since meeting him in June 1992 during a tank fight in a Sarajevo graveyard, had his arm in a sling from recent hand surgery. He was still shocked by the trauma of seeing the friends he loved dead on a road without their shoes – the rebels had stolen them – but he slowly recounted the story.

24 May. The rainy season had begun a few days earlier, but that day broke humid and clear. The Reuters team – Chisholm, Behrakis, Kurt – had woken early, as usual, taken eggs and bacon and juice and coffee at the Cape Sierra Hotel well before 8 a.m., and set out back up the road they had come from the day before – Rogburi Junction. A story had emerged in Freetown. Decomposed bodies had been found which were suspected UN soldiers. Kurt had also heard that a Sierra Leone Army (SLA) government offensive was underway, pushing towards the town of Lunsar.

Along the way, with Abdul, their driver, they stopped for cigarettes, pasta, bread, whiskey and tomatoes for the starving Sierra Leone government soldiers they had met the day before who asked them for food. In Waterloo, outside Freetown, they bought dried fish which the soldiers had requested. It made the car stink, and when Yannis went to relieve himself, Kurt planted something of Yannis' along with the fish, laughing as he did so.

'Typical Kurt,' Chisholm says.

They drove on, through dusty villages with small markets selling mangoes and onions. In the heat, Yannis fell asleep on Mark's shoulder in the back seat, and Kurt took a picture of it. They got a flat tire and had to stop. Eventually, they drove on, Kurt anxious about his deadline. Past Rogburi Junction, they took a left fork towards Lunsar. There, they saw Miguel Gil de Moreno Mora sitting under a tree, reading a book. A lanky, thirty-two-year-old award-winning cameraman for AP, Miguel had distinguished himself by riding a motorbike into Mostar's besieged East Side, as well as trudging into Grozny under heavy bombardment, and living with the Kosovo Liberation Army during a NATO bombardment. He informed Kurt, 'We arrived too late. The government troops left at 10 a.m. to take Lunsar.'

The friends decided to travel together in two cars, leaving behind their drivers. Kurt was in front, driving a dark blue Mercedes, with Mark next to him and Yannis in the back with two government soldiers. One, with a rifle, sat on the hood of the car. Miguel was in the second car, driving, with several other soldiers in his white Land Rover. 'I never spoke to Miguel again once we got into the cars,' Chisholm says. He recalls that the road seemed empty, deserted, and that there were shells of abandoned, burnt-out cars – 'obviously ambushed' – lining the road.

Suddenly, in the distance, further into the dense bush, they heard gunfire. Kurt's face lit up. 'Hey guys,' he called, 'we got a story.' They continued driving, weaving in and out of pot holes in the road, zig-zagging. Kurt, who had raced Porsches as an amateur racing driver in Limestone, Connecticut while living in Boston, was an accomplished driver. Miguel followed.

It was shortly before midday.

Arriving at a small village, they stopped. It was clear the SLA had come through and retaken the village and that the rebels had cleared out. There were a few soldiers left and Kurt asked if they could go ahead, if the road was clear. The soldiers nodded and said to go ahead. About 500 metres before they reached Lunsar, Chisholm recalls seeing a white Jeep, a UN Kenyan vehicle, that had been shot up and abandoned that morning. They decided not to take pictures of the Jeep, because there were no soldiers around. Instead, they headed another two kilometres down the road, to where Chisholm estimates was just over three kilometres north of Rogburi Junction – towards Lunsar.

Later, Corinne Dufka, who left Reuters to work for Human Rights Watch in Sierra Leone – and who travelled the roads frequently – would say, 'What were they doing on that road? All the burnt-out cars should have told them to go back.' Grieving, Dufka would add – because she loved her friend – that maybe Kurt had a self-destructive streak, 'because he sought to put himself in imprudent and dangerous situations'.

But others would disagree. All of the men were experienced and did not take unnecessary risks. Kurt, according to Geerte Linnebank, refused to go back to Chechnya after a friend, Fred Cuny, was killed there; he felt that the risks were not worth it. 'He didn't do anything he didn't want to and we didn't push him,' he says. Chisholm insists that, up until that point, the group had felt safe on the road towards Lunsar.

Then uneasiness descended like a dark cloud. Chisholm

had a flash of a unpleasant memory: one day, while working in Kosovo, when the same group had been together, he had experienced the same feeling. 'We turned back,' he said. 'We always had respect for each other's uneasiness.' That road in Kosovo turned out to be mined.

This road was far too quiet, Chisholm felt, except for distant shooting. They were trying to reach the SLA soldiers, who they reckoned were about two or three kilometres further north. 'We wanted to be reassured by the soldiers, so we kept on going.' Mark sat with his camera on his lap, trying to work out how to film the soldier on the hood who was weaving his rifle left and right towards the bush. They passed a flat bend in the road.

Five seconds later, the ambush started.

It started with the sound of incredible gunfire, coming from Kurt's side, from a gap between the road and the bush of about fifty metres. Bullets ripped through the car and the windows. Chisholm screamed at Kurt: 'GO! GO!' His instinct was to move forward towards the safety of the SLA soldiers further up the road. He could hear glass smashing and hunched down. When he looked over, Kurt, who had not said a word, was slumped over the steering wheel, sitting upright, eyes and mouth open. His head was titled slightly towards the left.

Chisholm knew his friend was dead. He saw blood, a bullet hole. Still, he believes that in the seconds before he died, Kurt had saved his friends' lives by driving closer to the bush, at least another thirty metres, so they could escape the shooting. Chisholm then took hold of the steering wheel and guided it towards the bush. 'It was mayhem,' he says. 'When I saw Kurt dead, I knew we were in desperate trouble.' He climbed out of the car and realised he had been hit by shrapnel in the hand and was bleeding badly. He ran into the bush.

In the back seat, Yannis, whose T-shirt was covered in Kurt's blood, caught a glimpse of the rebels in the bush and tried to get out of the car, but the door was jammed and the soldier next to him was dead. The other was frantically trying to climb out the opposite window and Yannis, trapped in the middle, made his way over the dead man and did the same. He followed Chisholm's trail of blood into the bush.

Each of the two survivors thought the other was dead. They did not see each other again for several hours as they hid from the rebels. It was terrifying. Night would fall in five hours, and every journalist in Sierra Leone knew what the rebels specialised in: amputations, torture, pouring gasoline on their victims and setting them alight. Yannis rubbed dirt on his face in an attempt to camouflage himself, and settled in a bush.

Chisholm, lying in a different part of the bush, tried to stop his bleeding by wrapping his T-shirt over his hand. 'I was freaked out, waiting to be killed,' he said. He had left his camera behind earlier because it was weighing him down, and he was 'terrified of being on my own. I didn't know what those guys would do when they found me, or how long it would take people to find me. I thought I would be hacked to death.' He heard fierce shooting getting closer and closer. He heard trees around him snapping. He lay on a log and put his head in his arms and waited to die.

That shooting, he later learned, was SLA soldiers coming back. They had heard the ambush and had found the bodies and were now spraying the bush, hunting down the rebels. Later, Chisholm watched through the foliage as the Mercedes burned. He realised how close he was to the road, and when he finally came out, he found chaotic SLA soldiers standing around the bodies of his colleagues. They raised their guns at him. He screamed out, 'Journalist!'

Then he saw the bodies. The young SLA soldiers. The journalists. Miguel, he recalled, was wearing blue socks. His glasses were next to him. Kurt had just had a fresh haircut. Both had had their shoes stolen, which upset Chisholm, who stared, overcome with grief. 'It was my way of saying good-bye,' he says. 'To look carefully at them. I thought . . . they had put on their blue socks that morning and did not know . . .'

On the road, Chisholm saw something shiny which he picked up. It was Miguel's – a devout Catholic – crucifix and bracelet on the ground. Later, he gave it to his family at the Barcelona funeral. Then he began walking back to the village, getting caught in another firefight.

Much later, Chisholm found Yannis. He said to the photographer, 'Miguel and Kurt are dead.' Yannis fell to the ground and began crying and punching the earth. The two, covered in blood and dirt, carried the bodies of the dead on to a truck. When they finally found a UN convoy, Mark called out, 'Please, please help us! We've been ambushed!' They began the long journey of taking the dead journalists home.

'I've asked myself hundreds of times – am I angry? Am I revengeful?' Chisholm says. 'I've come to the conclusion – I would do it again tomorrow if it were with the same people. It was just another day of doing our job.' He said that at the Washington Memorial Service, 'at least' ten people approached him and tearfully said that he had been 'honoured' to have been in the car with Kurt when he died.

Later, they found Kurt's computer. The story he was

writing was still on it. The image remains: Kurt bent over his laptop writing furiously; the old indignation.

UN STUMBLES IN SIERRA LEONE
By Kurt Schork
Rogburi Junction, Sierra Leone, May 24 (Reuters)

It took nearly 24-hours for a UN team of investigators to arrive at this site just two hours northeast of Freetown's capital where eight badly decomposed bodies wearing UN uniforms were discovered this week.

He went on writing, I could tell, enraged, for several paragraphs. But he never finished the story.

A fierce heat wave was wafting across the Balkans the day the second half of Kurt's ashes were laid to rest in Sarajevo. The sky was clear blue and cloudless. On 2 August 2000, Sabina brought the fifty-three-year-old war correspondent back to be laid next to the civilians that he had loved and lived among during the darkest days of the siege. Sean Maguire, who had married Dina Hamzic, a Bosnian working for the BBC, spoke about his friend. And there was music. Once, walking down a street in London, Kurt heard the Dire Straits song, 'Brothers in Arms', drifting out of a pub.

'Did you hear that?' he had asked, and suddenly he was pulled away from the London street back to the city he loved. 'It's the Sarajevo song.'

'Brothers in Arms' was played at his Sarajevo burial, along with 'Romeo and Juliet'. Kurt was laid in the earth. His grave on the hilly cemetery next to the 1984 Olympic speed-skating stadium – part of which had been a soccer field before the war killed 100,000 people – was dug big enough so that, when the time comes, Sabina could be buried next to him.

The Sarajevo government officials awarded Bosnian passports to both Kurt and Miguel for their dedication in reporting the war.

Dark Days in Sierra Leone

19 May, 2000

West of Petifu Junction, where the road turns to red dust and the bush grows darker, the villagers fly white neutrality flags over their mud shacks. It is their way of saying that they are peaceful civilians, a feeble protection from the Revolutionary United Front rebels, who are quickly advancing into this territory.

Further up the road that leads to Port Loko, there is real panic. The people who live in this bush are simple people who farm potatoes, grow rice and tap the palm trees for oil. This area was once held by the RUF, and the people know what the rebels will do if they come back. So they are fleeing, walking quickly in the heat of the day, or pedalling on rusty old bicycles, their children walking alongside them.

They are terrified; the fear is etched on the faces that pass me. These people are not political; most of them are uneducated. They do not know the statistics, nor the number of dead the RUF has left behind, but they understand the language of fear: the moment they heard shooting early on Wednesday they took their meagre possessions, bundled them on to their heads and began running.

'I'm afraid of those boys,' said John, who used to sell cans of cola and piles of onions at a small stand in his village. 'They cut people, or they kill them. They have guns. If they had sticks, I wouldn't be so scared.' They stopped running at the last British army checkpoint in Lungi Loi.

The British Pathfinders are calm, typical British soldiers, confident in the middle of the rebel advance. One of them, young, with a thick Liverpool accent, tells me that the villagers feel safer around a foreign army; it does not matter who they are as long as they are not rebels.

'When we arrived, they were terrified,' the young soldier says. 'Now they stand behind that wall and watch us.'

He said that 300 people a day wander into Lungi Loi from the eastern regions where the rebels were mounting more attacks. They began setting up makeshift tents and lining up cooking pots, fetching coconuts and water, getting their children into makeshift beds for the night.

Kadiatu Barrangura was leaning against a wall. She walked miles and miles because someone told her the British were nearby and would protect them, and before she left her hut, she put on her best green stone earrings and her beaded tribal necklace before she tied her two-month-old baby, Kanbebo, on her back and began walking. She hiked thirteen miles through the bush with her two other children before she found the British Pathfinders. 'I heard the first gunshots Saturday or Sunday. On Wednesday it got worse. The rebels are coming, and we had to run away,' she said.

Her daughter, Isatu Kamara, fifteen, had greater fears. She dropped her eyes as she explained why she is afraid. 'They take women away,' she said quietly. 'They do terrible things. And they cut off your hands.'

It is a sleepy place, this outpost. It looks like the Wild West, except for the people, exhausted, scared. Some are lined up on the verandah of a mud hut, silently watching the road leading east – as if they could see the rebels, believed to number a thousand, charging towards them. All of them saw the body of the young RUF soldier that lay on the roof of the battered car, the result of Wednesday's fire-fight with British and Nigerian troops. Someone finally took the body away, after it began to rot in the sun, but they can still see the deep, rust-coloured blood stains that line the bonnet of the car.

An older man, Alie Conteh, stood near the car, his eyes fixed on the blood. He quietly told his story: he had been captured and released by rebels near his village of Yakiba. 'They had already looted all the other villages, and they were carrying stuff on their shoulders,' he said. They took him and kept him with them for a day, making him carry their loot deeper into the bush.

The rebels, he said, were only teenagers. 'They were young boys, but they were frightening,' he said. He had managed to preserve his hands: he said they did not hurt him because they needed him to carry things. 'Then they let me go, but they had a commander called Gborie, who told me to go back and tell everyone that they were coming back,' he said.

Transistor radios are a real luxury here, so the real news is spread amongst people, a woman moving from group to group with the latest updates. Sia, who comes from Bombeh, has some news. She said that Lungi Loi was overrun with rebels on Wednesday. She said most of them came from

Mabonie, an RUF stronghold, and as dawn was breaking they pushed their way towards Lungi Airport.

'The rebels are trying to get to Freetown,' she said softly. She heard the news of Foday Sankoh, the rebel leader, being captured on a borrowed radio that she stopped to listen to as she was walking, and she says the rebels are advancing closer because they are desperate. 'They have nothing to lose,' she said. 'Now they have to cut their way into this bush.'

She, like everyone else, is running away because she does not want to get 'cut' – the infamous trademark of the RUF: to cut off either both or one hand, either 'long sleeves', cutting at the elbow, or 'short sleeves', cutting at the wrist.

An aid worker tells me that even the mention of the RUF is enough to clear an entire village. Everyone has seen the amputees. They can't work, they can't take care of their children, they can't gather water. If you are an amputee, you might as well curl up and die under a bush.

The aid worker says, 'People begin to run the minute they hear a mention of them. The worst thing that can happen to these people is to lose their hands or arms. It means they are dependent on other people, that they can't work. For them, it's worse than dying. The RUF know that. They spread that fear.'

As night falls, the people gather mangoes for dinner and prepare to sleep under the trees. A mother nurses a newborn baby and children play in the dust. But there is a strange silence and fear is heavy in the air.

'When you go to sleep in this country you do not know if you wake up the next day,' says Sia. She lies her head on her makeshift pillow. She tries to sleep, to forget the day.

A Slave in Freetown, 13 May, 2000

There's another girl called Sia, but this one has a secret, one that she tells with her eyes dropped, her voice soft. She says she was eleven when her elder sister was killed in front of her. She did not have time to weep. She was abducted by an RUF rebel soldier, taken to his commander and made a 'bush wife' – a sex slave who is kept in a command post and raped repeatedly by soldiers.

When they were bored, the rebels sent her into villages they planned to attack on 'missions' – to sleep with Nigerian Ecomog soldiers to find out information. She walked to the village wearing her best dress and seduced the Nigerians, officially the rebel's enemy, and as they were drifting off into gin-induced sleep got them to talk.

'I was a spy,' she says, a little bit proud. 'I gave them sex and they gave me information. Then we would come back the next day and kill them.'

Before long, the RUF realised Sia's value. She was a tough little operator, she didn't get soft on them. She did her job, went under the trees and had sex with the Nigerians, and then led the rebels back to kill them with no emotion whatsoever. So they made her a captain. She went through an initiation rite which included carrying out her first killing, eating the victim's heart and liver, being cut all over her own body with long knife slashes, and injecting her wounds with drugs. Sia is now eighteen. But she still has the scars, deep angry marks which run down her arms and neck.

At first she is embarrassed to admit what they are. Then she shows me: she lifts up her dress, shows me her arms, tells me the kinds of drugs they slipped inside the flap of her skin, drugs that made her run fast and talk fast and be strong to have more sex with lots and lots of rebels.

She spent seven years, her pre-pubescent and teenage years, with RUF before the UN found her in the bush, a wild kid, half-woman, half-animal. They brought her to St Michael's Lodge, a rehabilitation camp run by two Xavier-an priests. There are 152 former child soldiers there, all of them former killers, rapists, abusers and abused. Sia has been at the centre for more than one year. She still looks scary, her eyes still look wild. But the priests say that she has remorse. She is training to be a hairdresser. She reaches out and grabs a clump of my hair. 'It's thick,' she says. 'You should cut it.' I am not ashamed to admit that Sia frightens me. When I am near her, I still smell how many people she killed. She has not yet shed the past. But she looks solemn when she says, 'I'm tired of killing. I'm not taking drugs, so I don't feel the need to go out and kill.'

Around 5,400 children have been forced into combat in the Sierra Leone conflicts. The initiation to prove they are worthy of the job is brutal – beatings, indoctrination, torture and drugs. Some of them are made to kill a family member to prove their loyalty. According to one Unicef report last year, children often make better killers because their conscience is not yet fully developed.

Sia told me she knew that she would be a good soldier, so she got the best weapons training. 'I learned how to kill close up with a pistol. They gave me two pistols for close range. I always saw the people before I killed them. I checked if they were dead, then I gave them another shot in the head if they weren't.' She says that she was stoned when she did this. She snorted 'brown-brown' (cocaine), took 'red tablets' and 'white tablets' (believed to be amphetamines or crack), 'blue-boats' (crack), and was injected with 'medicine' (cocaine or speed) that 'made me strong and made me want to go out and kill'. She was so good at killing and cutting off limbs that she began to train younger children – captured five-, six- and seven-year-olds. 'She was a good teacher,' says Anthony, now eleven, a fat little boy who comes to speak with me. 'Sia told us to kill or she would kill us. So we killed.'

Although Sia talks willingly about the killings, she is embarrassed by amputations, which she calls 'cuttings'. She says that one of her other children would hold down the victims while she brought down the axe on their elbow or wrist. 'I cut people big and small, big and small. I couldn't kill everybody, so the ones I didn't kill, I cut.'

But all that is finished now, she says breezily. She wants to move into her own house in Freetown with her boyfriend, another child soldier, whose nom de guerre in the bush was Killer.

'Why Killer? How many people did he kill?'

Sia shrugs.

I go inside to look for the priests. Sia is beginning to frighten me now, even though she is skinny and not nearly as tall as me. From the outside, St Michael's looks like a run-down holiday camp in the middle of the bush. Outside the window of the bungalows where the boys live, the Atlantic Ocean breaks on an idyllic beach. The boys, drawn from all the militia factions, swim on Sundays after mass, where many now sing gospel in the choir. The girls live in another part.

The two priests, one Spanish, one Italian, spend months, sometimes years, trying to enable the former killers to function in the real world. The priests are protective of the kids, who sometimes get agitated when they speak of the old, murderous days. The Italian priest brings Momoh, who is seventeen, over to see me. Momoh spent five years as a soldier for the Sierra Leone Army (SLA). His dark eyes grow hostile when he recalls the cannibalism he committed, the murders and the rape.

'When he first got here, he used to complain that he needed to eat a human liver,' says Father Chema, a young, bearded priest who has long hair and wears shorts, a T-shirt and sandals. He says it calmly.

'Some of the other boys, when I try to break up fights, scream at me: You can't tell me what to do! I drank human blood!' They are not lying – all of the children speak of cannibalism and eating the organs of their first victim.

It usually takes three months for the children to trust the priests. 'We first make them feel safe and secure, then we talk to them all the time,' says Father Chema. One boy, Prince, aged nine, is so traumatised that he clings to the priest's legs and is unable to talk about his experiences at all.

Many of them are angry that in the bush, they lived like kings, with sex slaves, drugs and looted goods. At St Michael's, they live like the priests: in poverty. When they arrive, they get weaned off drugs. Then the chain of command that they established in the bush is broken. Then the priests talk to them, endlessly. 'But still, they scream at night for a long time.'

Although the priests will keep the children at the centre until they are eighteen, they are free to go at any time. But many of them know that they are not safe to leave. They can't go home to families because they have been identified as RUF or militia killers. The people in town might recognise them. They might see a former commander.

'They are never really safe again,' says Father Chema. 'They not only lost their childhood, they lost their future.'

When I leave, I see Sia watching me. She gives me a weak-looking wave, and says, 'Maybe see you in Freetown?'

I don't know, I say. Halfway down the road, I turn. Sia is still there, watching.

Life and Death in East Timor

22 September, 1999

You smell death before you see it. Inside the overrun garden of the independence leader Manuel Carrascalao, the sick, sweet smell leads to a corner where the well is full of bodies. The corpse at the top is covered with live worms. The body is bloated and discoloured, the skin leathery and burnt. The dead man's arms just in front as though he had tried to prevent himself from falling further down the well.

He is not alone there. The Australian soldier guarding the destroyed villa reckons that there are nearly thirty bodies thrown inside. I peer down. I don't know how many there are; there could be five, or there could be three or four times that, stacked one on top of the other. But judging by the slug-like colour of the corpse I saw, they have been there about two weeks.

All over Dili there are bodies. In a sewage tunnel in a remote and burnt-out shopping complex, a man in blue shorts, dead maybe two weeks, lies face up. You can see his ribs. His guts are ripped out of his torso and swim alongside him. His head is nearly skeletal. He floats among debris, sweet wrappers and moss. Pigs sniff the ground nearby.

Near the sea, overlooking the mountains, is a small river called Kampung Alor. In another time or place it might be idyllic; now it is contaminated. Floating among tin pots and long green weeds is a man of indistinguishable age, size and weight. He's wearing brown jeans. A crowd of children stand on the banks and stare.

Nearby there is more. Next to what once was the Prigondani restaurant in Hudi Laran district there is a vacant field. The corpse lying there for two weeks was buried yesterday by local people, who couldn't bear the dead man's indignity. 'He has no name,' one man says. 'Maybe he comes from Sami, a nearby village, but nobody knows for sure.'

This is day three of a liberated Dili but the militia who killed these men are still on the streets. Major-General Peter Cosgrove, the Australian head of the peacekeeping mission, called it 'a dangerous 24 hours'. Sander Thoenes, the *Financial Times* Jakarta correspondent, was killed on Tuesday night by soldiers who were possibly militia, possibly Indonesian Army. Early yesterday morning United Nations soldiers went to inspect the body. In the distance is a column of heavy black smoke coming from the vicinity of the Santa Cruz cemetery, where in 1991 an estimated 200 people died, protesting against Indonesian occupation.

Driving through ghostly streets, empty of people, it is clear that the militia has been at work. The houses are burning with freshly lit fires. Through the thickness of the smoke small groups of Indonesian soldiers getting ready to return to Jakarta are standing on corners smoking. Their barracks, as well as houses, are burning. It is clearly a scorched-earth policy designed to leave behind nothing that Indonesia built.

The soldiers are not friendly. Who started these fires? 'No comment!' they scream. One puts up a middle finger. Are they going back to Jakarta? 'No!' another one shouts.

In Aituri Laran, near Kuluhun, a pro-independence village and scene of numerous clashes before and after the referendum on independence, the town is on fire. Either the militia or the military started throwing grenades into houses at 9 a.m. and burning them in a last-ditch attempt to destroy. Thick columns of smoke rise from the houses; loud explosions come from within. Soldiers with the Indonesian Army Battalion 744, which is based there, stand and watch. They say they didn't do it; the villagers say they did.

'It's difficult for us to control the militias,' says one soldier weakly. 'We tell them to stop but they don't.'

Truckloads of Kopassus, special forces wearing red berets, drive by jeering at the flames. An old farmer emerges from his house: 'It was the army, not the militia, who started it,' he whispers. 'I saw them. They had red berets.'

'Today they're burning Julio Varres' house,' says Fernando da Cruz, a teacher who was shot in the hip by militia ten days ago. 'Even though the UN troops are here, the militias are still in control.'

Dead Men Tell No Lies:
Justice in Jamaica

May, 2001

A few hours ago, Daphne watched her twenty-six-year-old son take three bullets into his brain. She's crying and screaming and clutching the fabric of her dirty brown dress, as though she is trying to rip it off her own body. Her face is a map of pain, misery and submission to a life of hell. All she has ever known is poverty and childbearing and back-breaking work. Now her son, the one she says 'never gave me any trouble was never a bad boy', has been killed by the Jamaican police. Because he was in the wrong place at the wrong time.

'They took the wrong man!' a young girl in a yellow T-shirt screams. She witnessed the scene, saw the killing and is bursting with outrage. 'Chewie didn't do nothing! They got the wrong man!'

In places like this, places where the poor people live, they call the Jamaican police 'death squads'. That's because there are 140 cases a year of citizens being killed by them, the highest number per capita in the world. When you look at them like a line of numbers, it means nothing. But when you go to the funerals and walk through the dusty townships where these people lived and died, when you meet their families who try to find justice for their loved ones and rarely do, then you see people who died for nothing. This is an undeclared war, a war between civilians and the security forces. Amnesty International calls it a human rights emergency.

Daphne doesn't know statistics, and she hasn't thought about calling a lawyer. What good can a lawyer do? The police haven't come back yet to apologise to her for killing her son, and she is still in shock. In between animal howls of pain, she recounts Chewie's story. He was a simple man, a factory worker, a father to a small daughter and boyfriend to a pregnant young girl called Kay. Kay stands, hands on her belly, next to Daphne, wearing a look of sheer disbelief. She is beyond tears. Did Chewie have a gun, I ask. She looks at me hard.

'I knew him for nine years,' she says. 'He never had a gun.'

The crowd around Daphne, who have seen this too many times, are riled by the heat and the injustice of their situation. They are screaming and chanting: 'They kill him! Police kill him! Murder! Murder!' But they know no one is listening.

Kingston is going up in flames. For the entire month of May, violence has been rising and the police and the army are on the streets with APCs, flak jackets and helmets, with the intention, they say, of trying to separate turf wars. It looks like Bosnia or the West Bank. Every morning over my papaya at breakfast, the local paper, the *Daily Gleaner*, reports more killings, more havoc and more editorials about the police being out of control. WAR! the *Star* reports in five-inch high letters. Gangs trade bullets in West Kingston!

I was not standing on the corner watching when Chewie

was shot. All I know is what Daphne says, and I believe her. The police, led by a man she knew called Bobby Red, arrived at the boat factory where Daphne and Chewie worked. They were looking for a man who owed them money. The guy wasn't there. So Bobby Red got angry and they dragged Chewie, kicking and screaming and clinging to his mother's legs, outside and they beat him for a few hours.

She said it hurt, watching her baby get his head stomped in. Chewie was crying out to her for help and Daphne tried to intervene and then she saw a gun. Then she heard three bangs and Chewie slumped forward to the ground, dead.

Chewie died because he was poor, because he was powerless and because the police knew they would never be charged. Access to justice in Jamaica is like apartheid. It exists, more or less, for the middle classes. If you are poor, your life is cheap.

Carolyn Gomez, a softly spoken paediatrician who heads a grass-roots organisation called Jamaicans for Justice, says that the rate of police killing citizens – which is five times the number of another notoriously violent country, South Africa – is a human rights emergency. In her small office in Grants Pen, a crime-ridden inner-city neighbourhood where one hears the music of automatic gunfire nightly, Gomez sifts through a pile of manila files. Dead ends, cases of police killings that have been painfully unresolved.

'Our police force has been killing an average of 150 of our citizens for the past eight years,' Gomez says in a resigned voice. 'That's an emergency. That's 1,400 in eight years. And in those eight years, you can count on both my hands the number of policemen that have been held accountable.' Gomez sighs deeply, the breath of someone who believes they are fighting an impossible battle. 'It is an emergency if one more person dies.'

Jamaica is a schizophrenic paradise. North of Kingston, coming out of the grime and dust and traffic and heat, you drive through the Blue Mountains, acres and acres of velvety banana trees and fertile coffee plantations, before reaching the turquoise sea. The beaches are golden: miles of endless white sand, with hordes of sunburnt tourists piling in on charter flights from Europe and North and South America. They have no idea what is happening to the people who live and die here. I had no idea what was happening here when I stayed, one blissful winter, at the Jamaica Inn, reading Milan Kundera and drinking rum punch.

In the 1950s, elegant resorts like Round Hill lured the British aristocracy along with Hollywood stars. Noel Coward found the tranquillity to write; Errol Flynn had his own private island and used to run banana boats down the river to Kingston; Ralph Lauren still has a cottage near Montego Bay. There are golf courses and tennis courts and murals of Bob Marley, and quaint stands selling spicy jerk chicken. On the surface, it seems so cool and laid back, a lucrative tourist industry and a country of gentle, Rastafarian-insired people.

But the reality is much, much darker. Tourists tend not to leave their heavily secured resorts or the beaches of Negril or Ochos Rios. If they did, they would see this: inner-city barrios of Kingston with names like Havana or Trenchtown or Hannah Town or Denham Town, where the Jamaican army has to be called out. If they walked the 'lanes' (ghetto streets) of Olympic Gardens and got caught up in a shoot-out with a hail of nine millimetre bullets fired by police, they would understand. They would find a society that is believed to have the highest murder rate in the Western Hemisphere.

'There are only two ways out of the ghetto, one is to become a DJ, the other is to become a gunman,' one local journalist told me one night, over Red Stripe beers. Young men grow up fearing for their lives: if they don't die by the gun-fuelled gang wars, they could die at the hands of the police.

'The police have been able to kill with impunity,' says Yvonne Sobers, the founder of Families Aganst State Terrorism (FAST). 'Young men, in particular, are very fragile. They simply do not feel safe because there are too many people who have witnessed police brutality.'

What is perhaps most troubling is how under-reported and how unnoticed Jamaica's human rights offences have been. That began in 2001, when then-Secretary General of Amnesty International, Pierre Sane, met PJ Patterson, Jamaica's prime minister. Sane was assured that the government was committed to protecting human rights. But Sane returned from Jamaica concerned, not only about the death penalty – which still exists – and conditions of the jails, which are atrocious, but most of all, about the fact that so many seemingly extra-judicial killings were occurring.

Six months after Sane's initial visit, sixty-five more people were killed in police incidents. By the time Sane returned the following April, following the massacre of seven young boys who became known as the Braeton Seven, the Jamaican story had run out of control. In May, following the death of a local 'Don', West Kingston communities were trading bullets nightly and the Kingston General Hospital was full of bodies peppered with gunshots. A few weeks later, the government had to call out the army to restore order and over one single summer weekend, twenty-one people were killed. Helicopters patrolled the sky like black spiders and tourists cancelled their holidays. Paradise had become hell.

The motto of the Jamaican police force is to serve, to protect and to reassure. But this is often the last thing that they do. Growing up in Jamaica, children learn to fear the police almost as if they were an occupying force. In an attempt to handle an extremely violent country, they clamp down hard on civilians. When police do kill, when it is an accident, they are rarely held accountable for the crime. Often they act as if they are above the law. Sometimes, people fear, they act on the spot, not only as police but also as juror and executioner.

The roots of the current violence stem from the early 1970s, when, in the shadow of the cold war, Jamaica was pulled apart by pro- and anti-Western political factions. Later, Prime Minister Michael Manley and his People's National Party (PNP) would take a hard stand, aligning themselves with Castro and Cuba and alienating themselves from the United States, at a huge economic cost. In the 1980s, the country plummeted into depression and thousands of people emigrated to Canada, Britain or America. With the advent of more poverty, violence reached epic proportions.

Domestically, politicans from the PNP and its opposition, the Jamaican Labour Party (JLP), led by Edward Seaga, began the dangerous process of polarisation and began going into the teeming inner-city neighbourhoods and arming people to rustle up votes. This political tribalism was the beginning of the gang culture, which would increase the political divide and lead to more violence. Drug trafficking increased, and thousands of people died in shoot-outs and reprisal killings. Election times were particularly vulnerable: in the 1980 elections, more than 1,000 people were killed.

The police, whose roots were as an early protection force for the wealthy sugar plantation owners, were unable to control the gangs. They used a suppression of crime act, which gave them extraordinary powers of arrest and detention without charge and search without warrant. It was finally rebuked after twenty years in practice, but not before an entire generation of policemen grew up not knowing how to respect the rights of citizens. This is why the streets are now full of what the *Economist* deemed 'Killer Cops'.

Even now, with the police being trained by special British police forces sent over to educate the force in human rights abuse and how to arrest without shooting, Jamaicans are still coming to terms with this deadly legacy. The police commissioner, Francis Forbes, is a man who seems genuinely concerned with the situation, but is at a loss for how to control it.

'The homicide rate is the cause for serious concern,' admits Forbes, sitting in his colonial-style office with a map of Kingston behind him. 'We continue to have a problem with that.' But when pressed with specific cases, he seemed alienated from what was actually happening on the streets of Kingston.

Clearly, as the National Security Minister KD Knight angrily tried to point out to me when I confronted him with the human rights dilemma, the police do not have an easy job. Patrolling at night with a group of special officers through the twisted lanes of Grants Pen and Olympic Gardens is as frightening as being on patrol with the Israeli Defense Force in the Gaza Strip. Suddenly, you know what it feels like to be the enemy, to be hated, to be targetted, to be stuck between a rock and hard place.

The Jamaican police do not have armoured cars and the gunmen who want to get them have easy access to shoot at them from behind tin fences which hide their positions. According to Commissioner Forbes, twenty-six police officers have been killed in thirty-six months, and random killings, such as the shooting of two officers who were riding a bus, are not uncommon.

The gangs, meanwhile, shoot at each other from across gulleys – empty trenches – and violence erupts at any second without warning. Everyone seems to have a gun – British-made, American-imported or home-made. I began to joke that there were more guns in Jamaica than in Montenegro, where every family has a small arsenal. It is a culture bred on violence. The movies people love to see on Friday nights are films like Scorcese's *Scarface*, which features fifteen minutes of unadulterated shooting. You stay alive, I was told by one young boy, by following the way of the gun.

But even this extreme culture of violence does not excuse the police brutality. The Crime Management Unit, an élite crack force of the Jamaican police, is particularly notorious. Led by Superintendent Reneto Adams, a man whose name conjures fear in the hearts of most simple Jamaicans, these men have a record for operating with impunity and are usually sent in to do the dirtiest jobs. Created to crack down on the gangs and drug traffickers, their raids often end in bloody massacres. Adams, who sports a Mohawk-style coiffure and who excuses his men's behaviour as justifiable, has been likened to Dirty Harry. Despite the number of casualties, he says, casually, 'We have a job to do and we will continue.'

Francis Forbes tells me that Adams is respected by many Jamaicans who want to see crime squashed. But at what cost?

One steaming hot day, as Hannah Town was burning with riots and shooting, I sat in a car with a tiny woman, Millicent Forbes, whose little girl was killed by police in April, 2000. Millicent had just come from court where nothing had happened. Nothing is going to happen either, and she knows it. When a popular radio program led by 'Mr Perkins', a campaigning journalist, came on the radio and he began talking about Reneto Adams, Millicent cringed. Her entire posture shrivelled.

'Wherever that man goes, there is killing, killing, killing,' she cried, and her face crumbled. 'Wherever he goes, there is death . . .' Her voice trailed, defeated. Millicent is forty-three and raises chickens and lives in Trenchtown, and her story is beyond sad. Her thirteen-year-old daughter, Janice Allen, was shot in the back by police during a raid near her house. She was going out to buy rice for her mother with her older sister. She felt a bullet enter her spine, and died in a car en route to the hospital. A passer-by picked her up because the police had refused to take her to the hospital.

Millicent just wants to see the man who did it go to jail. Instead, her family is getting harrassed by police who want her to drop the case. When I asked Francis Forbes about Janice, he feigned ignorance and said he had no recollection. Strange, because he had talked to Carolyn Gomez about the case the day before.

'They are death squads, no different from death squads that operated in Latin America,' agrees Leonard Wilson, a trades union negotiator whose son, Tamoyo, was murdered along with six other boys by police on 14 March this year, in perhaps Jamaica's most infamous case of police brutality: the incident known as the Braeton Seven.

Like Millicent Forbes, Wilson is a father fuelled by injustice. He is not going to let his son's murder get buried. 'I am going to fight it until I can't go any further, until they try to stop me and there is only one way they can stop me,' he said. Wilson knows what it means to say something like that in Jamaica, but he insists he is not scared. 'No way, I am not going to let it rest,' he says.

The next day I met a man called Barrington Fox, a forty-nine-year-old plumber whose eighteen-year-old son Joel was rounded up into a police Jeep last October and was next seen with a bullet through his brain. His sister tried to stop them taking the screaming teenager away, because she knew he would never come back. He clung to her, begging her to save him. But once he was inside that Jeep, that was it.

Joel Fox was no angel; he was going the way of the gun, and Barrington is the first to admit it. But it doesn't mean the police have the right to play God, he says. So after Joel's death, Barrington co-founded Families Against State Terrorism (FAST) so that what happened to Joel will never happen to anyone else again. And he keeps Joel's ashes in a tall glass jar near him just to remind him not to quit.

'This is what keeps me going,' he says, pointing to the jar. 'That's my son there. And I want to see justice. And I am going to see justice.'

All the families' stories are horrific, but there is something about that of the Braeton Seven that leaves you with a sick feeling in your stomach. Braeton is a horrible story, a horrible crime with a horrible aftermath. It is a story that never should have happened, and worse, it is a story of men who killed who will never be punished. Sorting through photographs of the seven boys that died so violently on 14 March, as they played dominoes and ate a dinner of fish and flour dumplings, one cannot help but get the sense that their lives were halted so quickly, before they got a chance to grow into men.

Braeton is a middle-class community of hard-working Jamaicans. It's the kind of place where families aspire to send their children to university in Canada or the US, where Sunday afternoons are spent visiting relations or watering the rose garden. It is a quiet place and the small white house where the seven boys – none of whom had police records, and by all accounts of numerous witnesses interviewed, none of whom were gunmen or gangsters – were killed looks neat and clean. Four of them were teenagers, three had just turned twenty.

When you step inside the house where they died, it is clear that something evil happened here. Despite attempts by the police to scrub away blood in the back room where it is believed the boys were assassinated, you can still smell and feel death. If you think hard enough, you can still hear the boys screaming out for their neighbour, Mr Carpy, to come and help them, and hear their frantic pleas for their lives. Worse, you can hear them crying and saying the Lord's Prayer, which, according to witnesses, the police ordered them to do before shooting them with nine-millimetre revolvers.

The crime management unit arrived in full – sixty men – at dawn on 14 March. They had come on a tip-off that the house full of boys might be linked to the killing of a policeman and a high school principal. As the first light swept the sky, they crept up on the house. What happened next is sketchy. The police say the boys began firing at them – but there is no evidence of a shoot-out, and witnesses say they only heard one volley of bullets, police bullets. Bullet holes in the aluminium shutters of the house do not tally with the amount of bullets in the boys' bodies, or their positions. Some of the bodies had been shot from above, again suggesting execution.

All of this does not back up the official police version that the boys died in a shoot-out. 'It seems not possible that these lesions could have occurred just by random shooting,' reported an independent pathologist from Amnesty's Danish Medical Group, who came at the request of the families. Yvonne Sobers from FAST, who arrived a few hours after the murder with Barrington Fox and who collected parts of one boy's skull (suggesting he was killed at close range), is more blatant. 'It was execution,' she says firmly.

After the killing, the police removed the bodies without using body bags. They tampered with evidence (they claim they found a gun inside the house but they handled it without using gloves), performed seven autopsies in less than six hours and did not check the boys' hands for gunpowder residue to prove they were 'gunmen'. All this is standard procedure in Western Europe.

Yet, despite the lack of evidence, Reneto Adams still stood in front of the crowd of bewildered and grieving neighbours, who had known the boys all of their lives, and told them that the young men were gunmen and gangsters. To fathers like Leonard Wilson, who was proudly waiting for his son's acceptance letter to a Canadian university, this was a second assasination on his son's life.

For other parents like Valdene Beckford, whose fifteen-year-old son Reagon died in the house, taking nine gunshot lesions on his frail body, it felt like her heart was getting ripped out. Her son was dead; now his reputation was being destroyed.

'Reagon was no gunman,' she says, tears running down her

elegant face, unable to control her pain. 'He was my baby. He was tall, but he was still just a baby.' She shows a picture of Reagon wearing long shorts; he looks like a child. She shows his bedroom which is still full of his artwork. She says she is never going to remove it, never going to clean the walls.

When I left, the case was being investigated. But most legal advisors told me, straight out, that like the many other cases before it, it would be buried. Due to the sluggish judicial system, the Braeton case will die because it will be nearly impossible to finger one perpetrator. According to Jamaicans for Justice, it takes just under two years for the cases to trawl through the legal system just to reach the coroner's court.

Braeton has precedents, other cases that are clearly miscarriages of justice that have never been resolved. Another story in that catalogue of horror is Michael Gayle, a twenty-six-year-old mentally disabled man who rode his bicycle through a checkpoint manned by nine soldiers and four policemen in August, 1999.

Although Jamaicans for Justice say the curfew was illegally called, Gayle was thrown off his bicycle, kicked and stomped with clubs, batons, fists and finally, his ribs were smashed with his bicycle.

His mother, Jenny Cameron, heard that someone was being beaten at a checkpoint and rushed to see her son lying on the ground. She remembers him crying, 'Mama, Mama', and she could not believe that was her boy lying bloody on the ground.

Michael's internal injuries were massive. But the police would not let Jenny take him away. They told her to go to a police station and report that she had seen her son strike a police officer. Stunned, she refused. Michael was taken to a mental health clinic where he was given insufficient treatment and died several days later.

His case, according to Jamaicans for Justice, has gone nowhere, but his mother, like the families of the Braeton Seven and Millicent Forbes, is refusing to let it go. A former farmhand on the sugar planations, Jenny never learned to read or write. She lives in one small room in a 'yard', sharing a toilet and washing facilities with her neighbours, but she keeps her space neat and she treasures the gifts that Michael gave her for Mother's Day – two china figurines. She is not going to forget, no way, she says, shaking her head defiantly. 'Just because I'm some little woman from the inner city with six kids and they kill one . . . they are not going to get away with it.' At the age of fifty-three, she says, she wants to become a lawyer, even if it takes years.

Since Braeton, something has changed in Jamaica. Before, families of victims fell into complacency because they did not know how to fight back, or if they did, they were convinced they would never see justice. Organisations like FAST or Jamaicans for Justice, along with the awareness that Amnesty and the outside world are monitoring their story, have encouraged them to unite against the police and the justice system. The police, for the first time, are getting nervous.

'Braeton has changed something, definitely, in Jamaican society,' says Father Richard Albert, an American priest who has lived in Jamaica for forty years and who runs the St Patrick's Foundation, which organises various inner-city projects, as well as being active in Jamaicans for Justice. 'We now have good policemen and women who look at what is happening, and they feel ashamed.'

On a steamy summer night in Father Albert's church hall near Grants Pen, a group of families of victims are seated in a circle for a counselling session. You can tell that everyone in that room has lost someone because of their posture, their sadness, the heaviness in their faces. One by one, they speak: 'I lost my son', 'I lost my daughter', 'I lost my husband'. Their stories all sound similar and senseless.

A psychologist is talking to them about grief and about the circle of rage and sorrow that occurs when one person is killed by the Jamaican police: not just one person, but an average of eleven. Take that and multiply it by the number of people killed each year, and it is an ocean of pain.

As she speaks, I watch all of their faces. There is a kind of deadness to all of them, that deadness that comes when something or someone you love has been ripped from you, and you don't really know why. I have seen that deadness all over the world, from Kosovo to Grozny. The difference is, this is Jamaica – this is supposed to be a Caribbean paradise, not a country at war.

Finally, the counsellor lights a candle and asks each person to come up and remember their loved one and blow out the candle. One by one, they shuffle up to this small table – old women, young men, wives, a pregnant woman, all of them united by loss. Then, the strangest thing happens. Softly, and slowly, they all begin to sing the Jamaican national anthem. It is about freedom and beauty and how much they love this country, this place that has robbed them of family and of trust and of reassurance. I am stunned. If it were me, and I lost someone, I don't know if I would have that much generosity in my heart towards a place that had destroyed my life.

But afterwards, Jenny Cameron, whose beloved son Michael, who she says would never hurt anyone, who was kicked to death by fourteen men, comes up and touches my arm. She was singing loudly and now she has tears in her eyes. How can she still sing? I ask her, and she looks surprised. 'Oh yes,' she says quietly. 'I still love Jamaica. No matter what has happened. I always will.'

A few days later, I saw Leonard Wilson. He had a thick envelope, which he knew was his son Tamoyo's acceptance to a university in Canada. The boy had been waiting for that letter for months, it was his ticket out of Jamaica and into a different world.

Leonard hasn't opened the letter yet, even though he knows what is inside. He says he doesn't have the heart.

NOTE: *In November 2003, six police officers were charged in connection with the killing of the seven young men in March 2001, the Braeton Seven.*

However, the charges were limited to the lower ranks of officers who took part in the operation. The officer who commanded the operation was not charged.

And in February 2005, the six policemen charged with the murders were freed. Defence lawyers said there was no evidence to connect the accused with the shootings.

Small Voices in Zimbabwe

March, 2002

> *During the 2002 elections, a small group of people opposed*
> *to Robert Mugabe struggled to bring their country freedom.*
> *This is their story.*

Robert is listening to Stevie Wonder's track, 'Master Blaster',
on the car radio. He's singing along because in 1980, when
Stevie Wonder came along with Bob Marley to Zimbabwe
for the independence celebrations – effectively the end of
white rule – Robert was there, as a child, with his parents.

Two decades on, both his parents are dead, the result of
poor healthcare, and Robert, a former student leader for the
Zimbabwe opposition, the Movement for Democratic
Change (MDC), has been beaten and tortured and intimidated because he wants things to change in his country. But
for the moment, he's singing along with Stevie Wonder
enthusiastically until he reaches the line, 'Peace has come
to Zimbabwe'.

The car goes quiet. 'Peace has not come to Zimbabwe,'
Robert says, looking at the window where long queues of

angry people wait to buy sacks of corn meal, sugar and soap. 'My country is in chaos. My country is in trouble.'

It's the week before the 2002 presidential elections, and Robert is taking me to St Peter's, a village outside of Bulawayo, the country's second largest city, that has been burnt and looted by Zanu-PF teenage militiamen, the henchmen of President Robert Mugabe. For the past two months, the teenagers have been roaming the lush countryside, wreaking havoc on a civilian population who are being terrified into supporting Mugabe.

Mugabe, a former freedom fighter in the war of independence against white Rhodesians, has ruled the country for twenty-two years. Now, Zimbabwe is sliding into political and social anarchy. Despite the fact this is one of the most literate countries in Africa, the inflation rate is 117 per cent. The unemployment rate is sixty per cent; there is a deteriorating health and education system; and since Mugabe instigated land reforms, whereby Blacks confiscate the farmlands of white Zimbabweans who have lived in the country for generations, there is an added element of racial tension.

Mugabe, who is now eighty, is desperate to hang on to power.

'He's got an enormous amount to lose,' says David Coltart, a white Zimbabwean MP who is also the opposition's Shadow Justice Minister. 'He's not just going to ride off into the sunset.'

To lose the presidency would mean that Mugabe would lose his grotesquely high standard of living in a country where people are starving (for example, his young wife often borrows presidential planes to go on shopping sprees at Harrods). The full extent of his corruption will also be exposed and, perhaps more importantly, he could be called to a war crimes tribunal for the 20,000 or more civilians who were massacred by his élite troops in the Matabeleland region in the 1980s.

To hold on to power at any cost, Mugabe has encircled himself with thugs, like his Minister of Information Jonathan Moyo, who has banned foreign press such as the BBC from reporting inside Zimbabwe. He has enlisted 'war veterans' – supposed fighters in the war of independence, but many of whom were not old enough to fight – and the youth militia, the so-called Green Bombers. His election tactics, according to David Coltart, include intimidation to deter voters; manipulation of the way the vote is exercised, for example, taking people off who are dual citizens; and lessening the number of polling stations in urban areas where the opposition is higher.

'Votes should be equal,' says Coltart, who worked as a human rights lawyer for years and defended members of the opposition. 'People will be denied their vote as a result of that inequality.'

The hope for the country lies with the MDC's opposition leader, Morgan Tsvengerai, a former union leader who will celebrate his fiftieth birthday on the second day of voting and who is a kind of David-versus-Goliath folk hero. Tsvengerai has a degree from Harvard and has presented himself as offering a stable future in a country that is spiralling out of control. For this, he has been vilified by the government as a pawn of Tony Blair, as a man who wants to bring back white rule.

Surrounding Tsvengerai are thousands of supporters who are desperate not to see their country slide into destruction. This is their story – what it is like to live and fight against a regime – one week before the presidential elections.

St Peter's, a half-hour outside Bulawayo, was once a village of 2,600 farmers scraping by at poverty level. Now it shows the result of Mugabe's desire to hang on to power. These are poor people who live here. Farmers, labourers, simple people – 'the small but powerful voices', which is how Shari Eppel, a human rights worker in Bulawayo, describes them. People who are unable to defend themselves against a regime as powerful as Mugabe's.

Now the small voices have lost everything.

You get to St Peter's by driving down a dirt road, past a township where Zanu-PF youth sneer menacingly at our car, and past a dried-out field of maize, a metaphor for the drought and subsequent food shortages that plague Zimbabwe. At the end of the road is a village.

Here, the houses are primitive, mud with thatched rooves. Now only the walls remain, and the smell is reminiscent of the early days of Bosnia, after the Bosnian Serbs had razed a village. The aftermath of a village destroyed always smells the same: burnt houses, charred clothes and destroyed lives.

Most of the people have left, and St Peters is now like a ghost village, with a lone cow moving slowly down a lane surrounded by rubbish. In the distance, a man limps by. A house has all its windows broken, the result of stoning; from behind the shattered window a frightened face peers out.

Most of the villagers have gone to huddle in an abandoned school down the road that the militias plastered, as a final touch, with posters of an ageing Mugabe with his fist in the air. But some remain. They sit in front of their houses as though they are waiting for something to happen, fanning off flies with old newspapers. Their children squat in the dirt. One family has tried to reconstruct their home, using old bricks.

St Peter's is meant to be a stronghold for the opposition. But most of the people seem too poor, too apolitical to care about anything other than getting their next dish of corn meal. Still, they have been punished.

This is what the witnesses, and two Norwegian election observers who were the first on the scene, say happened here.

The Zanu-PF militias came late in the afternoon, hundreds of them, wielding clubs and whips. First one wave of several hundred youths trained by the hundreds of militia camps that have been set up throughout the country since November. Then another wave.

The villagers saw the militias approaching from the bush, running down pathways and chanting Zanu slogans, their heads wrapped in scarves of the Zanu colours. It must have been terrifying. The ones who could run and hide did; the ones who could not stayed behind and met their wrath. They beat a handicapped man, they bashed in the head of another, they slashed an elderly woman. They burned, they stole, they broke the cheap blue ceramic plates that now lie in a pile outside the huts. They burned the food supplies and people's life savings. They threatened and screamed and ranted, and when everything was destroyed, they went back to the bush.

They scared people, part of the election tactic. But perhaps the most important and chilling thing was that they destroyed these people's right to vote. When they burned their houses, they also burned their ID cards. 'In Zimbabwe,' says Shari Eppel, 'if you don't have an ID card, you don't have a vote.'

Maggie Moyo, a fifty-year-old mother of four and the wife of a labourer, is standing outside her hut wearing a green, button-down, 1950s-style coat. Despite the heat, she is wearing a wool cap pulled low over her forehead and she is wandering in front of her burnt hut with the look of someone who has just been in a recent car crash.

Maggie says, 'I had very little to start with in life, now I have nothing.' She stares at her hands, then at her feet, still in shock. She has come back to the ruins to see if anything is left to salvage.

I ask if it is true that the village is said to be an MDC stronghold, and Maggie says that she is a supporter, although now she – like everyone else in the village – cannot vote. 'They took my ID and burned it,' she says.

Then she does something unreal. Even though she has nothing left, not even her birth certificate, Margaret still breaks into a huge grin when she talks about Morgan and the opposition.

'I love them, I love them,' she says. 'Without them, what hope is there for my country? Without them, my children would be herding donkeys.'

The next day at the Bulawayo Cathedral, the Archbishop of Bulawayo, Pious Ncube, sits in his office surrounded by portraits of saints and martyrs, listening to the story of St Peter's.

'Evil, evil, selfish people,' he says, shaking his head, referring to the regime.

On this afternoon, a few days before voting begins, the bishop is bad-tempered because he is losing optimism that the opposition will win. If they lose, he will continue being an outspoken voice against Mugabe.

'I don't like doing it,' he says. 'I don't like being critical. I don't like being outspoken. I wish someone else would do it, but we have to speak out against a government that is selfish, evil, corrupt.'

He takes a boiled sweet from a bag on his desk and pushes his papers aside.

For many years, Ncube has spoken out against the Mugabe regime. He was instrumental in launching investigations into the massacres in Matabeleland in the 1980s, and he has accused the government of corruption while the people starve. He says his real troubles started when he spoke out against the land invasions in 1999.

'I wrote Mugabe a letter saying what he was doing is wrong,' he says, as if he is referring to a badly behaved child. 'I pointed out that what he was doing is wrong, that he was planting the whole country with intimidation.'

Ncube continued to speak out, during the parliamentary elections in 2000 and during the run-up to this election, when the level of intimidation and violence spiralled out of control. He speaks out, knowing that nothing and no one will protect him if Mugabe wants to get rid of him. He says they started a smear campaign against him, and they started threatening his eighty-six-year-old mother recently.

'I said to them, come after me,' he says. 'It's my problem. Leave my mother alone.'

The fact that the archbishop is sitting in this room surrounded by books in Italian, English and German is a testament to his own strong character. Ncube grew up poor, the son of peasants, on a farm outside Bulawayo, and put himself through Jesuit school, university and training in Rome. He says he continues speaking out because he wants to help the helpless. It is with the poor that he identifies and he bristles, for instance, at Mugabe going in front of a war crimes tribunal.

'It will do absolutely nothing,' he says. 'What matters is that the people have food.'

He sees a bleak future for his country. He does not think the Zimbabwe people will rise up once Mugabe takes power again, as the Filipinos did against Ferdinand Marcos.

'It won't happen, they are too timid. This is a country with a literacy rate of eighty-five per cent, but the people are still scared and threatened.'

He seems saddened by the prospect of the next few years in Zimbabwe. 'Such a selfish, self-centred government that is running this country,' he adds, taking another sweet, before going to prepare for mass.

Down the road from the cathedral where the archbishop lives are the offices of David Coltart, another opposition fighter. Born and bred in Zimbabwe, the former student leader and activist demonstrates that the opposition is not divided on ethnic grounds.

Coltart calls himself 'a thorn in Mugabe's side for the past eighteen years'. Like Ncube, he is frequently ridiculed in the newspaper or by government officials. He is also threatened with death and intimidated, and since the election campaign has heated up, it has become worse.

Along with Shari Eppel and Ncube, Coltart is responsible for initiating a report, 'Breaking the Silence', that exposed the atrocities of Matabeleland. He knows the extent of Mugabe's corruption, which is what inspires him, 'along with my faith', to keep going.

But he also knows what Mugabe is capable of. For the past few months, Coltart, who now moves with large bodyguards, has had death threats and has been harassed by youth militias. In January, returning from New York where he met with members of the United Nations, he was returning home with his wife and children, including an infant, when he saw a youth militia camped in front of his house. He reversed, fled and called the police. They never arrived.

When he returned home several hours later, the police finally arrived. But it was not to protect him, but to arrest him, for allegedly firing at the youth militia. 'I don't even own a gun,' he says wryly.

Coltart, like others here, has a contingency plan for escaping if things get very bad. But he insists he will only use it if he is desperate. Like all of the people I met fighting the Mugabe regime in Zimbabwe, he does not want to leave, does not want to go into exile.

'I passionately love this country,' he says. Despite the odds, he believes that there is still tremendous capacity for change. 'If a country like this, highly educated, with resources, can't function – what hope is there for the rest of Africa? If Africa is going to remain a perpetual basket case, what hope is there?'

I first met Mark Chavunduka, editor of the *Standard* newspaper, at the Amnesty International Awards in May, 2000, when we both received awards. I listened to his story, but the impact of what he had undergone did not hit me until I met him again at his office, in a block of flats in Harare, several days before voting began.

Chavunduka grew up a middle-class Zimbabwean. His father was the first black veterinary surgeon in the country and had been educated in Scotland, where he met Mark's mother, a nurse. Mark rose quickly through the journalistic ranks, from reporter to chief reporter to editor by the time he was twenty-nine.

He began running stories that irritated the government;

one in particular drew the attention of the secret police. When they came for him, he went peacefully, believing that he would be released shortly.

For nine days, they held him and his chief reporter, Roy Choto, who wrote the story, and brutally tortured them. The manner – electrocution, drowning, beatings, suffocation – and the specifics of what his torturers used is so horrific that his face is still pained as he talks of it, and he says that he wakes up screaming from the memories. 'I didn't think I would get through it,' he says. 'I kept begging them to shoot me. To this day, I don't know how I got through it.'

Despite three months' treatment at the Medical Foundation for Victims of Torture in London, he still says, 'the physical scars have healed, the emotional ones have not.'

Chavunduka is lucky in the sense that the international community, largely through Amnesty International, got word of his ordeal. Afterwards, he received the prestigious Neimann Fellowship at Harvard University, and although he opted to leave his wife and three children in America for safety, he decided to return home to Zimbabwe to continue his work.

'What else can I do?' he says. 'I try not to worry, because what is the alternative? I have to work.'

He is aided, he says, by the courage of his convictions. 'What I am doing is fair. We're doing proper work. I have to continue for the youth, the young people that are watching what we are doing, as role models.'

Shari Eppel, a forty-one-year-old clinical psychologist and mother of three who runs the Amani Trust for victims of torture with a kind of ferocious energy and passion, says the same thing. For eighteen months, she has been living on her nerves and in the run-up to the election, the week before, she seems on the verge of total exhausted collapse. But she still arrives at her office, an old colonial house behind a gate in a suburb of Bulawayo, early in the morning and stays until after dark.

Eppel is one of those characters who is so committed to bringing justice and truth to light that her face seems to change when she talks about her work and her country. She says she will never go, 'unless it is life or death'. 'Mugabe can't last forever,' she says. 'The rats will abandon the sinking ship.'

But it is not easy. Like Chavunduka, she has sent her children away to safety, in South Africa, to be with her parents. 'I don't want them to be there if the police come for me in the middle of the night,' she says.

One day, she brings four young men who have been tortured by Zanu-PF to her office. All four move slowly, their eyes dropped to the ground, almost as if they are ashamed of what has happened to them. Slowly, they lift their shirts and show the marks of the cruelty that has been inflicted on them. It is unthinkable, staring at the skin that has been broken over and over by bullwhips, the cigarettes put out on soft flesh, the bones broken and the backs kicked and beaten, that human beings can do this to one another.

Later, Eppel tells me that one of the torture victims told her that all he wanted to do was vote, because he still believed enough in democracy, that his vote would matter. 'He didn't want vengeance,' she says slowly. 'He just wanted to vote, even after being tortured. He still believed in it.'

It never occurs to Eppel to stop her work, to do something else, even if she admits that during the investigation into Matebeleland massacres, she often woke up in tears, 'found myself wandering around the house in the middle of the night crying, unable to stop'.

She says she keeps doing it for the small voices.

On the third day of voting, I go to the high-density areas of Harare with Gordon, a young Zimbabwean journalist, and wait at voting stations to talk to people who have tried three days in a row to vote.

Gordon, like Robert, is young and hopeful and desperate for his country to change. He takes a risk every day by supporting the MDC, by helping foreign journalists, and by writing anti-government articles. Or rather, simply writing the truth about the government.

When I meet Gordon, I remember something David Coltart said when I remarked on his courage. 'Courage?' he said in a surprised voice. 'The real guys with courage are these guys . . .' He pointed at Robert who sat smiling proudly at the compliment. 'These young black student leaders, the rural guys with no profile. If you're white, people have more sympathy. Because of our white profile, we are protected. Our black colleagues can be murdered and the government has immunity.'

On the first two days of voting in Harare, some people queue for twenty-five hours. Women are pushed and shoved out of the line and on the third day they divide into two lines, one for each sex. There is some violence, but not as much as we expected. Instead, there is the quiet determination of the people who want to use their rights and who know, deep down, that they are getting cheated.

In Chingeweza, a commuter 'suburb' outside the city, the results of Mugabe's greed are evident. Here, people are truly poor. Some have tattered shoes; some are barefoot; the women look ancient and carry their babies strapped to their backs. Near the polling station, at the OK Bazaar, the Southern African equivalent of Sainsbury's, a massive food queue snakes around and around the store. People are desperately trying to buy a bag of mealy-meal, or corn meal, the national staple, but they are also queuing for sugar, oil and soap. All of life's necessary items are impossible to come by in Zimbabwe if you are poor and powerless.

'I'm voting so I can eat,' says Petronella, who is a student. She won't say who she is voting for, but it is clear.

No one will tell me who they are voting for, but I know they are all voting for the MDC. A man, a brave one, gives me the open-palmed five-fingered greeting, the MDC sign as opposed to Mugabe's aggressive Zanu fist.

'*Chengwa*,' a man whispers to Gordon. '*Chengwa*,' Gordon answers back, triumphantly. *Chengwa*, change.

In the next few days, a lull descends over the city as it becomes increasingly clear that the elections are rigged. The majority of the election observers – with the exception of the Norwegians who have been the real heroes of this election because they dared to tell the truth – basically stood by and did nothing. The South African observers in the room next door to me appeared to do nothing more than observe the swimming pool, drink cases of beer bought on their per diem money, and close their eyes to the ballot-stuffing and intimidation.

Morgan Tsvengerai gives a press conference (which I am unable to attend due to the presence of the secret police), but a young journalist called Hilarious, who is working with me, goes, wearing a button-down shirt and tie for the occasion. He comes back telling me that Morgan was practically in tears, begging the international community to intercede and declare the elections unfair.

Gordon is putting on a brave face. He says that the MDC are still 'sure to win'.

I say sharply, 'I don't want to burst your bubble, but it's high time you thought about what's going to happen when Mugabe wins again.'

Gordon looks doubtful. 'We will win,' he says in a strong, steady voice. 'Maybe not now, but in three months, six months. Mugabe cannot go on forever.'

Maybe not forever, but at least for the moment. By the end of the week, after the 'counting' is over, Mugabe has declared a victory and the Zanu followers party in the streets. Meanwhile, MDC leaders such as Welshmen Ncube are caught trying to flee the country to bring their children to safety, and are put in prison.

'My God, the witch-hunt starts now,' says Gordon. This time, he does not sound so confident.

After a while, the paranoia becomes too much, and I am tired of escaping down the back staircase of the hotel, or waking in the night with a panic attack. It is time to go. Not even in Algeria during the massacres – when reporters needed ten bodyguards to prevent Islamic fundamentalists from slashing our throats in the night – had I felt so exposed.

When I reach South Africa, a gust of hot wind hits me on the airport runway, and I am flooded with a sense of relief at being out of Zimbabwe. The tension of the elections, of working under the shadow of the secret police, of the frustration that democracy did not prevail under the noses of the international community, was more powerful than I had thought.

As I wait for my luggage, I get a text message on my phone, then another. It is from Robert in Bulawayo. The first one says: JANINE, PLEASE CAN I COME TO YOU, I HAVE NOWHERE TO GO. As I am contemplating what this means, the second one comes in: PLEASE CALL ME. VERY IMPORTANT.

When I reach Robert, he sounds panicked and scared. 'I can't go home,' he says. 'The Zanu militia are everywhere, around my house. They're picking up anyone who was active in the opposition . . .' His voice breaks.

'Where are you?' I say.

He is hiding somewhere downtown. I make some calls, we arrange for him to go somewhere safe, and he is calmer when I phone in an hour.

The next day, however, there is another text message. This time, he is trapped inside the MDC headquarters on 14th Street in Bulawayo with his colleagues, and his voice is high-pitched with fear.

'They are outside with combat gear and bazookas!' he screeches. 'Please call the cameramen, the photographers! Let them know what injustice looks like!'

I put down the phone, feeling utterly powerless.

I think Robert will be all right for the moment, but for how long, I do not know. The same for David Coltart, or Shari Eppel, or the archbishop, or Mark Chavunduka or any of the 'small, powerful voices'. I wonder how long they can keep going before they are tracked down and forced to stop what they do. Or worse, how long they can last before they are forced to leave the country that they love, that they have bled for.

As Gordon remarked dryly a few days earlier, the witch-hunt has begun.

NOTE: *Mark Chavunduka died after a long illness in November, 2002. He was thirty-seven years old.*

Lotti's War: Abidjan, Ivory Coast

November, 2002

Rene was found in a dustbin. His thirty-kilogram body was covered in worms. Red ants were coming out of his mouth and his ears. He was still alive, but barely.

It took Rene eight days to die, as the final stages of AIDS racked his body. He drifted in and out of consciousness, sometimes aware of a slight, Swiss woman in a white coat sitting by his side holding his hand.

'Why are you doing this?' he asked the blonde-haired stranger who had picked him up off the streets and placed him in her car. 'You saved me from hell.'

'Because I love you,' she replied without hesitation. A few hours later, the thirty-four-year-old seaman from Cameroon, a stranger in the Ivory Coast, passed away. Latrous wept – as she does when any of her patients die – but she also had a flush of fulfilment.

'Rene died wearing clean clothes, in a bed, surrounded by love and warmth,' she says. 'We gave him back his dignity.'

It is a strange journey that took Lotti Latrous, a forty-nine-year-old from Zurich, from the life of a wealthy expatriate to the slums of Adjouffou, a suburb of Abidjan. She once lived in a grand villa with a pool and servants; now she lives in one room with a few books and photographs of patients she loved who have died. The tennis club and smoked-salmon cocktail parties are another life.

Latrous has given away all of her clothes, her gold jewellery, her possessions. She told her husband – a wealthy Nestlé executive – never to give her a gift again. Her husband and three children have left Ivory Coast for a new life in Egypt, and while they find it difficult to be apart from her, they support her choice. Her own mother thought she had lost her mind.

'I feel guilty sometimes,' she says. 'My daughter was only nine years old when I chose to come and live here. But my children have everything. They are loved. These people have nothing.'

For five years, Latrous has spent her days and nights caring for AIDS sufferers in the last stages of the disease, guiding between the window of life into death. The AIDS rate in the Ivory Coast is one of the highest in West Africa. Twelve per cent of the population – thirty per cent in the slum areas – suffer from it, but it is still a grave taboo, a shameful secret. Relatives try to poison sufferers to kill them faster. Often they are tossed out on the street to fend for themselves.

'They die like animals,' Latrous says. 'It's not fair for people to die like dogs and others to live in luxury.'

Every Wednesday, Latrous, along with Dr Germaine Gnode, a thirty-six-year-old Ivorian who, like her, works for free, combs the gutters and sewers, the shacks and tenements. They bring the sick, often covered in sores, bloody wounds, starving and incontinent, to Centre d' Espoir, which Latrous built from funds she gathered from friends and supporters in Switzerland. Before she had the centre, she worked from under a mango tree. 'I knocked on a lot of doors to build it,' she says.

For many of the sick, it is too late to be treated, and the expensive anti-viral medicines are not available. Instead, Latrous – called Mama by the patients – feeds them three big meals a day, gives them antibiotics to ward off secondary infections, clean clothes and a bed made up with colourful sheets. She then showers them with love and attention. When they die – which is anywhere from days to months – she is by their side.

'I have never been happier in my life,' she says. 'I do it not just for them, but for me. I am satisfied. It gives me back something.'

Some of the patients do respond to her care and manage to ward off death for some time, and are even able to live outside the hospice, returning for meals. But more often, they are desperately ill and die in her arms. It is then that rage overcomes her.

'When I am holding a dying child in my arms who might have been saved, I sometimes get so angry I could kill someone,' she says. 'Why do the rich only get successful treatment? Why is the world so unbalanced?'

The Centre d'Espoir is a simple, one-storey building that cost around $25,000 to build. Latrous and her husband – who comes with the children twice a year to visit – painted it yellow because she thought it was more hopeful.

'I didn't want it to be sterile, like a hospital,' she says. 'I wanted it to be serene.' She has painted the words from the Torah – 'He who saves one life saves all of humanity' – on one wall, beside the long table where those who can get out of their beds come to share communal meals. On the wall of the morgue, she has painted a lush green painting of the Garden of Eden.

'When someone dies, the others are scared,' she says. 'I try not to lie to them about their own fate. I try to help them accept it.'

She spends most of her day moving from bed to bed. Since September, seventy-seven people have passed through the hospice and twenty-five of them are dead. Yesterday, it was fifteen-year-old Virgine, who contracted AIDS from a blood transfusion. Today it is Agnes, who had held Latrous' hand the night before in fear.

'I might not be here tomorrow,' Agnes told her.

'I know,' Latrous replied quietly. 'But you will not be alone.'

She passes through the three wards, joking with Vincent who is so thin that he can only lie on one side. She picks up a year-old baby, Eric, whose mother, Eloise, sitting silently by his side, has infected him with AIDS by breast-feeding. She checks the IV drip of Adele, who has had a bad night, kisses and cuddles her, then wanders into the kitchen to make sure that the lunch is being properly prepared.

Latrous wants to build more hospices all over the country, but she is not obsessed, she says, with saving the world. She is content with her small patch in the middle of a slum where children crawl through dirt and their tiny bodies are covered with angry sores. In another part of the complex, she has set up a medical centre to treat other sicknesses in the slum: malaria, malnutrition. She scoops up a smiling two-year-old, Ramatou, with a tumour bulging out of her forehead and a patch over her left eye. The eye has just been removed. Latrous is trying to get the baby sent to Switzerland to see a neurologist.

With a war breaking out in Ivory Coast, and the country effectively split in three parts by various factions, her job has become harder. Food is more expensive. She cannot get medicine as easily. She is thrilled when someone donates an old television set. 'But I don't want money,' she protests. 'I just want people to be aware of how fortunate they are to be privileged. I want them to be grateful. To know how other people suffer.' She is not particularly religious, she says: 'I did this more out of rage.'

Her goal, she says, is that when someone dies, they go knowing they were loved in their last hours. 'That is my motivation.'

Sitting at her tiny desk, going over her accounting books – she has no secretary or computer and begins work every day at 6 a.m. after a few hours' sleep – it is hard to imagine her as an affluent housewife with 'everything you could dream of . . . carpets, cars, paintings . . .' She says when she sees old friends now, her presence disturbs them. 'I make them feel guilty.'

Suddenly, an AIDS afflicted teenager, Julien, reaches up with frail arms and hugs her. He calls her Mama. Latrous' eyes grow wet.

'Here, we have saved thousands of lives,' she says, kissing Julien on the forehead. 'I feel so privileged. Not many people get to see what I see.'

Nobody's Children: Mogadishu, Somalia

February, 2002

Early morning, Mogadishu. The wet equatorial heat is rising from the chewed-up streets, and the gunmen are already working. Truckloads of militiamen, hanging off the backs of pick-up trucks, cruise the neighbourhoods of South Mogadishu. They chew quat, the bitter narcotic leaf imported from Kenya; they wave Kalashnikovs above their heads and stand defiantly in position behind anti-aircraft guns chained to the backs of the trucks.

The American marines used to call them *Skinnies*, and it still makes the gunmen laugh, because it makes them seem innocent and sweet, like a cappuccino at Starbucks, which they are not. They are young men, some of them boys. They wear dark, Gucci-style sunglasses, bandannas around their heads and homeboy gear – jeans slung low, T-shirts, flip-flops. Some of them are barely into their teens, their weapons bigger than their tiny frames, but they know how to shoot and kill and ambush and raid. *Figli di nessuni*, someone scrawled on a shot-up wall near the former Italian Cultural Centre. Nobody's Children.

'With the lack of government,' says General Ahmed Sahal Ali, who runs the Mogadishu prison, 'the militias are uncontrolled. At least three people are killed a day, wounded uncounted.'

But who cares? This is Somalia, a totally forgotten war, a forgotten country.

Still, this is what it looks like, smells like, sounds like; the pop of bullets is frequent. The smell of decay permeates through the haze of heat. The trash lies heaped up in a pile, smouldering, like an apocolyptic vision. A few children and veiled women wade through it, ankle-deep, searching for scraps of food. If you try to take away the trash, you get shot for it. My friend Abdi says someone from Unicef tried it once, but they tried to shoot him.

No one wants to get shot and no one wants to work for Unicef. Or any UN organisation for that matter – Somalia is too high-risk. Aid organisations are generally staffed by locals, who still get kidnapped or killed. 'It's OK for NGOs or diplomats to go in for a few days,' is how one regional aid worker puts it. 'But a permanent presence, forget it.' So the misery spreads.

Abdi is one of the *figli di nessuni*. He tells me a story. He's one of seventeen children. One day in 1995, he's casually walking down the street with a brother when he hears a bullet whizz by. He looks down, sees it's gone through his sleeve. *Lucky again*, he remembers thinking.

Then he notices his brother, no longer by his side.

The brother, who was seventeen, takes a few steps, stumbles and falls. Abdi tries to lift him. But the boy doesn't move. Abdi finally rolls him over. He sees the same bullet that went through his sleeve had cleanly entered his brother's heart.

Abdi tells me the story one night as a form of comfort. A

close friend, a war correspondent, had killed himself in Bolivia. I have contained myself all day and then burst into tears. Abdi tells me that in the midst of life we are in death. He gives me a cigarette lighter as a present, to cheer me up. Then, one by one, the hardened gunmen who have been sent to protect me shuffle up and clap me on the shoulder.

'We are all on that train, moving closer to death,' Abdi says. 'It's just that in Somalia, it happens so much faster.'

There is a war here, but not a war as we know it. Somalia is a failed state, driven by conflict.

'It is always dangerous here,' says one surgeon, Dr Sheikhdon Salad Cilmi, who struggles to keep a small hospital running with virtually no aid money. 'There is no law. There are no police. Kalashnikov is the rule here.'

Troops do not patrol the streets like in Kabul or Grozny; there are no real, defined front lines. There are no trenches or snipers posted on hilltop positions. But clan battles break out without warning, and Mogadishu is carved up by warlords, essentially into two fractured parts but, within those, dozens more frontlines.

Mogadishu Cathedral is destroyed and if you wander around there, sooner or later you get pinned down in a fire-fight between militias. The first foreigner, an Italian bishop, was murdered here in 1989 as President Ziad Barre's security forces spun wildly out of control. Then he was dug up and his teeth ripped out of his skull for gold.

The cathedral lies on the Green Line. From there, the city is divided into two, north and south, split between the militias of the Transitional Government (TNG) and the various warlord factions of the Samal and Sab clans and their numerous clan families and sub-clans, such as the Abgal

of North Mogidishu and the Habr Gedir of South Mogadishu. Battles begin quickly here, so you don't linger on the
streets. One minute, a fisherman proudly shows off a sixty
kilogram shark pulled from the Indian Ocean. Then the
stillness is shattered, people scatter. The rattle of machine
guns; civilians caught in crossfire; the hospital floods with
broken bodies. Doctors begin treating the wounded under
the trees because there are not enough beds. You look around
some days, at the utter chaos, and feel as though you have
landed on a planet inhabited by extras from a Mad Max film.

To reach this other world, you take an early morning
quat flight from Nairobi, slipping down between hemp bags
of the leaves. The real president of Somalia is quat, a pilot
told me. One and a half tonnes of quat come into Somalia
each day. Each sack sells for $200 to dealers, who then sell
small bundles, a day's worth, for $7. The Mogadishu port
and the airport are technically non-operational, but Musa
Suudi Yelehov, one of the most notorious warlords, con-
trols the armed positions that overlook them. So he gets lots
of quat.

While Musa Suudi's big guns scope out everything on the
horizon, the grizzled warlord prospers. From here, he can tax
quat and food exports. As the prime minister told me in a
tired voice one afternoon, 'There are so many people who
gain from the chaos here.' Musa Suudi, who is a member of
the government opposition, the Somali Reconciliation and
Restoration Council (SRRC), is one of them. Still, even he
admits Somalia is a disaster. 'Any terrorist can arrive here,'
he says, meaning Osama bin Laden. 'You're a witness. Did
you come here with a visa? There are no consulates, no
control. Anyone can get in, or get out.' He is right. In the
Bakara Market, I purchase a Somali passport for $20. It

takes under thirty minutes to fill out the paperwork. For an extra $30, I could have got a diplomatic one.

The TNG, described by Western diplomats as 'well-intentioned but weak', does not extend past Mogadishu, and the SRRC, who see themselves as the Northern Alliance was in Afghanistan, waiting to topple the Taliban, are viewed by many as warlord thugs. An umbrella group of several fractured parties, they are most visibly led by Hussain Farah Aideed, son of the notorious late Mohammed Farah Aideed.

There are two breakaway republics in the north, and a battle raging in the south, where TNG forces clash with the opposition. Islamic fundamentalist groups feed off the lawlessness and the only aid that comes in comes from the Arab world with a price tag on it: take this, pray to Allah, build an Islamic state. There is no justice system, no courts, no law. Somalia is a black hole on the map, a vaccum in the Horn of Africa, as well as being a humanitarian disaster.

Until September 11, however, Somalia was a distant disaster, someone else's problem. America was aware of al-Ittihad, the Islamic movement on the Pentagon's list of terrorist groups with links to al-Qaeda. But even the knowledge of Osama bin Laden having some foothold here was fairly irrelevant. It was too remote, too messy.

But in the past six months, Somalia has moved up on the foreign policy agenda. Such a vast political vaccum has left room for a radical Islamic movement to flourish. While it is believed that al-Ittihad was crushed in the early 1990s by Ethiopia, which has its own agenda for wiping out fundamentalism in the Horn of Africa – it shares a long border with Somalia – there are regional analysts who fear that by allowing Somalia to sink into chaos, we allow al-Ittihad and its satellite organisations to grow.

There is a feeling that Somalia could evolve into an Islamic state, ready to turn towards the only hand that is feeding it. And while Osama bin Laden would probably not find shelter here – as one Somali put it, 'We have no secrets here, he could never hide' – what is likely is that a radical, Taliban-like government could gain a foothold. As one Western diplomat put it, 'If you have an Islamic state, will they move beyond the borders? Somalia is a regional concern, but it's also a US concern.'

According to Andre Le Sage, an analyst who has been watching Somalia for a decade, the problem is more pressing. 'The threat of al-Ittihad is its potential,' he says. 'Potential to infiltrate weak Somali institutions in the future. Al-Ittihad *still* exists and there is still a cause. But there is nothing tangible to target but individual leaders.'

Targetting those leaders, or the entire country, is the dilemma. A certain block in US government, led by Paul Wolfowitz, believes that following the success of Afghanistan, a new template for global military action against terrorists is needed. Iraq is the primary target, but there are other concerns and Somalia is one of them. If it is created, it would involve American special forces and air power supported by local opposition. But while the TNG is unacceptable, for various reasons, pushing them out using the SRRC as a Northern Alliance is dangerous. 'The SRRC are composed largely of insidious warlords who at one time or another had relations with al-Ittihad,' says one Somali working closely with Washington.

Ken Menkhaus, an American expert on Somalia, also cautions against any kind of immediate intervention, including bombing campaigns, snatch operations or proxy wars against the TNG, 'which may appear to the rest of the world as *assassination sans frontières*'. He writes, 'If the United States is going to assume the role of judge, jury and executioner within the borders of other sovereign states, it will have to weather fierce criticism.'

So temporarily, the TNG will remain in place. Pushing them out at this vulnerable moment is not an option. 'It would simply fuel another civil war,' sighs Le Sage. 'Which would only push people further into the arms of al-Ittihad.'

In its darkest days – following the disaster of the American-led humanitarian mission which culminated in the 1993 street battle of Black Hawk Down – Somalia slipped into obscurity.

To Somalis, Black Hawk Down had its own consequences which Ridley Scott's film chose to ignore. In a run-down block of flats in central Mogadishu, a fourteen-year-old girl called Kifah, blinded by shrapnel from an American rocket, sits quietly in a chair. Even though her family hid when they heard the first whirr of the helicopters, Kifah lost her thirty-eight-year-old father, three brothers and a cousin. Her mother, Binti, survived with a broken leg and relatively little bitterness for someone whose family was wiped out in the course of a street battle.

Binti does say, however, that she was 'pleased' to hear that the American helicopters crashed that night and the pilots were dragged through the streets. 'If someone kills your children, that's how you feel,' she states. As for September 11, she shrugs. 'It's good for them to experience the pain we have felt.'

Before that, she did not hear much about Osama bin

Laden. Now she says, 'If he was around that night of the helicopters to help us, I would have supported him.'

After the withdrawal of UNISOM in 1995, Somalia faded from television screens. With a lack of any real funding from Western NGOs, the Muslim humanitarian aid organisations quickly moved in. Money from Saudi Arabia and Kuwait flooded the schools and the hospitals. It was inevitable that organisations such as al-Ittihad – listed by the US as one of the terrorist organisations linked to al-Qaeda – and, to a lesser extent, groups like al-Islah, al-Tablik and al-Takfir – all of whom call for an Islamic state – would mushroom across the country.

Like al-Qaeda, al-Ittihad inhabits a shadowy world. There is little tangible information about the leadership, but there are believed to be fifteen core leaders and an unknown number of rank and file. Sometime around 1995, Osama bin Laden was said to have paid a visit to northern Somalia and its training camps, although whether or not he got to Mogadishu is unclear. Others say he was in Somalia after the 1998 US Embassy bombing in Kenya.

The SRRC labels various government members – including President Abdulkassim Salad Hussein – as al-Ittihad. And while it is believed most active members have gone underground, Musa Suudi argues that their operations continue.

'Somalia is a feeding ground for these terrorists,' the warlord says from his headquarters, a villa surrounded by a small army in North Mogadishu. He says, 'The government is completely al-Ittihad. Abdulkassim is the head. They have direct relations with al-Qaeda.' Then he adds ominously, 'Who do you think was behind the eighteen US Marines that were killed?' The suggestion is that Islamic extremists were arming the warlords from the beginning.

During the civil war, Musa Suudi, a central player in the Mogadishu turf wars, was controlling Medina. His main battle was against Mohammed Farrah Aideed. 'It was my men, in fact, who killed Aideed,' he says proudly, hooting with laughter at the suggestion that Aideed died of natural causes.

It is difficult now to find people in Bakara market who profess support for bin Laden. Initially, in the early days post-September 11, there was condemnation of America as Islamic factions tried to mobilise public support. But soon after the bombing of Afghanistan began, 'they realised what a danger it was exposing themselves to American scrutiny'. According to Andre Le Sage, 'They saw the military reprisals to terrorism.'

Organisations like al-Islah, which hails itself as a society for businessmen, still operate openly, supporting Koranic school and harvesting Arab money to build mosques. Dr Ibrahim Disuqi, a softly spoken cardiologist and member of the Transitional National Authority, is not afraid to speak on behalf of al-Islah – whose name roughly translates to reconciliation or mediation – but he chooses his words carefully.

It's all harmless charity work, he intones, which is funded by generous Muslim backers. He does not mention their primary objective: to build an Islamic state. 'Building mosques is natural,' he says. 'Ten per cent of Somali children are now being educated. None of the schools are strictly Koranic. That is a myth.' He adds that 'the Arabicists have no political interest in Somalia.' Pause. 'Anyway, most Somalis regard themselves as Arabs.' As for Osama bin Laden in Somalia, he scoffs at the idea. 'Somalis talk too much, Osama could never hide here,' he says.

Still, with American ships patrolling the Kenyan–Somali

coast and observation planes circling the skies ahead, not to mention rumours of American land invasions, there is increased paranoia. Like Kabul after the Northern Alliance overran the Taliban, everyone is metaphorically shaving off their beards.

Al-Ittihad originally came into being as a military movement in the early days of the civil war, with a strategy of trying to build power by seizing key economic installations. At first, they tried to capture airports and administer towns with porous borders, such as Luuq and Dolo in the Gedo region. Here, arms and supplies could flood in, and they could court support from local clans. But when it became clear that they could not hold these towns, they began an alternative strategy. Like the Taliban, who also set about initially trying to 'clean up' a broken society, they consolidated their support base by setting up social services, healthcare and schools. 'But always with strings attached,' says Andre Le Sage.

Al-Ittihad then established themselves as protection for the business community, much in the way that the *camorra* operates in southern Italy. While the businessmen grew fat on money from the banana trade, the sugar trade, or simply *bagash* – the market fodder of plastic sheeting, flip-flops and other trinkets that make up the Somali household – they needed al-Ittihad for protection.

By 1994, al-Ittihad had affiliated themselves with the sharia courts. Their modus operandi was to infiltrate and take over weak public administrations. Thus, the businessmen and the traders found themselves under the common banner of an extreme Islamic faith, and one that overrode the rival clan system. Al-Ittihad had essentially become the Rotary Club of Somalia.

But according to Le Sage, al-Ittihad began losing power prior to September 11. In the wake of the creation of the TNG in Djibouti in August, 2000, they began to become politically marginalised. In towns such as El Waq, in the Gedo region, they no longer had the money to pay their militias and were forced to join forces with the clan militias, selling their technical equipment and weapons and moving back to Mogadishu.

Which still does not erase their threat.

'Somalia is a dangerous place to itself, to its neighbours and to the world, because it could easily be a terrorist breeding ground,' says Dr Sheikdon Salad Cilmi, a surgeon at Medican hospital, as he tries to dress the wound of a ten-year-old with abdominal gunshot wounds. 'Any terrorist who comes here can recruit as many people as they like because of the poverty. Mr bin Laden would get plenty of followers. Anyone he can feed.'

Merca, a languid, sultry coastal town with a flourishing banana trade, is a place renowned for beautiful prostitutes and rabid fundamentalism. Here, Mr bin Laden is still popular. There are even said to be Osama impersonators who dress and walk like him, in the fashion of Elvis impersonators.

One week after a seventy-year-old Swiss aid worker was gunned down by machine-gun fire in Merca, I sit in a café, drink a Coke and gaze upon the portrait of Osama bin Laden. His photograph is pinned on the wall underneath the late King Hussein of Jordan, and above a youthful Saddam Hussein. The owner of the café, Ali Musa, reverently calls Osama, 'Something for the Gods. All the most powerful nations on earth are looking for him, but no one can find him. He is working with God.'

Abu Bakar Shekil Ali, a twenty-seven-year-old local, calls bin Laden 'the hero of Islam'. Ali's got his own personal portrait of bin Laden, that he bought in Bakara market in Mogadishu for $1. He flashes it, and says, 'I love Osama because there is evil in the world and Osama does not allow aggression.' About the acts of aggression on September 11, Ali looks puzzled.

'That wasn't aggression,' he says. 'That was something right. An eye for an eye. Think of the suffering of the Palestinians.'

If the TNG see them as warlords, the SRRC on a good day see themselves as something far more noble – knights in shining armour ready to carry a bleeding Somalia off on horseback. On a bad day, they see themselves as a less efficient – if it is at all possible – Afghan Northern Alliance. Based in Baidoa in the south of the country, they include infamous leaders such as Hassan Mohammed Mur, aka General 'Red Shirt'; Hussein Aideed; and General Morgan, aka 'The Butcher of Hergeisa', who is responsible for levelling the northern city at huge civilian costs.

'It must be very clear that the SRRC are warlords, the people who ruined Somalia and waged war,' stresses Dr Ibrihim Dusuq from al-Islah.

Although they deny it, their operations appear to be based out of Addis, where they are tacitly backed by Ethiopian money and arms. Ethiopia does not recognise the TNG. Instead, the regional strongman throws its weight behind the SRRC which was founded in March, 2001, as a buffer against the threat of Islam.

'Ethiopia sees the TNG as a nest of Islamic extremists, another al-Qaeda,' says a diplomat in Addis. In return, the

TNG sees the SRRC as a tool of Ethiopia, who has long had an interest in the Somali borders. Of their relationship with Ethiopia, the SRRC will only admit to a 'security arrangement to rid the region of al-Ittihad'.

This comes from the most controversial, if not the strongest player in the SRRC, Hussein Aideed. Hussein is the son of the late warlord, Mohammed Farah Aideed. His son is the co-president of the SRRC and president of the United Somali Congress – his father's former party.

On a rainy weekend afternoon, Aideed answers the door of his dreary cottage at the Hotel Gion in Addis, wearing a starched shirt and tie. Outside, an Ethiopian wedding is in full swing, complete with women ululating and a band picking up tempo. Aideed makes the mock gesture of covering his ears. 'It's the wedding season now,' he says, annoyed.

His bodyguards linger in the shadows. Since he has taken up this high-profile position in the SRRC, and since he is his father's son, Aideed says he has suffered assassination attempts, the closest call being Mogadishu, May, 2001, when a battle broke out between his militiamen and his attackers. He got away, he says, just barely.

Aideed is tall and honed, with high cheekbones. The thirty-eight-year-old civil engineer speaks English and Italian, the result of an early education at the elite Vatican school in Mogadishu. He later graduated from Corvino High School and California State University, Long Beach, and served as a US Marine in the 1990s. He sees no irony in his being a soldier in the First Division California Marine Expeditionary Forces in Mogadishu while, at the same time, his father was being hunted down.

'There was no conflict of interest. I was trained to defend

the US,' he insists. 'We were soldiers, helping a small country, delivering food.'

One wonders what his father would make of him now, an advert for the American way. His wife, mother and children are still in California (one detractor claims his wife collects welfare there), and he calls his youth there 'the best days of my life'. Indeed, listening to Aideed is like hearing the American involvement in Somalia rewritten.

His father – a former diplomat and advisor to Ziad Barre, who helped oust the dictator in 1991, thus sparking the Somali civil war – did not steal humanitarian aid. UNISOM soldiers were not dragged bleeding through the streets after being gunned down by his men. 'My father was a historic myth,' Aideed says. 'The most respected military man. Even his enemies respected him. He opposed Islam in Somalia. He would oppose it now.'

Perhaps, but at the height of his father's powers in Somalia, 300 people were dying each day of starvation. The aid that arrived was quickly 'liberated' by clan checkpoints, and the money pocketed by warlords such as Aideed. The UNISOM forces, which began arriving in December 1992 as part of a New World Order, a political experiment, quickly found themselves embroiled in a war against fanatics. The battle of Black Hawk Down was a failed attempt to try to snatch-and-grab Aideed Sr.

That negative image of his father, Aideed claims, was fostered by the UN, in particular by Boutros-Boutros Ghali, whom he loathes. The former Secretary General is an Arab who had other intentions for Somalia, he says.

'The UN targeted my father,' he says bitterly. 'Not the United States.' Somalia today, he argues, is being hacked up by Arab states who want to enforce Wa'habism.

The SRRC are the only option, he says. Controlling eighty-five per cent of the country, they have the public support. He estimates 'thousands' of troops are at his disposal. 'We don't think in terms of troops; they are more militia, like the movie *Patriot* starring Mel Gibson,' he explains. Their main agenda, he says, is to squash al-Ittihad.

As part of his mission, he prepares endless drafts to the American embassy in Addis and the CIA, as well as producing documents linking various individuals – most of them well-placed TNG members – to the terrorist organisation.

'The threat is not those old men running the TNG,' he sniffs. 'The threat is al-Ittihad. Go and look in Mogadishu. Look at them teaching eleven and twelve-year-olds in the *madrassas* about the jihad.'

Aideed is fond of dropping frequent euphemisms from Machiavelli's *The Prince*, and appears confident that he is indispensible to the Americans. At the same time, the Americans do not see him in quite the same light.

'This is a man who is a primitive smooth talker,' says one diplomatic source in Addis. 'It was clear he was not going to be the solution.' Another analyst scoffs: 'He was never going to be able to fill his father's shoes.' A diplomat in Nairobi calls him a 'lightweight'. His own cousin, a member of the TNG's cabinet, says in a condescending, honey-dripped voice, 'Ah, Hussein. Isn't he a handsome boy?'

Meanwhile, in Mogadishu, in the midst of what Aideed calls 'the nest of al-Ittihad', is Abdulkassim Salad Hussein, the President of the TNG. A Soviet-trained biologist and a former minister in the regime of dictator Ziad Barre, he was appointed president during the Djibouti conference.

A natural linguist, he switches easily from Somali to English to French to Italian and, although I did not hear it, Russian. Although the SRRC accuses him of being in the heart of al-Ittihad (Musa Suudi even supplied documents allegedly linking him to the organisation), one American diplomat described him and the TNG as ineffectual but 'well-intentioned'.

Abdulkassim's view is a standard TNG line: the warlords have destroyed his country, looted it, caused the disintegration of all state institutions. He believes the United States 'ignoring' Somalia after the UNISOM withdrawl was a grave mistake. He does not recognise the SRRC, other than as a bunch of warlord stooges backed by Ethiopia.

'The SRRC does not exist,' he says simply. 'It is the Ethiopians.' His cronies, seated around him, guffaw.

As for terrorism, the only terrorists are the warlords. 'I am a Sunni Muslim,' he says. 'We do not believe in extremism. We even forbid the killing of animals or the cutting down of trees.' He simply laughs at the al-Ittihad charges against him.

Then, suddenly, he drops the defensive tone. He sounds almost vulnerable when he talks about the chaos that Somalia has descended into. He pleads for help, saying that Somalia has something to offer: huge resources that could be managed in a free market economy. But first, steps must be taken.

'We must disarm the militias,' he says. 'We need the international community and that means the United States. If they really want to fight terrorism, they should help Somalia and the TNG. Otherwise, it will be difficult to fight terrorism.'

As a parting note, he throws in a warning: 'If Somalia is divided and insecure, then we will have a breeding ground for terrorism. Al-Ittihad may appear dormant, but they could easily resort to violence.'

The sky has darkened when I leave the president's villa. My own freelance militia – who cost $5,000 for two weeks' protection – are waiting outside patiently, high on quat. Stoned or not, their protection is essential, especially after dark; when – if it is at all possible – the broken-down city becomes even more spooky and lawless.

What has been done in Somalia post-September 11 is marginal. Al-Barakat, the bank and the main telecommunications facility in Somalia (and, according to Aideed, one of the 'places where Islamists dwell') has been closed down because of alleged links to al-Qaeda. But all that has done is fuel resentment amongst the locals who have lost their jobs and their ability to send emails and use their mobile phones.

Conferences on Somalia are frequently called, symposiums organised. Privately, analysts have little hope that it will achieve much. Twelve reconstruction conferences have already failed.

'About the only thing Somalia has going for it at the moment,' admits one diplomat, 'is a willingness to get going.'

While much focus has been on the formal structures of the TNG – such as the cabinet, the parliament and even the constitution which the Swiss are helping to re-write – no one is focusing on the bigger issue of territorial control. What is not being looked at is how a dysfunctional bureaucracy such as the TNG can survive in the violent atmosphere of Mogadishu. At the moment, their entire future rides on their ability to service the interests of the Somali business cartel. Without them, they sink.

In 2000, when General Tommy Franks visited the region searching for al-Qaeda, Somalia briefly hit the headlines again. But to most Somalis, it doesn't make sense. The threat of reprisals hanging over the heads of the Somalis does, in some ways, make the country uninhabitable to al-Qaeda. So does establishing a quarantine around Somalia – stepping up intelligence-gathering flights to monitor al-Ittihad movements – in addition to forging strong regional agreements with neighbours such as Ethiopia and Kenya. In other words, to limit Somalia's potential to be used for terrorism.

But it does not stop the clan warfare or the humanitarian disaster. Everyone knows that America, still wounded from its eighteen dead soldiers, will never really return to help this dying place. The question is, who will?

Abdusalam Omer, a Somali UN consultant puts it this way: 'The only people who can defeat the warlords are the fundamentalists. And it would have to be a unifying force, like the Saudis.' Even those who don't support an Islamic state will support them, he says, to rid the country of the warlords.

'It wouldn't be a big deployment,' he says with a straight face. 'Five Apaches could wipe out the warlords.'

Until then, Somalia bleeds. Sheik don Salad, the surgeon from Medina Hospital, spoke for many ordinary Somalis when he said in a defeated voice, 'Afghanistan was lucky. They got the intervention of the international community.'

Somalia will not. But it will unravel, although how is difficult to predict. Over lunch in a lush Nairobi garden, one Somali sighed. 'There should be no illusions of Somalia solving its problems alone,' he said.

And we are leaving it alone. Meanwhile, Abdi keeps getting older, keeps dodging the bullets. In 2003, I managed to get him a week-long scholarship with the Reuters Foundation in London, thinking it might get him out of the country, maybe set him on the trail of a new life.

Abdi was ecstatic. Such excitement! He telephoned me from a call centre in Mogadishu, and with borrowed mobile phones belonging to the odd aid worker who passed through. He wondered what to pack, and what kind of food would he eat? It was the first step towards a new life.

Except it never happened. Abdi managed to get to Kenya, and then was meant to go on to London. But the Kenyan authorities would not give him a visa. Somalia does not really exist and no one would take responsibility for him, this child of nobody. Reuters and I both tried to help but it was senseless. A mass of red tape and restrictions; laws and customs officials who gave us a steely 'no'. Abdi stayed in Nairobi for a week then his money ran out and he flew back to Mogadishu.

I hear from him from time to time, though it grows less frequent. The last time he said he was surprised he was still alive.

Hope Wanted: AIDS in India

August, 2004

One night in April, 1986, Suniti Solomon, M.D., an American-trained microbiologist working for the Indian government in Madras, received a late-night phone call. She assumed it was an emergency for her husband, a cardiac surgeon. But the call was for her. And it was one that would alter not only the course of her life but ultimately the future of India.

On the phone was Nalini Ramamoorthy, Solomon's research assistant at the Madras Medical College. For six months, ever since the news of AIDS had burst upon the international medical horizon, the two women had been hunting for evidence of HIV in India. That night Ramamoorthy confirmed that six prostitutes – sex workers, as they are more correctly called – were HIV-positive. None of the women had had sex with a foreign client. The implication was clear: the disease was well-rooted inside the country.

Solomon is now sixty-five years old and runs the Y. R. Gaitonde Centre for AIDS Research and Education (YRG CARE), the largest AIDS clinic in Southern India. She has devoted the past two decades not only to research but also to enlightening the Indian public about AIDS, trying to destroy a stigma so fierce that even doctors and healthcare workers often refuse to treat HIV sufferers. In a country where a televised kiss is shocking, it's difficult to get people to talk about sex, let alone AIDS.

The AIDS problem in India is now catastrophic, not just for Asia but for the entire world. According to the Joint United Nations Programme on HIV/AIDS (UNAIDS), India ranks second only to South Africa in the number of people infected by HIV. There are an estimated 5.1 million people in India infected with HIV, the virus that causes AIDS. Of that figure, approximately 1.9 million are women aged fifteen to forty-nine. And those may be low estimates – some experts believe the real number of cases now exceeds South Africa's. Because of the stigma, many people are too ashamed to come out and report their illness.

The situation is so grave that on the eve of the Indian elections last April, the *Economist* reported, 'Indians start voting next week to choose a new government. Its first priority should be AIDS.' At the XV International AIDS Conference in Bangkok last July, AIDS in India was one of the main topics. (Sonia Gandhi, president of the Indian National Congress Party, was a featured speaker at the closing ceremony.) And according to Judith Auerbach, Ph.D., the vice-president of public policy for the American Foundation for AIDS Research (amfAR), 'With India poised to overtake China as the most populous nation on Earth in the next thirty years, its AIDS epidemic has the potential to jeopardise the stability of the region, indeed the world.'

World economic growth is increasingly dependent on India, Auerbach points out. Solomon feels this oppressive weight on her slight shoulders. At one time, she was named India's 'Woman of the Year', and Richard Gere publicly called her a hero, but Solomon still gets teary when she talks of the HIV-infected children who are left abandoned at her clinic, or mothers who beg her 'to kill their AIDS-infected son, who makes the room smell'. Hers is the sort of work for which one never really feels a sense of accomplishment. Since the virus was discovered, Solomon says, she has finished only one quarter of what she set out to do.

After her AIDS discovery in 1986, Solomon was awarded a grant from the Indian Council of Medical Research. She spent a decade tracking the virus, and one of her most important findings was its presence in pregnant women who had a single partner. But during those ten years, the virus continued to spread, and today in Chennai (formerly known as Madras) alone there are an estimated 20,000 HIV-infected people. The number of HIV pregnancies is also steadily increasing. Sometimes Solomon thinks she should have spent her time on the streets instead of in the lab.

'I wish I had been out talking to people,' she says wistfully. 'In terms of awareness or the discrimination of HIV sufferers, we have not come far.' She remembers one night in 1996 driving for hours around Chennai with an HIV-positive woman who was in labour. No hospital or clinic would accept her to deliver the child. Solomon finally got her admitted, only after 'neglecting' to tell the staff at one clinic that the woman was positive.

The disease has not yet reached a plateau. Instead, there is fear that within ten years, the number of HIV sufferers will be five times what it is now. Particularly vulnerable are women. At the Bangkok conference, attention was drawn to the fact that 'as the AIDS pandemic spreads, it has assumed a woman's face, with almost six out of ten new HIV infections occurring in women.' (Auerbach says women are two to eight times more likely to contract HIV from men than the other way around, in part because of the greater vulnerability to infection of the female genital tract.) But there are other reasons why, worldwide, women are more susceptible to AIDS, a heady combination of social and physiological factors. Cultural practices such as early marriage and gender discrimination contribute to women's economic dependence and their lack of resources to protect themselves. In India, middle-class married women are particularly at risk: while they may be monogamous, their husbands are often not. Men have sex with commercial sex workers, and married couples do not generally use condoms.

'The painful irony in India is that marriage and monogamy can actually increase a woman's vulnerability to the HIV infection,' says Auerbach. Here it is estimated that eighty per cent of HIV is spread by heterosexual, mainly married couples, and Solomon reports that ninety per cent of her patients are married with a single partner. And despite the wide swathe the disease cuts across all levels of society, the subject is still a huge taboo. 'Rich people get it,' Solomon says. 'Actors, lawyers, doctors get it.' Last year, two HIV-positive children were kicked out of their school in Kerala State, even though Kerala has the most progressive sex-education programmes in India. 'The problem is that pro-minent people who have it don't talk about it,' she says. 'We don't have a Rock Hudson in India.'

This is a worrying concept, particularly for women. India is still a deeply traditional society. Women usually marry by the time they are eighteen, and most are virgins. The mar-riages are more than likely arranged, and the man, who customarily marries at an older age, will probably have visited one or more of the 2 million sex workers who operate throughout the country. If he has the virus, he is still unlikely to wear a condom.

'A sex worker can tell a client to use a condom, but when it comes to family, an ordinary Indian woman must oblige her husband's wishes,' Solomon says.

One sweltering summer morning, I arrive early at the Madras Medical Mission to see Solomon lecture on how to prevent transmission between pregnant HIV women and their infants. There's an ob-gyn trade fair going on outside the auditorium (start your own sperm bank!), and the audience is packed with mainly female doctors, who listen attentively. Solomon is a softly spoken woman, but when she stands on the podium in a neat navy-and-gold sari, her dark hair carefully brushed into a flip, she speaks with a sense of urgency. 'These are the dilemmas faced by Indian women today,' she says, using a projector to highlight her points.

    arranged marriage
    wife faithfully submits
    man does not want children (knows he has hiv)
    but society frowns on 'barren' woman
    she gets pregnant
    hiv
    the woman is voiceless

There's silence in the room; then people ask questions. Solomon instructs them on how much nevirapine – the drug that reduces transmission between mother and child by fifty per cent if given during labour – to administer, and doggedly insists that HIV women must not breast-feed.

'There is HIV in breast milk,' she says staunchly. 'They must use formula.'

Later, she tells me this is not so easy to ensure. 'It's OK for an HIV doctor with a good salary to use formula to feed her baby, but for a woman from the slums, it's too expensive.' When I comment later on the surprising number of women obstetricians in the room, she regards me carefully.

'Yes, but if I asked how many of them would deliver an HIV woman's baby, none of them would do it,' she says.

Solomon comes from a privileged background – her father ran a successful leather business – and in 1994, her elder brother started a foundation that helped her open the YRG clinic, which is named after her father. Housed in a former leprosy unit, it has so far treated 17,000 patients and conducts extensive research as well as counselling. When I walk through the wards, I see very sick people – mostly men tended by their wives, who probably also have the disease – but these patients are the lucky ones. Those who can't get to a place like YRG go to government hospitals, where doctors see up to 1,500 patients a day and where they are subjected to moralising lectures.

'Women with HIV who live in the slums are really isolated from society,' Sethu Lakshmi, an ethnography coordinator at YRG, tells me. 'There's no support from their immediate or extended family. If they aren't educated, there's no way of earning a living. They have no access to HIV treatment.'

Rochelle D'Souza Yepthomi, an aide who works with Solomon, says that the burden of care in the family always falls on the woman. If both the man and the woman are sick, she will care for him and often give him her share of medication, rendering her own utterly ineffective.

'There is an unwillingness to help a woman who's going to

die anyway,' Yepthomi says. 'They don't see her as a bread-winner; they see her as a liability. Women are not as empowered here as in other parts of the world.'

There is some work being done on a grass-roots level. Groups like the Positive Women Network, founded in 1998 in Chennai, now has branches throughout India. They offer counselling, training and support groups, mainly to lower-income women. In theory it sounds good, but the reality is often not that effective. When I set out to visit their offices, I have trouble finding them: they are located in the back of a crowded tenement block and there is no sign on the door. The Positive Women Network's brightly coloured brochure tells women, 'We dream of a life not secluded; free from stigma and discrimination; with all rights intact.' But one of the project managers tells me that when they send out letters to members, they don't mention the name of the organisation. 'If the woman can't read, the postman must read it out loud, and then everyone would know her situation.'

Lavanya Vijayshankar, a social worker for PWN, explains to me that an HIV-positive woman in India has no rights. 'Often respondents feel that human rights or legal rights are entities beyond their comprehension,' reports a survey from the Indian Network of Positive People. 'Most respondents suffered from low self-esteem due to lack of information about human rights and life after infection.'

Even death brings complications, Vijayshankar says. 'If her husband dies, the woman loses all rights of joint property and is usually, quite unfairly, blamed for his HIV. Her dowry is not returned.' Legal battles take too long to contemplate, and as Vijayshankar wearily points out, most of her patients are illiterate.

'We've got to fight against fear,' she tells me, closing a

large stack of files that she has on her desk. 'The information given out to society is that you get HIV, you die. We've got to teach women that you have to be careful: even when you go into marriage, you have to be careful.'

A few days after I meet Solomon, I visit an orphanage for HIV children, run by an unusual Indian couple, Patrick and Victoria Samuel, who say they are working for a Christian organisation based in Omaha called Word Made Flesh.

The Samuels are half-dressed when we arrive at 2.00 p.m., and furious that Alex, the photographer, and I have arrived without an appointment. As they pull on rumpled, dirty clothes behind a screen, I take stock of the place: it is filthy; the children are barefoot, dressed in rags. Three dogs bark shrilly. The sitting room is strewn with papers, old books, mouldy clothes and half-eaten food. Containers of dirty water serve as the water supply. It is appalling.

The couple refuse to answer questions about the children's healthcare and order us to leave the property, but not before giving me a pamphlet to send money 'to the children', addressed to 'The Director' – i.e., Mr Samuel. His last words express concern that the neighbours would find out he was housing sick children.

The following day, I drive to the outskirts of Chennai, to the Community Health Education Society (CHES) orphanage, which houses thirty-three children, from nine months to fourteen years old. All but one are suffering from HIV. After my experience with the Samuels, the CHES orphanage is a pleasant surprise. The smell of good food drifts through a room flooded with sunlight. The children are dressed in colourful clothes, and the older ones diligently help feed their younger companions. There is much laughing and hugging with the four babysitters. In a corner a group of infants are taking naps on the floor. Some lie on their stomachs; others are curled around pieces of vivid sari cloth.

Then I see Dilli Babu.

I assume Dilli Babu is around nine months old, but, in fact, he is four years old. Stick limbs, covered in boils and open sores, jut from his cotton shorts, which dwarf his emaciated body. He weighs no more than twelve pounds. His head is large, his hair falling out so that only a few wisps cover his scalp. Unlike the other babies, Dilli Babu sleeps fitfully, trying to find a comfortable position for his knobbly spine. Natarajan Rajeshkannan, a volunteer with CHES, whispers that Dilli Babu is terminal, 'in the last stages of his life'. I find it hard to comprehend that a four-year-old is in the last stages of his life. I find it hard to comprehend a four-year-old weighs less than my own six-month-old baby. I have seen many sick and disturbed children all over the world, victims of war and disaster, and have visited many AIDS hospices in Africa, but it is harrowing to watch Dilli Babu struggle to breathe. It is the moment when I really understand what AIDS does to a human being, and how enormous the problem is in India.

Dilli Babu wakes, opening expressionless eyes, and motions for water. He drinks with a shaky hand. It takes him forty-five minutes to chew a slice of white bread. When one of the babies tries to pull his food dish away, Dilli Babu makes weak yelps, like a bird. He cannot stand on his stick legs. The virus has affected his hearing. When I call his name several times, he turns to me and regards me with the air of a very weary old man.

'He doesn't have the energy to show his emotions,' Rajeshkannan explains. I ask why the other children leave Dilli Babu alone in a corner. Do they sense that he is going to die?

Rajeshkannan thinks for a moment. 'No. He just likes loneliness.'

The day before, I had sat with the CHES director, an efficient paediatrician named Pinagapany Manorama, M.D., who told me that most of the children are not aware of their status until they are about fourteen – if they live that long. She talked about stigma, fear and how medical personnel need to learn how to touch AIDS sufferers without fearing they will catch the virus.

She talked about life expectancy for AIDS children. 'When we started, they told us they could live five years,' she said. 'Now we have some kids who have been with us fifteen years.' But most of all, she talked about how India desperately needed to face up to the AIDS problem in order to overcome it.

Then she showed me a video called *The Last Minutes of a Dying Flower*. It was a stark, home-made film of an eight-year-old boy dying of AIDS. Tubes ran in and out of his nose. White stuff came out of his mouth. In the background, mournful Hindi music played. It was the AIDS equivalent of a snuff film – horrible, but horribly effective. Manorama told me she hopes to get it released on Indian TV. She hopes it will shock the public out of their fear, their unwillingness to take responsibility for the spread of the disease. She thinks that if they watch this, instead of Bollywood musicals, it might start educating people. She showed me the end of the video. Should children get AIDS? it read in large black and white letters. Are we not responsible for this?

The big question is, what can be done to halt this epidemic? Experts agree that considerable resources must be devoted not only to drugs and to treatment but also to raising awareness. 'Preventing new infections is the only truly effective way to stem the emerging epidemic in India,' says Auerbach of amfAR. 'HIV prevention, including educational interventions and male and female condom distribution, must be a priority.'

The Bill & Melinda Gates Foundation has committed $200 million to HIV prevention in India. But with the rapidly rising rate of infection, India also has to improve its healthcare structure, produce low-cost drugs and train doctors. In a country that spends $10 per capita per year on healthcare – and less than six cents per person on AIDS research – that's asking a lot. Also, as Vijayshankar points out, certain sectors of the population are extremely hard to reach: for example, HIV-positive women from the slums. One afternoon, I accompanied Geeta, the midwife at YRG, on a home visit to one of her patients, a nineteen-year-old woman called Raj, who had given birth nine days before. Raj was raped when she was thirteen by her brother-in-law, who infected her with HIV. Despite that, she married a man who did not have the disease, and she got pregnant, delivering by Caesarean section. During labour she – and later the infant – was given nevirapine to reduce the risk of transmission.

Geeta was concerned that Raj's neighbours – who don't know she is infected with HIV – would grow suspicious if foreigners visited her, so she gave us stethoscopes, and we pretended to be doctors. Raj lived on a squalid street, and her home lay over an open sewer and up four flights of narrow stairs. She and her husband, who sometimes worked as a street cleaner, lived in a small, stiflingly hot room with one little window near the roof.

Raj lay on a mattress on the concrete floor, with her baby, who was still unnamed, covered in a pink towel. There was a small gas stove in the room, some clothes and bedding piled on open shelves, and a plastic bag of used baby clothes, which Raj proudly showed off. There was also a baby bottle and a tin of formula, on which 'mother's milk is best' was written in Hindi.

Raj had been firmly told not to breast-feed. But formula costs a lot, and her neighbours keep asking her why she is not feeding her baby herself. As Geeta snaps on rubber gloves to remove Raj's stitches, the young woman wonders out loud how the couple will get by, feeding their daughter. 'We'll manage,' she finally says. Her daughter can't be tested to see if she has HIV until she is eighteen months old, and Raj is hoping that she has not passed on the disease. 'She's so tiny,' she keeps saying, stroking the baby's cheek, 'so little'.

But Raj, who has accepted her disease and has acted responsibly giving birth, is a rare exception. Sethu Lakshmi had told me that the biggest obstacle for workers in the slums is denial. 'Most of them won't come to be tested, even if the test is free and anonymous,' she says. 'They just can't accept what happens. To an Indian in the slums, HIV means you are immoral. And that you will die.'

Another section of the population that is essential to reach is the truckers, who are believed to be the main transmitters of the virus, along with sex workers. Most of us live in countries where much of our freight is delivered by air or rail, but in India, truck routes are the lifeline of the country. Until you've seen an Indian truck-stop, it is difficult to understand what a huge part of the culture this is. There are an estimated 5 million truck drivers who race up and down the subcontinent, serving every kind of industry. And the HIV virus also runs up and down these truck routes as truckers and sex workers spread the virus north to south, east to west.

One night, as a gentle rain slicks the road, I drive to Red Hills, a truck-stop an hour outside of Chennai on the Kolkata highway. The Gates Foundation recently gave millions to a trucking-education project dubbed 'Healthy Highways', and a social worker takes me to a kind of flophouse where the men rest between road trips. The place reeks of curry and unwashed flesh, and men lie on the floor, sleeping, playing cards and watching Hindi DVDs.

We climb up an unlit staircase until we reach a small room at the top. It's an office with logbooks from counselling sessions and cartoons of men putting on condoms. 'A lot of the men don't know how to use them,' the embarrassed social worker says. 'We have to tell them that the penis must be erect.' He also says that a prostitute takes the risk of losing a customer if the man refuses to use one. There is always another sex worker he can go to who won't insist, he tells me.

We next walk down a muddy alley to a small stall selling sweets, magazines and toiletries. There is a packet of condoms, costing one rupee – about two cents. A prostitute charges around fifty rupees – $1. Has anyone bought condoms today? I ask the man behind the counter. He flushes and shakes his head.

Many of the men at the flophouse will probably go out to the highway and spend time with a sex worker before getting back on the road. Some of them will have heard of AIDS, some may not. Because many of the truckers won't take the responsibility, it is often up to the women to practice safe sex.

For the 2 million sex workers, this means a total re-education. Many are concerned about losing business, but others now realise that it is a matter of life – their own life – or death. In Kolkata, for instance, the Sonagachi Project is led by sex workers to pass information about the infection and ways to access care. The women discuss power relations and negotiating techniques to encourage clients to use condoms. The group sessions sometimes include regular clients.

But what about the ones who already have the disease? They are the modern-day equivalent of the untouchables. I drive out to Pallavaram, on the outskirts of Chennai, to a bungalow housing a dozen HIV-positive former sex workers. It is run by Zonta Resource Centre, which was founded in 1990 by three Chennai women as a refuge for women who had no other place to go. One of the founders is a gynaecologist who introduces herself as 'Dr Mrs Ida Lobo'. Born in Zanzibar, then part of British East Africa, in 1927, she speaks in a clipped British accent reminiscent of the days of the Raj.

On the trip to see the 'children', as she calls them, she tells me about how difficult it was growing up in those days as a woman, struggling to get educated. Widowed at the age of forty-seven, she raised her five children alone. She now devotes herself to caring for these women and speaks about the faults of governmental care for AIDS sufferers with a passion and anger I have not yet heard.

When we arrive, the women rush forward with great excitement. 'Children! Say your prayers!' Lobo says bossily, sitting down like a pasha in front of them. The women are originally from Chennai but were taken by pimps when they were ten and eleven years old to Mumbai. When they were discovered to have HIV, they were discarded both by the pimps and by their own families.

'So we gave them a place where they could live peacefully, and eat nutritious food and feel safe,' Lobo says. The 'children' come forward and show their 'medical boxes' – plastic cases full of brightly coloured pills and Ayurvedic powders. Lobo explains each of their individual problems:

one is deaf – mute; one is nearly blind; one ate a forbidden curry and had to be rushed to the hospital ('we almost lost her; their stomachs just can't take spicy food'); another died the week before. Most of the women have TB, jaundice and constant diarrhoea. I ask Lobo how long most have; she tells me in extremely lucky cases they have ten or fifteen years, maximum.

As the women scurry around, excited to have a visitor from the outside world, Lobo suddenly breaks into a contralto, a song from her childhood: ' "Bless this house, O Lord we pray./Make it safe, by night and day./Bless these walls, so firm and stout,/ Keeping want and trouble out." '

I think the irony of 'Bless This House' is lost on the 'children' who sit gaping at her and me. They remind me of teenagers in a girls' boarding school. I ask if they miss men or just a normal life where they can live and work freely.

'They do,' says Lobo cheerfully. 'Sometimes they climb a wall. Then we find them by the highway, starving. No one wants them. They end up coming back.' When we leave, Raymond, Lobo's son, who drove us to the home, gives me some of the embroidered hankies that the girls made as a gift.

'It's something they do to pass the time,' he says. 'Because they know they are going to pass away. They all know it.'

Dr Solomon knew she wanted to become a doctor when she was four years old and was given a vaccination for smallpox. 'I asked my father what it was, and he showed me pictures of what smallpox could do without that vaccine,' she says, 'I decided then and there I wanted to give injections. That was my dream.' But one Sunday morning, I meet her at her spacious home for tea and ask her if the weight of her task ever feels unbearable. In India, it is estimated that two adults become infected with HIV every minute. How can she possibly fight a statistic like that? The doctor is usually an optimistic person – she often talks of drug trials and therapeutic vaccines that bring the viral load down to an undetectable level – but at this moment, she sighs. She's wearing a gold and white sari that catches the light, and as we talk she's trying to calm her hyperactive two-and-a-half-year-old golden retriever, Lara. 'I tell Lara everything, all the sad stories,' she says. She begins to tell a few of them: about babies being left on the doorstep of her clinic; about suicides and rapes; about women being turned out on the street. But she also tells me about AIDS babies being adopted and brought to America, and sex education in schools growing, and young people being much more aware than when she herself first stood before them and talked about condoms and AIDS.

We walk to her small garden, with a lily pond filled with dark green water; I ask her if she ever feels like giving up. She says no, but there are days that are harder than most. 'When it comes to individuals, you feel hopeless,' she says. 'Poverty. They don't have food – how can we give them drugs?'

During my time in Chennai, I saw many people and places that brought back the horror and shame of AIDS in India. But there was one woman in particular who struck me because she seemed to be an Indian Everywoman. She had a job she loved, she was a mother, she was middle class and worried about her weight, her children and her complexion. The only difference between her and me is that she is HIV-positive – she caught the virus from her husband – and she knows that some time in the near future, she will die.

Latha is twenty-eight, with skin the colour of coffee and long, thick eyelashes. She's educated and from a wealthy family. She was a nineteen-year-old virgin when she married a man from a similar background to hers. He was her first and only partner, and he gave her HIV. We meet at her office, and she asks me not to mention where she works and to please change her name. After she fetches us iced water, she returns to the room and locks the door. She sits very close to me and speaks in a barely audible whisper. 'If people knew I had HIV, I would be discriminated against,' she says. 'It's still shameful.'

She tells me about when she discovered her husband had AIDS and how she begged him to use a condom to protect her. He refused. She tells me how he continued going to prostitutes after their marriage and how painful it was for her and how ashamed she felt when he laughingly told relatives, 'She doesn't like sex, so I have to go to sex workers.'

She has a daughter who is 'thankfully, negative', whom she adores. But Latha is aware – even though her CD4 (immune cell) count is now above average – that she probably has a limited time on earth to spend with her. Still, she wants the time she has left to be better. One day, she gathered courage and left her husband. Her own family took her back, which is rare. When her husband died, she said, she did not feel sadness, only relief. This spring, she married again. Her new husband is also HIV-positive, and they were introduced by friends. It may sound like a macabre sitcom, but in a culture that still relies on matchmaking, it was a perfect solution. Latha says her new husband caught his HIV from his wife, who died last year. Although he would love to have a child, both of them feel too responsible to risk transmitting the disease to an infant. Latha's daughter is still young, and she does not know what her father died from, or what her mother's sickness is. Latha is not sure how she will tell her or when. But she is adamant that she will tell her one thing, and this one thing is a small step on the ladder to preventing AIDS. 'When it comes time for her to get married,' Latha says, 'I am going to tell her to marry a man that she loves.' She drops her voice and smiles slightly for the first time. 'And when she is a little older, I am going to tell her about condoms.'

Latha was a small ray of light in a dismal landscape. But, a few months after I left India, more darkness: word came through from the CHES orphanage that Dilli Babu had breathed 'his last breath'. His closest surviving relative, a maternal uncle, refused to claim his AIDS-ravaged body.

'Please do pray for him,' wrote Dr Manorama, 'that his soul rests in peace along with his mother and father.'

THREE: PRIVATE WARS

Tough Love

December, 2003

On holiday recently, a friend's ten-year-old son was given a toy gun so well constructed, it could have been the twin of the Magnum my husband, Bruno, keeps at our house in the Ivory Coast. It's been under the bed since a violent coup d'état broke out in September, 2002. We both hate the gun in the same way we hate the six-inch steel door that separates our bedroom from the rest of the house – the door people jokingly call the 'rape door'.

I watched as Bruno pulled the small boy aside and said quietly, 'Be very careful of that gun. It's a very powerful thing.' Then, pausing, he added, 'I've seen people die from guns.' It was a strong thing to say, but it's true. Bruno and I, both reporters, were the only people in the room who had actually seen people die from bullets, or suffering from terrible injuries – children crying in agony, their intestines ripped apart; women shot in the knees by snipers. All of this is as much a part of our collective memory as the moment we both fell in love.

Bruno and I met in Sarajevo in 1993. We both had other

partners at home, but we fell for each other the way people do in war zones: hard. We parted, miserably, a few months later, but not before he had hiked for two days with Kurdish Peshmerga guerrillas to find a working telephone line to send me a love letter by fax. For five years, we had no contact because we felt it was best to forget each other.

But in 1998, I was given an assignment in Algeria and we met again by accident. That encounter would set in motion a love affair that would play itself out over five different continents, a dozen different conflict zones and the vast space of time. Thank God the mobile phone had just been made accessible to the general public.

It was me who started it again. I had called Bruno before I left for Algeria, breaking our wall of silence, to get the names of some contacts. He sounded sad when he heard my voice. He told me that he had just left his long-term girlfriend. Three days later, while I was sitting in the faded dining room of the St George Hotel in Algiers, where General Eisenhower had based his desert campaign during World War II, Bruno walked through the door. We stayed up all night, talking, in a perfumed rose garden.

Our official love affair began, but we weren't living together and we were working in different places so, for the next five years, we were mostly apart. When we were together, it was either in Paris at his apartment in the Marais, or in a war zone when we were lucky enough to be posted at the same time. But it didn't always work out like that. We spent a lot of time and a lot of money communicating on satellite phones. Even so, we managed to speak several times a day, always in the morning and always before we fell asleep at night. And we never went more than a month without seeing each other, no matter how far apart in the world we both were. It involved an inordinate amount of juggling, but we did it. I remember flying extraordinary routes, for example Iraq to London via Senegal, to meet him in obscure places, even for a few days. But it was always worth it.

In 1999, the war in Kosovo broke out. We were separated – I following KLA soldiers, Bruno in northern Albania. For three terrifying days in May, my unit came under fierce aerial bombardment. Many of the soldiers were killed. I slept in a ditch, carried the wounded and mopped up blood. I had no communication with the outside world as the Kosovar commander banned me from using my satellite phone: he was afraid I would report how many of his men had been killed.

Bruno, ten hours' drive south, heard about the bombing. He was afraid I was one of the many casualties. Through a friend, he enlisted the help of a French secret-service agent to find out if I was still alive. When I walked through his door a week later, he did not recognise me because I was so matted with dirt and grime, and wearing an ugly hat that a soldier had given me. Gradually, I saw the recognition and joy spread over his face as he jumped up to embrace me.

I began to book my assignments with long stopovers in Paris. I was flying all over the world to work, rarely at home in Notting Hill. East Timor in August, Africa and Israel in the autumn, Chechnya in the New Year . . . When Grozny, the Chechen capital, fell in February, 2000, and I was one of the only reporters inside, the Russians had completely surrounded us and were pummelling the place with helicopter gunships and tank rounds. I was sure my luck had finally run out.

My satellite phone's battery was nearly dead, but I called Bruno. He was very calm. 'You must find a way to stay alive,' he said. 'The best reporter is the one who lives to tell the story.' He told me he would see me very soon in Paris, and not to be afraid: 'You have angels all around you.' His voice, his belief that I would be all right somehow, got me through that terrible night.

Six months later, in Sierra Leone, two of my reporter friends were killed and my car was surrounded by hordes of stoned teenage soldiers. I narrowly escaped being raped. It was a terrible time, and I had not seen Bruno in months. He was in Burma, making a film, undercover. Later, he told me he was on a remote train when he pulled out a small bottle that he always carried of the scent that I wore. It was a perfume I had found in New York made by Tocca, but he called it 'the smell of happiness'. 'What a big mistake to take the cap off that bottle,' he later wrote to me, 'because suddenly you were sitting with me on that train and I could not concentrate on my work.'

In Afghanistan, we met in Tora Bora. There were more tearful goodbyes in Third World airports; more joyous reunions in the Gare du Nord or Zimbabwe or Guadeloupe. The drama was high, and we were never bored, but we were getting tired: we wanted to live like normal people who argued over who bought the milk. So when Bruno was offered a job as Africa correspondent for France 2 television, based in the Ivory Coast, I went along to work on my book. He fixed up a wing of the house for me to work in, overlooking a cocoa tree. For a while, it was a quiet life of dinner parties, Sundays at the beach and lying by the pool.

But the idyll did not last. One night, home alone in Abidjan, I heard a grenade. Then a mortar. Then machine-gun fire. I turned off the lights and crawled to the window to see red tracer rounds. I hurriedly sealed the rape door. Violence had come to our home. Later, our car got shot at, with Bruno in the front seat, by teenage soldiers with AK-47s. It was one thing to report from a war zone, another to live inside one permanently. Bruno physically loaded me on a plane to Paris. Once again, we were back to the telephone and obscure airports, and the satellite phone. From December, 2002, I spent nearly four months in Iraq before we met up in Senegal for my birthday in late April.

But finally, we got married. In August 2003, on the French feast of St Amour, our close friends and family gathered in the village in the French Alps that Bruno's ancestors had built 500 years before. It was nearly ten years to the day since he had stopped me in the lobby of the Holiday Inn Sarajevo.

Soon, I was pregnant. And, with marriage and impending motherhood, something strange happened: I developed an emotion that had lain dormant in me for many years: fear. The numbness that had been my protective shell for more than a decade while I reported war seemed to have evaporated. Suddenly, I did not want to risk getting incinerated by bombs in Iraq or Afghanistan. But mostly, I feared for my husband, who was wandering around lawless places in Africa. One night last autumn, a colleague of his was assassinated on the street in cold blood by the police. I felt physically ill.

'Must you go to Liberia?' I would plead after another friend of ours was shot and nearly died there. I would never have done that before. And he would never have forbidden me to take assignments in dangerous places, or ordered me to stay away from the malaria and war-riddled Ivory Coast while I was pregnant. We had both changed.

I finished my book, Madness Visible, in London, not in Africa. It's about war, but also about life. I sometimes have to explain it to other people, but I have never had to explain it to my husband. Despite our years apart, he knows me and my life better than anyone. He is the only person I have never had to tell how agonising it feels to see a child lose both arms because of a bomb, and not be able to do anything about it.

Of course, nothing was ever straightforward with our lives, and we had to spend the first seven months of my pregnancy apart. But we spoke three or four times a day. It must seem strange to other people, but it's the way we live.

Before Bruno went back to Africa, we had a routine ultrasound. As the tiny baby appeared on the screen, my super-macho husband, who had lived among guerrilla soldiers for weeks and had abseiled down the Eiffel Tower with a camera on his shoulder, burst into tears. 'I was so touched!' he said. 'The baby was so big!' But I knew it was more than that. When you have seen so much destruction and chaos, the purity of life really is a miracle.

Goodbye To All That

February, 2004

I am not a big television fan, but recently a friend rang and told me to watch *Prime Suspect*. It was a two-parter in which Helen Mirren was investigating the murder in London of a Bosnian refugee who had witnessed a brutal massacre during the Balkan conflict. I watched it. The next night I stayed at home to watch the second part. There was an actor I knew from Sarajevo playing the bad guy, and there was Helen Mirren, slowly going mad as she became more and more embroiled in the case. Eventually, she became obsessed. She disobeyed her boss, sacrificed her job and flew to Bosnia at her own expense to investigate the massacre. Strange behaviour. But I recognised that look in her eyes.

My friend rang me after the second part ended. 'What was it with Bosnia,' he asked, 'that made people so obsessive?' I could not answer, but I have been thinking. I began reporting the Bosnian war in 1992, and while I am fortunate enough not to have been injured or to suffer from post-traumatic stress disorder, not a day goes by in which the conflict does not enter my mind. I met my husband in Sarajevo. I forged some of my closest friendships in Bosnia. And, in a horrible way, my most powerful memories come from those years.

One of my colleagues from Bosnia recently said, 'Reporting the war in Bosnia was the highest point of my life.' I understood what she meant – that the intensity had never been surpassed – but it was an odd statement.

After all, 250,000 people died in that war, and 3.5 million from a pre-war population of 23 million were displaced. If you asked their families what the high points of their lives were, they would surely not be the years 1991–95.

But, of course, what my friend meant was that she could never duplicate that passion, even in another war. She went on – as most of us reporters did – to work in other war zones, but nothing could match the wars that ripped the former Yugoslavia apart in the last decade of the twentieth century.

I do not believe journalists report war for adrenalin rushes, unless they have some sort of psychological problem. And Bosnia was not the most brutal or dangerous war that I have reported (for that, Chechnya or the wars in West Africa take the unhappy prize). But the injustice and cruelty of it haunted me for many years, even more than the piles of bodies I saw by the side of the road in Zaire, or the blind people I encountered trapped in a bombed-out house with no food, water or assistance after the fall of Grozny.

While I rarely spoke of my experiences in Bosnia, I would dream about them: vivid, technicolor dreams, like drug-induced hallucinations. People I knew and loved would return as perfect as a colour photograph. Snatches of forgotten conversations would be replayed. I wondered if it was because I was so young when I began working there, or so impressionable. But this was not a coming-of-age war. I was even younger when I reported from the Middle East, and later, Rwanda or Liberia. Yet those conflicts did not move me to the same extent or provoke the same outrage.

I began writing *Madness Visible* in 1999. The book had a strange genesis.

During the Kosovo war, I got caught in a Nato bombing raid on a KLA (Kosovo Liberation Army) front line in which many men died. While trapped there, I wrote a long, stream-of-consciousness piece which did not just stick to those gruesome days, but which drifted back and forth in time to years of conflict and memory. The piece won a prize, and the prize got me publishers.

I wanted to write the book in a detached way, so that it was not a book about a journalist's experience, but the experiences of others. There is one scene in which I and two other reporters are captured by a drunken Serb paramilitary and made to march in the woods in mock-execution style. It took me ages to write the scene because I didn't want to overdramatise it.

After all, I am still alive and I emerged without having been raped or beaten. But, after reading it and commenting on the detached style, an American critic kept pressing me, 'But how could you write about this in such an impersonal way?' The answer was that it was not my book. It belonged to the people who allowed me to write about them. I wanted to capture what war smells and feels like, what it looks like, what it is like to sit under a bombardment. Most of all, I wanted to write about what it feels like to die.

Before I began reporting war, I thought death came with dignity, with angels descending poetically from the heavens, with the strains of Pachelbel's Canon or the Albinoni Adagio; with closure. But that is not death. Death is a room full of old people in Sarajevo dying from the cold, while I was unable to help them. Death was the Rwandans who collapsed at my feet vomiting some disgusting green substance during a cholera epidemic.

Death was the naked men, their hands tied behind their backs, who I found by the side of the road near my house in the Ivory Coast after the coup d'etat.

Recently, I and a small group of colleagues were interviewed by a Canadian psychiatrist for a three-year study on the effect of war on journalists.

'How many dead bodies have you seen?' was one of the questions the shrink asked me. 'I have no idea,' I said. I wasn't being glib. I have spent a lot of time in Africa. I have stared into many mass graves, and seen bodies stiff with rigor mortis stuffed down wells. I honestly did not have a clue.

'Don't you think that's an odd answer?' he said. After all, he added, most people just see their grandparents' bodies at funerals. I tried always to keep that in mind as I was writing *Madness Visible*. I wanted the people I wrote about – a cast of characters ranging from teenage soldiers to mass murderers – to speak through me and tell their stories.

But getting back to Bosnia: why did it etch itself so deeply into so many people's souls? Martha Gellhorn once wrote of the Spanish Civil War, 'You can only love one war; afterwards, I suppose, you do your duty.' My colleagues and I did fall in love, in a gruesome and horrible way. We fell in love with a country not far from England, one which we could fly to in less than three hours, then drive overland through the dark fir forests and mountains to a city that was enduring a medieval siege. There, we found poets burning their books and doctors operating without antibiotics and opera singers going mad and children still playing in the snow, despite the constant thud of the mortars.

Recently, I saw Nic Robertson, the talented CNN correspondent, being asked by some naive anchor back in Atlanta whether Baghdad was as dangerous as Sarajevo. I saw his face twitch and I knew what he was thinking – 'You moron! How can you compare the two?' Because nothing really compared to Sarajevo.

'No, Sarajevo was far worse because it was dangerous just to go outside your door,' Roberston replied patiently. This was true. There were kids who were shot in front of their houses having been allowed out to play because their parents simply could not keep them confined any longer. There was an old man who was shot between the eyes when he went out to chop wood because his friends were freezing to death. Sometimes, even those who had not ventured outside found themselves in danger. I knew of a family whose mother was shot by a sniper while washing dishes at the sink.

No, nothing else compared to Bosnia.

Sometime in 1993, I made an unconscious decision to record the war as dispassionately as a stenographer. Almost every day I climbed the hill to the morgue to count the bodies. I wrote down the recipes people used to make cheese and wine from the rice in their humanitarian aid packages. I recorded conversations and images carefully: like the dog seen running near the Bosnian presidency building with a human hand in its mouth. Or walking through makeshift graveyards reading the markers: born 1971, 1972, 1973. There was a poem by a Sarajevo poet, 'Beginning After Everything', that I read over and over following the war:

After I buried my mother (under fire, I sprinted from the
    graveyard)
After the soldiers came with my brother wrapped in a tarp
    (I gave them back his gun) . . .
After the ravenous dog feasting on blood (just another corpse
    in Sniper's Alley)

The writer and historian Misha Glenny once wrote about the
seductive spell that Bosnia cast: 'It is through the middle of
Bosnia that East meets West; Islam meets Christianity; the
Catholic eyes the Orthodox . . . Bosnia divided the great
empires of Vienna and Constantinople . . . it is both the
paradigm of peaceful, communal life in the Balkans and its
darkest antithesis . . .'

I and many others were caught up in the dangerous spell. It
was not just the fact that this was our generation's Vietnam,
as someone pointed out, or that we felt, initially, a strong
obligation to report the evil that was happening so close to
home just fifty years after the Holocaust. It was not even the
draw of the multi-ethnic, cosmopolitan city, or the heartbreakingly beautiful country ripped apart by war. It was
more a question of what had driven these people, in these
neat villages with pretty church steeples and pretty rivers
winding through them, to destroy each other's lives? From
where did this evil come? That is what drove all of us, I
believe: the desire to find out how humanity could plunge to
such darkness.

Sometimes, it came at a huge cost. One weekend early into
the war, my incredibly tolerant long-term boyfriend took a
weekend trip to Zagreb. His plan was that I would leave
Sarajevo by one of the UN humanitarian flights and stay a
few days in a nice hotel with him. I was uneasy: I was worried

the aid flights would shut down, as they always did, or that a major event would happen in Sarajevo and I would miss it. I also felt terrible guilt that I was going to be pampered while my Bosnian friends were stuck inside the siege. But he was persistent and finally, one Friday lunchtime, I flew to Zagreb.

It was a grey, drizzly day. We ate schnitzel and drank heavy red wine at a faux-Hapsburg restaurant, then walked the streets. But I was miserable. I felt as though I was missing a limb. I wondered what was happening in the Reuters office, or if my Bosnian godson, Deni, had got over his fever. I spent most of the day shopping for supplies to take back to friends. I worried the whole weekend that the Sunday flight would be cancelled and I would never get back.

My then-boyfriend – who has since died young – and I had been together for several years. He was an uncomplicated person who wanted to live quietly, get married, have kids, watch *Match of the Day* and read the newspapers in peace in the morning over his breakfast. He had it in him to be happy.

I, on the other hand, was complicated. On day two, he said brightly, 'When you get back, we'll have a great holiday and then try to start a family!'

My heart sank. If I had kids, I would never be able to go to Sarajevo again. What kind of life would that be? The thought was intolerable. I smiled and said, 'We'll see.' But on that wintry Sunday morning, he went back to Notting Hill, I went back to Sarajevo, and I did not come home again for a very long time.

A few years after the war ended, and before the war in Kosovo erupted – around 1997 – I burnt all my Bosnian notebooks. It was a strange thing to do, an act of defiance and rebellion against the past. Every morning I had woken up staring at those notebooks which were on an open bookshelf in my bedroom. They represented war and misery. I had begun to hate them. Letters, documents, diaries – all went into the raging fire. I wanted to move on. I did not think of them again for some time.

Then, a few years later, a researcher from the war crimes tribunal at The Hague rang. They wanted me to testify about the siege of Mostar.

During that siege, I lived on the east side of the Neretva River, the Muslim side, in a bombed-out apartment with two young soldiers. We spent our days on the front line, where my friends were snipers with a small unit, and the nights trying to avoid being hit by shrapnel. What do I remember from that time? Lying on a mattress at night watching red tracer rounds; the sound of the bombing; eating cherries and cold beans for dinner, the only food available; my soldier friends laughing over some silly joke. But most of all I remember the feeling that there was no life outside that room, that front line, that city. In that limited, dangerous world, I was strangely happy. How could I report that to the war crimes tribunal? Instead, I told the startled researcher that I had burnt my notebooks – the documentation of Croat atrocities, the count of the dead, the interviews with witnesses. 'You did what?' she gasped. Only then did I realise what I had done.

But it had not erased the memories. I could not forget the dead. They were everywhere I looked. And when I went back to Sarajevo over and over after the war, they were still there – hanging around the brand-new Benetton shop or the Internet café or the Mexican restaurant that served bad margaritas.

They followed me around like warm, grey clouds. Only my friend Dragan, who had been with me during the war, understood. One day he drove me to the airport and told me to get a life. 'Get married, have kids, forget this place,' he said. 'Say Dovidjenja Bosna (Goodbye Bosnia).'

But in the end, only writing did that. As I gave all the characters, living and dead, the freedom to roam around my book – because it reads more like a novel than a work of non-fiction – I liberated them, and, ultimately, myself. Only when I finished the last page, printed it, and sent it off to my editor did I finally begin to forget about them.

The sadness did not go away. It still pricks at me, like a sharp pin. But it gets duller, with the years passing and my memories fading, more and more, into some lost place in time.

Conclusion

Luca, Rising

December, 2004

I was born in late April in the year of the Ox. A Taurus bull meets an ox – a fatal combination in terms of grinding one's heels into the mud and refusing to budge.

I have been stubborn all of my life, and described as such in various languages. My husband refers to me as '*tête de mule*', accompanied by much Gallic hand language. My mother was kinder. 'Determination is your middle name,' she would say. But for many of my friends and family, that determination is a maddening quality.

In one instance, though, I am eternally grateful. This is the case of a little boy who – had I listened to nearly every doctor I spoke to – was not meant to be born. He is on this earth simply because long ago, I developed an allergy to someone telling me I could not do something.

In this case, it was listening to many, many doctors. Most of us are timid when it comes to obeying doctors' orders: we are brought up to assume they are always right, that they stand next to God. Until I defied them all, I believed it too.

The story begins shortly after my thirty-fifth birthday, on a routine visit to a doctor. I had chosen this particular woman because my friend Susan said she did not pressure women to have babies. I had left my last doctor because he drove me insane with his questions. 'When are you going to get pregnant?' he kept prodding, every time I went for check-ups. Every minor ailment, every disfiguration – from a mole on my cheek to a chronic cough – would be 'sorted out once I had babies'. I began to hate him.

Which is why I liked this new doctor. Single, childless, rather plump and plain, in her late forties, she had a matronly bedside manner and a calm, quiet air. She never mentioned the dreaded biological clock. She simply checked me, took my blood pressure, wrote out prescriptions and smiled blandly.

It was not that I disliked children. I was simply not ready. Having been one of seven children in a large, strange family, I was in no rush to become a mother. I was more in the process of discovering what had gone wrong in my own immediate family, and how – when the time came – I would not repeat those mistakes.

Besides, I loved my work, my friends, my boyfriends, my freedom, my financial independence. I hated the fact that society pressured women to feel unworthy if they did not have children. I once read a novel that stated that a woman who did not have a child was incomplete, akin to a soldier who had never killed anyone. That thought kept me awake one night but oddly comforted me. I was not a soldier but I had been in plenty of wars and never felt the urge to kill anyone.

I saw the kind doctor for a check-up. The topic turned to fertility. She became gloomy and talked about declining birth rates with the air of a meteorologist describing an approaching typhoon. She began quoting statistics and facts. Whenever this subject came up, I tuned out and prepared mental shopping lists.

'My mother had me at forty-two,' I chimed in, already drifting away.

She shrugged and said it was probably luck. She asked me if I would ever consider an egg donor.

Here I will admit it. So ignorant was I of fertility options – I assumed one just stopped using birth control, got pregnant and that was that – that I did not know what an egg donor was. I did not know what IVF (*in vitro* fertilisation) really was – I thought it was probably something women did if they could not get pregnant, and you did it once and it worked. I naively assumed that one went to a doctor to get problems fixed. A prescription was written, and *voila!* you were healed.

That day, the lady doctor shot me a terrifying look. 'And what happens when the child wants to see her real mother?'

'I don't know,' I said. 'I hadn't thought about it.' (I wasn't even sure why an egg donor *wasn't* the real mother).

We had something of a dispute over this – the morals of egg donors – with me arguing something I knew nothing about. Then she said it:

'What ever made you think you could have a career like yours and become a mother?'

I looked up. Her face was twisted with rage. There was an awful silence.

'Oh,' I finally said. I felt slightly wounded, as though she had delivered a fierce blow to my ribs. I climbed down from the table and dressed. I picked up my shoes and walked outside to put them on in the waiting room, and only then did I begin to feel panic.

Proustian questions are often reprinted in magazines, asking celebrities secrets about their lives. When and where were you happiest? Who or what is the love of your life. One of the questions is, 'What is the depth of human misery?' To which the celebrity usually responds with the obvious or the profound: starvation, the Holocaust, lying, the massacre at Srebrenica.

If I were asked, I knew what my answer would be. It is entirely selfish. It was a few years after the lady doctor and I parted ways, and I *did* want to have a baby. But, racked with Catholic guilt, I was sure she had cursed me in some way. I was not having much luck. I stood outside gates of St Mary's Hospital, Paddington, on a clear spring day, crying into a mobile phone. I was talking to my mother, more than 3,000 miles away. Above the din of lorries passing and buses screeching to a halt, and a screaming maniac who emerged from the hospital and spat at my feet, she spoke words of comfort.

'Darling,' she said, 'don't believe everything doctors say!'

But it was difficult for me not to. I was brought up in a culture where a doctor's word is respected and not challenged. On that particular day, I had emerged from a consultation with Britain's foremost expert on miscarriage, a thin, attractive and utterly bloodless woman. In less than one year, I had suffered three, and was beginning to crack under the strain of the hormonal roller coaster, not to mention the profound sense of loss.

One miscarriage would have been tough. Two was agonising. Three was unbearable. The doctor's advice was sombre; in fact, she had no advice other than to tell me to continue getting pregnant. Eventually, she said, in a crisp, no-nonsense voice, statistics were on my side. I might have a healthy baby.

According to studies done at St Mary's, a woman who had four miscarriages had a sixty-two per cent chance of having a live birth. A woman who endured five miscarriages had a forty-eight per cent chance. 'The reality is if they stick at it, they'll have a healthy baby,' she said briskly. It might have been true but it was not exactly comforting. And for someone like me who spent a lifetime being pro-active, passively waiting for the one pregnancy which might work was a prescription akin to torture.

The doctor had spent time showing me charts and graphs and lines on her computer. She did not mean to be heartless. But my case was less dramatic compared to other women she treated: women who had miscarriages in the double digits; women who tried for years to get pregnant, then had IVF and lost those babies. In fact, she cheered me slightly as I was leaving: 'Be grateful you get pregnant at all. Many of my patients are infertile.'

I never thought someone else's bleak misfortune would make me feel any better. But life's like that sometimes.

Much as I intended not to, I did have another miscarriage – my fourth – while on holiday in Austria. This one was particularly traumatic. The scan showed that I had lost the baby, but my hormonal levels kept jumping up and up like an excited rabbit. The doctors were baffled and kept taking more blood samples. They concluded it was an ectopic pregnancy – when the embryo settles in the Fallopian tubes – but they weren't sure.

'Medicine is not always perfect,' one of my many doctors once said to me. 'You would be surprised to see how much we have to guess.'

This would have meant surgery and possibly the removal

of one of my Fallopian tubes. These were added complications I did not need.

As I sat stunned, wondering what I could have ever done in a past life to bring such misfortune on myself, the kindly Austrian doctor – at this point, I had seen doctors all over the world who examined me and tended to think of them as either kind or not so kind – said, 'You should really do something about this. Have you thought about having IVF?'

I didn't have a problem with infertility, I told him. In fact, my problem would have been easier if I was infertile – at least people could pinpoint what was wrong. There was a known and tested treatment for it, even if the odds of it working for anyone over thirty-five weren't exactly encouraging. Still, I had many friends who had taken the IVF route and had several children, all healthy, as a result.

'No, but at least they could monitor your pregnancy better,' he said, leading me to the door. 'Think about it. You're losing time.'

The four words a woman trying to have a baby does not want to ever hear are: you are losing time. Back in London, feeling shaky, I made an appointment with a famous IVF specialist. He was famous for getting a fifty-six-year-old teacher pregnant with twins.

More importantly, a close friend with serious gynaecological problems had gone to him and emerged triumphant after two IVF attempts, also pregnant with twins. Seven months into it and glowing with her good fortune, she generously offered to take me to my appointment.

'He's got a weird manner,' she said when she picked me up. 'So don't get hurt if he says something strange.'

She told me that when she woke up after having exploratory

surgery with the odd man by her bedside, he had chortled, 'I haven't taken out your Fallopian tube – yet!' while my friend, reeling from anaesthetic and anxiety, burst into tears.

At his Harley Street office, I thumbed through old copies of *Vogue* with some extremely nervous women. They were both young, in their early thirties, but looked wrecked. One was in the process of chewing through her nails, another was yanking out her hair in clumps. I realised, not for the first time, how desperate people feel when they want a child and cannot have one.

First I met with one of the odd man's partners, an Egyptian doctor who had a quiet manner. He took a detailed case history and genuinely looked concerned when I described the miscarriages. Then the man burst in. He pulled a chair between my friend and me, listening carefully to the Egyptian doctor's briefing. 'Miss di Giovanni has suffered four miscarriages . . . blah blah blah . . .' The doctor rambled on and on. The specialist looked bored. He did not look at me at all.

Then he turned. His eyes were strange. 'It would be easier if you were infertile. The miscarriages are probably because of your age and there's nothing we can do about that.'

He then babbled about egg quality, statistics, failed hormones, injections, trials of drugs.

I felt nauseous.

'Maybe you should try an egg donor,' he said. 'Or a surrogate mother.'

I sat back in horror. A surrogate mother! What the hell was that? 'I'm not even forty years old!' I said.

'Still, you might have left it too long,' he said, scratching his chin. He spent the next ten minutes regaling me with more bad news about miscarriage rates and inferior eggs. It was barely a week after my fourth miscarriage and my hormones took over. I burst into tears. The room went quiet. The Egyptian doctor looked horrified. My pregnant friend's own eyes filled with tears. The specialist sighed.

'Oh dear, I've done it again,' he said. 'My big mouth. My wife left me because of it, you know.'

Back home, I called the miscarriage authority and informed her of miscarriage number four.

'Should I try IVF?' I asked in a desperate tone.

'The success rate is extremely low,' she said coldly.

'So there is nothing I can do?'

'I'm sorry,' she said. 'Nothing.'

I genuinely think she meant it.

Some time passed before my black depression cleared and I had the energy to bound back into activity. In that time, my boyfriend (now husband) brought me to a teaching hospital in Dijon, France, where his younger brother was a research haematologist. He thought I might have an auto-immune disorder.

This did not come as a surprise. In my early twenties, while studying for my Master's degree, I slept very little and ate even less. After a few months of this, I noticed spontaneous bruises the size of grapefruits on my legs and arms. My GP thought I might have leukaemia. He announced this before he had even done a blood test.

I did not have leukaemia, it turned out, but I had a genetic blood-clotting disorder called factor 12 deficiency. He sent me to Charing Cross Hospital. For one year, while I was writing my Master's degree thesis on whether or not Katherine Mansfield plagiarised Chekhov, I was poked and prodded and finally told I wasn't going to die from this blood-clotting disorder. I could go through my life and not even know I had it.

'Just remember if you need surgery to ask for fresh frozen plasma,' one of the doctors told me finally. 'Remember: FFP.'

When I was in my early thirties, I had my appendix removed. It was emergency surgery and I was coherent enough before they put the anaesthetic in my arm to ask for the FFP.

'What?' shouted the surgeon, the expression behind his green mask growing dark. The surgery was halted. I lay on a cot in the hallway until the haematologist arrived. She examined me and vetoed the plasma. The risk of HIV was too high. We went ahead with the surgery. I did not need FFP after all.

A few weeks later, the haematologist, Dr Catherine Ozanne, contacted me. She said she had my blood results and wanted to run more tests. 'Something is strange,' she said. She wanted me to take part in a study at University College London Medical Centre. She arranged a meeting with a famous haematologist she was working with.

But none of this happened. By the time the meeting rolled around, Dr Ozanne had diagnosed her own leukaemia. She underwent chemotherapy and radiation, but died a short time later. My records disappeared.

It took several years and four miscarriages later until I found out why my case was so interesting.

To be fair, the miscarriage authority and the other scores of doctors whose doors I passed through also gave me blood tests. But the doctors in Dijon, France concluded that I weirdly had not one, but two blood-clotting disorders: antiphospholipid syndrome, which can cut off the supply of oxygen to the growing embryo thus triggering a miscarriage; plus the factor 12 deficiency.

Once diagnosed, the treatment was simple enough – daily injections of a blood thinner and baby aspirin. Even then, when I presented her with these facts, the miscarriage authority seemed oddly dismissive of my condition, telling me that depending on the lab and the test itself, the results changed. The problem, she implied, was my age, to which she could offer no solution; no alternatives; no encouragement. The miscarriages were probably all chromosomal. That was her parting shot.

In retrospect, I wasted a lot of time with doctors who did not help the condition, or, more importantly, my spirits. The terrible thing about miscarriage is that you are given a beautiful gift, then for no reason at all, it is yanked from your grasp. The American doctor, Jonathan Scher, who eventually gave me the courage to change my destiny, described it as 'heartbreaking', and stressed that women who have my experience – and I believe there are many – need a doctor who will 'be pro-active and enthusiastic'.

But those doctors are very, very hard to find. During pregnancy number three, I consulted a fashionable and expensive north London doctor favoured by supermodels and wives of rock stars. I sat in the waiting room with a very pregnant Jasmine Guinness and was given a tour of the pool where Kate Moss gave birth. I willed myself to believe this pregnancy would yield a healthy baby and registered for a private room with a double bed. I took the telephone numbers for Indian head massage and natural childbirth midwives. But a few weeks later, I called the fashionable doctor in desperation because I knew I was in the throes of another miscarriage. It was the same thing – the pain in the back, the bleeding, the headache, the chills.

'Is there anything you can do? Can I check myself into the hospital?' I pleaded.

'No', he said. 'There's nothing you can do.' (Later, my American doctors would disagree with this diagnosis.)

I remember it was my birthday, a cold spring day. I was forty years old, and I was utterly alone. My boyfriend was far away, in another country, another continent. I spent that night in bed, knowing that life was seeping away, powerless to do anything. As a final insult, my radiators burst and water poured all over my wooden floors. No plumber would come because it was Easter weekend. My close friends were all away.

This is the worst it will ever get, I told myself. If you get through this, you can get through anything.

But it got a little worse. A few days later, I found myself in the same waiting room in which I had happily sat with Jasmine Guinness, but this time to have the remains of a miscarriage removed.

As for the super-trendy doctor, he might have been a great communicator with Elle MacPherson, but I experienced a remarkable lack of compassion. When he examined the scan which confirmed I had lost the baby, he told me to wait for him in a room upstairs. I waited and waited. The sky grew darker. It began to rain. The room was freezing cold. I dialled my friends one by one with the terrible news. One and a half hours later, the doctor arrived.

'Sorry, I was just delivering a baby,' he said matter-of-factly, not considering that for someone who had just lost their fourth baby, this news might not be met with joy. 'The poor mother was having a terrible time. It was a breech birth.' Although I liked his cheerful hospital and his birthing room with the Kate Moss memorial pool, I never went back to him again.

I was on the verge of giving up when my niece called me from the States. The daughter of my eldest sister, she is only three years younger than me. When she was only twenty-nine, she lost a baby at twenty-one weeks. She went from doctor to doctor who gave her grim diagnoses until she met Dr Jonathan Scher who specialised in high-risk pregnancy and fertility disorders.

My niece was diagnosed with an auto-immune disorder called anticardiolipin syndrome. It is hereditary, which means I probably had it, too. She was monitored carefully and treated with drugs and eventually went on to have three healthy babies under this doctor's care.

'I have seen so many doctors, I don't ever want to have another blood test again,' I said. She quietly reminded me that her own doctors had told her that her eggs were too old when she was in her early thirties. Another doctor told her she was going through early menopause. A third told her to consider adoption.

'You can't give up,' she said.

I booked a ticket to New York.

Most of the women Dr Jonathan Scher sees have had numerous miscarriages or failed IVFs. Some of them have a dozen. He never tells them it's impossible. He does in-vestigations into auto-immune diseases, which he says ac-count for fifty to sixty per cent of recurrent miscarriage.

He ordered for me a battery of tests. My husband was put on antibiotics – he was living in Africa and had recently had malaria. I was sent to a drugstore on Third Avenue to stock up on blood thinners and progesterone. He sent me to a fertility specialist and a haematologist.

I rented an apartment overlooking Central Park during a rainy month, and spent the time having tests. My husband flew out from Africa. We drank martinis and went to diners to eat cheeseburgers and went to the movies and to hear jazz. And then a few weeks later, when I was back home, and very relaxed, the doctor called me on my cell phone. 'Congratulations,' he said. 'You are pregnant.'

But this time, it was different. I stayed in bed for nearly five months. I reread *War and Peace*, *Anna Karenina* and Herodotus. I sorted through my old diaries. I watched a lot of afternoon television.

It was often not easy but at every single crossroad, every time I felt like I wasn't going to make it, I thought of what pleasure I would get taking my baby to see the stone-faced miscarriage authority. My stubbornness kicked in. Things began to go wrong, but I would not let it happen this time. At twenty-one weeks, I was given a cervical stitch. It was made of steel and I knew I was having a baby as stubborn as me. Stay in there, I told him.

The daily injections of heparin, a blood-thinner that I injected into my belly, left me black and blue. I thought I would pass out the first time I stuck myself, but then I got used to it. The nurse who taught me said, 'Pretend you're sticking a knife in butter.' I jabbed myself hard and she turned white. 'Uh, that's a bit rough,' she said, 'be gentle.'

Until fourteen weeks I had horse injections of progesterone in my hip. I forced my friends to give them to me. One of my girlfriends shook so much she missed the muscle, hit a blood vessel and it bled and bled. She apologised profusely. But I, who once feared needles, just laughed and laughed. It was such a small price to pay.

Two weeks before I gave birth, I developed a weird cough which was so violent I nearly fractured two ribs. At this point I was living in France, and my French doctor put me in the high-risk unit for observation. Scores of doctors from every department – immunology, haematology, gynaecology, infectious diseases trooped in and out of my room, lifting the sheet, touching my belly and my ribs. It hurt to breathe. They thought that I was too weak to give birth. They thought I had picked up a rare ailment from the dirt in Iraq.

But at thirty-four weeks, labour started before they had time to take the steel stitch out. The contractions pushed against the stitch, which strained. We took an ambulance to the hospital and a terrified French paramedic tried to console me while the other careened around corners, blowing through red lights. My husband rode alongside on his motorcycle, at 120 mph.

At the hospital, I screamed and screamed at the poor midwife not to touch me when I saw her coming at me with an enormous pair of scissors to clip the stitch. My husband was mortified. 'Your manners!' he hissed, French to the end. But the birth itself was easy, and the baby came into the world to Julie London singing 'My Heart Belongs to Daddy'.

The doctor said, 'He's going to be a blues man,' and passed this small bundle to me. We called him Luca Costantino. Luca, for light, because I knew he was going to be sunny; and Costantino for my Italian grandfather who grew fig trees and climbed the roof of his New Jersey home trying to trap fat pigeons which he would later cook. He thought he was back in the Old Country where he hunted squab; he never quite got used to living in the New World.

I often wondered if I had not been so stubborn, so determined, and so angry at the response I had from doctors, what might have happened. If I had listened to the miscarriage authority and simply kept repeating the awful cycle of pregnancy, miscarriage, pregnancy, miscarriage . . . I am sure Luca would not be on this earth.

So I went back to see the miscarriage authority when Luca was nine months old, and she was as professional as ever, speaking of translocation of chromosomes and showing me more charts which showed the difficulty of implantation. She was genuinely happy about my baby, but said of my case, 'You were lucky. Some people get lucky, like at the fruit machines.'

A fruit machine! I had won the fruit machine! I left her office on a cold autumn afternoon, passing through the gates of St Mary's feeling much better than when I had wept down the phone to my mother, who had told me, 'Darling, don't believe everything those doctors say!'

For once, I was awfully glad I had listened to my mother.

As I write this, my son is nine months old, weighs twenty-four pounds and has two and a half teeth. He is in the next room laughing and laughing at his father, who is playing peek-a-boo with him. He is beginning to walk. He smiles all the time. The French call him 'sage' – a high compliment meaning quiet and content. Every mother thinks their child is extra-ordinary, but I know my baby is more – he is a miracle.

Because of the treatment I got in New York, I believe in science and medicine. I believe in not taking no for an answer. But I also believe in something else, something higher.

When Luca was tiny, and I was still very nervous about taking him outside (thinking I would drop him, leave him in a taxi, or what if he cried and did not stop?), our first excursion outside was to a beautiful church, St Roch, near our home in Paris. The church was dimly lit by candles and smelt of old wax and lemons. A choir was practising for Sunday mass. I sat with my little boy – a little boy who nearly was not born – and cried and cried. The tears dripped over his stripy cashmere blanket, a gift from my friend Charlotte, and he regarded me with his milky newborn eyes. I just could not stop the tears. It had been a long road.

Later, I asked a friend who is very wise why that happened. 'I just felt overcome by emotion,' I said. 'It was the strangest thing.'

My friend was quiet for a moment. 'It's because you see your son as a miracle,' he said gently. 'And at St Roch, you were in the presence of whoever granted you that miracle.'

A NOTE ON THE AUTHOR

Janine di Giovanni is senior foreign correspondent for
The Times and contributing editor for *Vanity Fair*. She
has won Granada Television's 'Foreign Correspondent
of the Year' award, the National Magazine Award and
two Amnesty International Media Awards. She is
the author of three books, *Madness Visible*, *Against
the Stranger* and *The Quick and the Dead*.
Janine di Giovanni lives in Paris.

A NOTE ON THE TYPE

The text of this book is set in Linotype Sabon, named after
the type founder, Jacques Sabon. It was designed by Jan
Tschichold and jointly developed by Linotype, Monotype
and Stempel, in response to a need for a typeface to
be available in identical form for mechanical hot metal
composition and hand composition using foundry type.

Tschichold based his design for Sabon roman on a
font engraved by Garamond, and Sabon italic on a font
by Granjon. It was first used in 1966 and has proved
an enduring modern classic.